DISCRETE EVENT SIMULATIONS – DEVELOPMENT AND APPLICATIONS

Edited by **Eldin Wee Chuan Lim**

Discrete Event Simulations – Development and Applications
http://dx.doi.org/10.5772/2585
Edited by Eldin Wee Chuan Lim

Contributors

Giulia Pedrielli, Tullio Tolio, Walter Terkaj, Marco Sacco, Wennai Wang, Yi Yang, José Arnaldo Barra Montevechi, Rafael de Carvalho Miranda, Jonathan Daniel Friend, Thiago Barros Brito, Rodolfo Celestino dos Santos Silva, Edson Felipe Capovilla Trevisan, Rui Carlos Botter, Stephen Wee Hun Lim, Eldin Wee Chuan Lim, Igor Kotenko, Alexey Konovalov, Andrey Shorov and Weilin Li

Published by InTech

Janeza Trdine 9, 51000 Rijeka, Croatia

Publishing Process Manager Mirna Cvijic
Technical Editor InTech Prepress, Novi Sad
Cover InTech Design team

Additional hard copies can be obtained from orders@intechopen.com

Discrete Event Simulations – Development and Applications,
Edited by Eldin Wee Chuan Lim
p. cm.
ISBN 978-953-51-0741-5

For EU product safety concerns:
IN TECH d.o.o., Prolaz Marije Krucifikse Kozulić 3, 51000 Rijeka, Croatia,
info@intechopen.com or visit our website at intechopen.com.

Meet the editor

Dr Eldin Wee Chuan Lim is a Lecturer in the Department of Chemical & Biomolecular Engineering at the National University of Singapore (NUS). He is a Member of the Editorial Boards for the Elsevier journal, Advanced Powder Technology, the American Journal of Fluid Dynamics published by Scientific & Academic Publishing, and the Journal of Chemical Engineering & Process Technology published by OMICS Publishing Group. Some of the academic awards that he has received include the HPC Quest Silver Award presented by IBM and the Institute of High Performance Computing Singapore, ERS-IASC Young Researcher Award presented by the European Regional Section of the International Association for Statistical Computing, two Best Paper Awards presented at the 2010 SECAU Security Congress and the Frontier Award presented by the Fluid & Particle Processing Division of The Society of Chemical Engineers, Japan. He is also a recipient of the Teaching Commendation award presented by the Faculty of Engineering of NUS.

Contents

Preface

With rapid advancements in computing power, computer modeling and simulations have become an important complement to experimentations in many areas of research as well as industrial applications. The Discrete Event Simulation (DES) method has received widespread attention and acceptance by both researchers and practitioners in recent years. The range of application of DES spans across many different disciplines and research fields. In research, further development and advancements of the basic DES algorithm continue to be sought while various hybrid methods derived by combining DES with other simulation techniques continue to be developed. This book presents state-of-the-art contributions on fundamental development of the DES method, novel integration of the method with other modeling techniques as well as applications towards simulating and analyzing the performances of various types of systems. This book will be of interest to undergraduate and graduate students, researchers as well as professionals who are actively engaged in DES related work.

There are nine chapters in this book that are organized into three sections. The first section comprises three chapters that report recent studies on fundamental development and analyses of the DES method. In Chapter 1, Pedrielli and co-authors introduce a distributed modeling approach that allows complex discrete event systems that would otherwise not be practicable to model using conventional simulation techniques to be modeled efficiently. Wang and Yang discuss in Chapter 2 various approaches for fast event scheduling for simulations of large-scale networks. They report the results of computational experiments that demonstrate the performance of a cache aware algorithm to be better than that of a conventional Calendar Queue. In Chapter 3, Montevechi and co-authors present the application of factorial design statistical techniques for identifying significant variables in discrete event simulation models with a view towards speeding up simulation optimization processes.

The approach of integrating DES with various modeling techniques has also attracted the interests of several researchers throughout the world in recent years. In the second section of this book, two chapters on work conducted in this area are presented. Ortega discusses in Chapter 4 a simulation platform that combines DES with stochastic simulation and multi-agent systems for modeling holonic manufacturing systems. Brito describes in Chapter 5 a decision support system that was developed by combining DES with Multiple Criteria Decision Analysis. The application of such a hybrid decision support system towards analysis of a steel manufacturing plant is illustrated.

The final section of this book is devoted to contributions reporting applications of DES towards various systems. Lim and Lim describe simulations of human evacuation processes using a discrete approach for modeling individual human subjects in Chapter 6. Kotenko and co-authors report the development of a DES based environment for analyses of botnets and evaluation of defense mechanisms against botnet attacks in Chapter 7. In Chapter 8, Li proposes a comprehensive DES model that is able to capture the various complexities associated with new product development projects as well as take into account engineering changes that arise stochastically during the course of such projects. In the final chapter of this book, Klug focuses on project management issues that are of relevance to simulation projects in general.

This book represents the concerted efforts of many individuals. First and foremost, I would like to take this opportunity to acknowledge the efforts of all authors who have contributed to the success of this book project. I would also like to thank the support provided by Ms. Mirna Cvijic of InTech Open Access Publisher, without which the publication of this book would not have been possible. Last but certainly not least, and on behalf of all contributing authors, I wish to express my sincere appreciation and gratitude towards InTech Open Access Publisher for transforming this book project from inception to reality.

Eldin Wee Chuan Lim
Department of Chemical & Biomolecular Engineering,
National University of Singapore
Singapore

Section 1

Fundamental Development and Analyses of the Discrete Event Simulation Method

Chapter 1

Distributed Modeling of Discrete Event Systems

Giulia Pedrielli, Tullio Tolio, Walter Terkaj and Marco Sacco

Additional information is available at the end of the chapter

http://dx.doi.org/10.5772/50350

1. Introduction

Computer simulation is widely used to support the design of any kind of complex system and to create computer-generated "virtual worlds" where humans and/or physical devices are embedded (e.g. aircraft flight simulators [20]). However, both the generation of simulation models and the execution of simulations can be time and cost expensive. While there are already several ways to increase the speed of a simulation run, the scientific challenge for the simulation of complex systems still resides in the ability to model (simulate) those systems in a parallel/distributed way [35].

A computer simulation is a computation that emulates the behavior of some real or conceptual systems over time. There are three main simulation techniques [23]:

- *Continuous simulation*. Given the discrete nature of the key parameters of a digital computer, including the number of memory locations, the data structures, and the data representation, continuous simulation may be best approximated on a digital computer through time-based discrete simulation where the time steps are sufficiently small relative to the process being modeled.
- *Time-based discrete simulation*. In this case the universal time is organized into a discrete set of monotonically increasing timesteps where the choice of the duration of the timestep interval changes as a result of the external stimuli, any change between two subsequent timesteps must occur atomically within the corresponding timestep interval. Regardless of whether its state incurs and changes, a process and all its parameters may be examined at every time step.
- *Discrete event simulation* [5]. The difference between discrete event simulation and time-based simulation is twofold. Firstly, the process being modeled is understood to advance through events under discrete event conditions. Second, an event (i.e. an activity of the process as determined by the model developer) carries with it the potential for affecting the state of the model and is not necessarily related to the

progress of time. In this case, the executable model must necessarily be run corresponding to every event to accurately reflect the reality of the process.

Since continuous simulation is simply academic and cannot be reproduced on real computers, it is important to comment the difference between time-based simulation and discrete event simulation.

Under time-based simulation, the duration of the timestep interval is determined based on the nature of the specific activity or activities of the process that the model developer considers important and worth modeling and simulating. Similarly, under discrete event simulation, events for a given process are also identified on the basis of the activity or activities the model developer views as important. Whereas time-based simulation constitutes the logical choice for processes in which the activity is distributed over every timestep, discrete event simulation is more efficient when the activity of a process being modeled is sparsely distributed over time. The overhead in discrete event simulation, arising from the additional need to detect and record the events, is higher than in the simpler time-based technique and must be more than compensated by the savings not to have to execute the model at every time step.

A fundamental difference between time-based and discrete event simulations lies in their relationship to the principle of causality. In the time-based approach, while a cause may refer to a process state at a specific timestep, the fact that the state of the process is observed at every subsequent time step reflects the assumption that the effect of the cause is expected. Thus both the cause and the effect refer to the observed state of the process in time-based simulation. In discrete event simulation, both cause and effects refer to events. However, upon execution due to an event, a model may not generate an output event thus appearing to imply that a cause will not necessary be accompanied by corresponding observed facts.

Discrete Event Simulation (DES) has been widely adopted to support system analysis, education and training, organizational change [43] in a range of diverse areas such as commerce [13], manufacturing ([14],[38], [79]), supply chains [24], health services and bio-medicine ([3], [18]), simulation in environmental and ecological systems [6], city planning and engineering [45], aerospace vehicle and air traffic simulation [40], business administration and management [16], military applications [17].

All the aforementioned areas are usually characterized by the presence of complex systems. Indeed, a system represented by a simulation model is defined as complex when it is extremely large, i.e. a large number of components characterize it, or a large number of interactions describes the relationships between objects within the system, or it is geographically dispersed. In all cases the dynamics can be hard to describe. The complexity is reflected in the system simulation model that can be characterized according to the following concepts [23]:

1. Presence of entity elements that are dynamically created and moved during a simulation [62]
2. Asynchronous behavior of the entities

3. Asynchronous interactions between the entities
4. Entities which concur for the use of shared resources
5. Connectivity between the entities

The simulation of complex systems through the use of traditional simulation tools presents several drawbacks, e.g. the long time required to develop the unique monolithic simulation model, the computational effort required for running the simulation, the impossibility to run the simulation model on a set of geographically distributed computers, the absence of fault tolerance (i.e. the work done is lost if one processor goes down), the impossibility to realize a realistic model of the entire system in the case several subsystems are included and the owners of each subsystem do not want to share the information.

Most of the aforementioned problems can be effectively addressed by the distributed simulation (DS) approach which will be the focus of this chapter.

The chapter will be organized as follows: Section 2 presents the main concepts and definitions together with a literature review on applications and open issues related to distributed simulation. Section 3 delves into the High Level Architecture [1], i.e. the reference standard supporting the distributed simulation. Section 4 shows an application of distributed simulation on a real industrial case in the manufacturing domain [77]. Finally, Section 5 presents the conclusions and the main topics for future research in the field of distributed simulation.

2. Distributed simulation

Traditional stand alone simulation is based on a simulation clock and an event list. The interaction of the event list and the simulation clock generates the sequence of the events that have to be simulated.

The execution of any event might cause an update of the value of the state variables, a modification to the event list and (or) the collection of the statistics. Each event is executed based on the simulation time assigned to it, i.e. the simulation is sequential.

The idea underlying the distributed simulation is to minimize the sequential aspect of traditional simulation. Distributed simulation can be classified into two major categories: (1) parallel and distributed computing, and (2) distributed modeling.

Parallel and distributed computing refers to technologies that enable a simulation program to be executed on a computing system containing multiple processors, such as personal computers, interconnected by a communication network [20].

The main benefits resulting from the adoption of distributed computing technologies are [20]:

- *Reduced execution time*. By decomposing a large simulation computation into many sub-computations and executing the sub-computations concurrently across different processors, one can reduce the global execution time.

- *Geographical distribution*. Executing the simulation program on a set of geographically distributed computers enables one to create virtual worlds with multiple participants that are physically located at different sites.
- *Integration* of simulators that execute on machines from different manufacturers.
- *Fault tolerance*. If one processor goes down, it may be possible for other processors to pick up the work of the failed machine allowing the simulation to proceed despite the failure.

The definition of distributed modeling can be given by highlighting the differences compared to the concept of parallel and distributed computing as presented by Fujimoto [20]. If a single simulator is developed and the simulation is executed on multiple processors we talk about *parallel* and *distributed computing*. Whereas if several simulators are combined into a distributed architecture we talk about *distributed modeling*; in this case, the simulation execution requires the synchronization between the different simulators.

The *distributed computing* can be still applied to each simulator in a distributed simulation model [60], but the complexity related to the synchronization of the different models can be such that the performance of the simulation (in terms of speed) can be worse than when a single simulation model is developed. This drawback related to the decrease in the efficiency in terms of speed of simulation leads to the following question: "Why is it useful to develop a distributed simulation model?". The following benefits represent an answer to this question ([57], [77]):

- *Complexity management*. If the complexity of the system to be simulated grows and the modeling of each sub-system requires various and specific expertise, then the realization of a single monolithic simulation model is not feasible [65]. Under the distributed modeling approach the problem is decomposed in several sub-problems easier to cope with.
- *Overcoming the lack of shared information*. The developer of a simulation model can hardly access all the information characterizing the whole system to model, again hindering the feasibility of developing a unique and monolithic simulation model.
- *Reusability*. The development of a simulation model always represents a costly activity, thus the distributed modeling can be seen as a possibility to integrate pre-existing simulators and to avoid the realization of new models.

The feasibility of the distributed simulation concept was demonstrated by the SIMNET project (SIMulator NETworking [73]), which ran from 1983 to 1990. As consequence of this project, a set of protocols were developed for interconnecting simulations and the Distributed Interactive Simulation (DIS) standard was the first one. Afterwards, the High Level Architecture (HLA) standard ([1], [15], [27]) was developed by the U.S. Department of Defense (DoD) under the leadership of the Defense Modeling and Simulation Office (DMSO). The next sub-section presents a general overview of the HLA standard for distributed simulation, whereas Section 2.2 gives an overview of distributed simulation in civilian applications.

2.1. HLA-standard: An overview

HLA (IEEE standard 1516) is a software architecture designed to promote the use and interoperation of simulators. HLA was based on the premise that no single simulator could satisfy all uses and applications in the defense industry and it aimed at reducing the time and cost required to create a synthetic environment for a new purpose.

The HLA architecture (Figure1) defines a *Federation* as a collection of interacting simulators (*federates*), whose communication is orchestrated by a *Runtime Infrastructure* (RTI) and an interface. Federates can be either simulations, surrogates for live players, or tools for distributed simulation. They are defined as having a single point of attachment to the RTI and might consist of several processes, perhaps running on several computers.

HLA can combine the following types of simulators (following the taxonomy developed by the DoD):

- *Live* - real people operating real systems (e.g. a field test)
- *Virtual* - real people operating simulated systems (e.g. flight simulations)
- *Constructive* - simulated people operating simulated systems (e.g. a discrete event simulation)

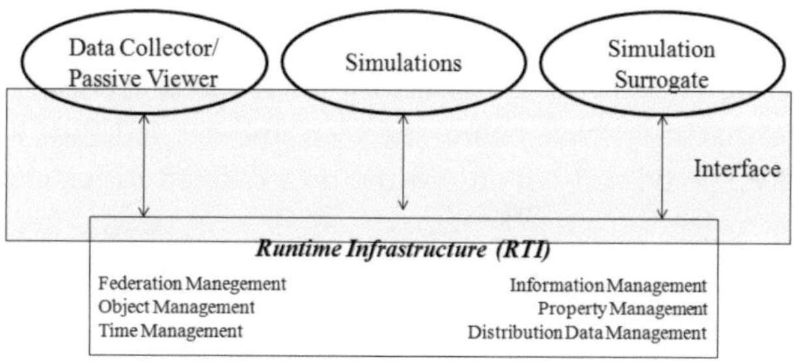

Figure 1. HLA Reference Architecture

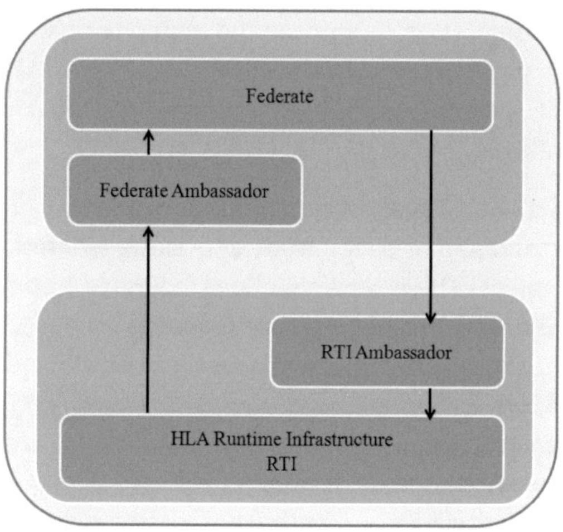

Figure 2. RTIAmbassador and FederateAmbassador

The HLA standard provides four main components for the realization and management of a federation:

- HLA rules (IEEE 1516.0, 2000) representing a set of 10 rules that the simulators (federates) have to follow in order to be defined HLA-compliant.
- Federate Interface Specification (FIS) (IEEE 1516.2, 2000) defining how simulators are supposed to interact with the RTI.
- Object Model Template (OMT) (IEEE 1516.1, 2000) specifying what kind of information is communicated between simulators and how simulations are documented. Following the OMT each federate defines the data that it is willing to share (publish) with other federates and the data it requires from other federates (subscribe). The resulting object models related to each federate are called simulation object models (SOMs). The federation object model (FOM) combines the federate SOMs into a single object model for the federation to define the overall data to be exchanged within the federation.
- Federate Development Process (FEDEP) (IEEE 1516.3, 2004) defining the recommended practice processes and procedures that should be followed by users of the HLA to develop and execute their federations.

The federates cannot directly exchange information throughout the federation, instead the RTI plays the role of the operating system of the distributed simulation, providing a set of general-purpose services for federation management and enabling the federates in carrying out federate-to-federate *interactions*. In particular interactions represent an explicit action taken by a federate that may have some effect on another federate within a federation execution, such action can be tied with a specific time defined as *interactionTime,* when the action takes place.

Each federate is endowed with an *RTIAmbassador* and a *FederateAmbassador* (Figure 2) to access the services offered by the RTI. Operations on the *RTIAmbassador* are called by the federate whenever it needs an RTI service (e.g. a request to advance simulation time). In the reverse direction, the RTI invokes an operation on the *FederateAmbassador* whenever it needs to pass data to the federate (e.g. to inform the federate that the request to advance simulation time has been granted). Six classes of services (Figure 1) have to be provided by the RTI to be defined HLA-compliant. These classes are specified within the FIS and they can be summarized as follows:

- Federation Management. These services allow federates to create and destroy federation execution and join or resign from an existing federation.
- Declaration Management. These services allow federates to publish federate data and subscribe to updated data produced by other federates.
- Object Management. These services allow federate to create and delete object instances, and produce and receive data.
- Ownership Management. These services allow federates to transfer the ownership of object data during the federation execution.
- Time Management. These services coordinate the advancement of simulation time of the federates.

- Data Distribution Management. These services can reduce unnecessary information transfer between federates by filtering out irrelevant data.

HLA overcame the shortcomings of the DIS standard by being simulation-domain neutral (it was not developed referred to any specific language, therefore HLA provides means to describe any data exchange format as required and specifying functionalities for time management and bandwidth control (see the FIS module).

HLA provides Application Programming Interfaces (APIs) for all the classes of services just mentioned, but the RTI software and algorithms are not defined by HLA. Also the operations in the *FederateAmbassador* need to be implemented at the federate level, as part of the federate code or some interface service (*adapter*).

These facts have caused the growth of multiple HLA-RTI implementations (e.g. [80], [81]) and the development of *ad-hoc* solutions for the adapters on the federate side [25]. In particular the last aspect represents one of the most relevant criticalities in applying HLA for distributed simulation: the lack of a standardized approach to adapt a simulator within an HLA-based distributed architecture, makes a distributed simulation project time expensive since a lot of implementation is required in addition to the effort to build the simulation model.

This consideration represents one of the leading arguments for the research community in the direction of the development of additional complementary standards (Section 3) to ease the creation and management of an HLA-based distributed simulation.

It is the objective of the next section to analyze the state of the art on the adoption and advancements in the use of HLA-based distributed simulation technique.

2.2. Distributed simulation in civilian applications

Herein the attention is focused on distributed modeling of complex systems in civilian domain.

HLA constitutes an enabler for implementing the distributed simulation. The standard, though, was conceived for military applications and several problems arise when trying to interoperate heterogeneous simulators in civilian applications (the terminology Commercial off-the-shelf discrete-event simulation packages CSPs [62] will be used to describe commercially available simulators for the analysis of Discrete Event Systems).

Boer [12] investigated the main benefits and criticalities related to the industrial application of HLA by interviewing the actors involved in the problem (e.g. simulation model developers, software houses, HLA experts, [9]-[11]). The results of the survey showed that CSPs vendors do not see direct benefits in using distributed simulation, whereas in industry HLA is considered troublesome because of the lack of experienced users and the complexity of the standard. In addition, as suggested in [49], although the approaches and general methods used in military and civilian simulation communities have similarities, the terminology turns out to be completely different [36]. For instance, terms like live simulation and virtual emulator are rarely used in civilian applications although equivalent techniques are commonly applied.

The major difference between military and civilian domain resides in the way simulation models are developed and what are the goals to meet when starting a simulation development process. In the military community where time and budget constraints are not the key elements leading the building process of a simulation tool, languages such as C++ and Java are usually adopted because of their flexibility. On the other hand, in the civilian simulation community, the use of commercial simulation tools (e.g. Arena, Automod, Simio, ProModel, Simple++, SLX, etc.) is the common practice. These tools satisfy the need of rapidly and cost-effectively developing the simulation models.

The use of commercial simulation tools hinders the applicability of the HLA standard for the realization of a distributed simulation model, because the direct access to the HLA APIs (Section 2.1.) from the commercial simulation software tools is not usually possible. Therefore, the enhancement of HLA with additional complementary standards [51] and the definition of a standard language for CSPs represent relevant and not yet solved technical and scientific challenges ([25], [49], [50]). Recently, the COTS Simulation Package Interoperability-Product Development Group (CSPI-PDG), within the Simulation Interoperability Standards Organization (SISO), worked on the definition of the CSP interoperability problem (Interoperability Reference Models, IRMs) [74] and on a draft proposal for a standard to support the CSPs interoperability (Entity Transfer Specification, ETS) [61].

2.2.1. Literature review

The application of distributed simulation in the civilian domain has been studied by reviewing the available literature with the purpose to individuate which civilian domain distributed simulation is generally called, which motivations underlie the adoption of the distributed technique, which technical and scientific challenges have been faced and which solutions have been proposed so far. More than 100 papers have been analyzed and classified according to three criteria:

- *Domain of application*, i.e. the specific civilian sector where the distributed simulation was applied (e.g. manufacturing domain, health care, emergency, etc.).
- *Motivation* underlying the adoption of the distributed simulation, i.e. the main problem leading to the adoption of the distributed simulation architecture.
- *Technical issue* faced, i.e. the solutions to integration issue or enhancement to services of the HLA architecture proposed within the considered article.

Most of the articles can be classified according to more than one criterion and Figure 3 shows the percentage of articles falling in each category.

The bibliographic search was carried out by considering the following keywords: Distributed Simulation, Operations Research and Management, Commercial Simulation Packages, Interoperability Reference Models, High Level Architecture, Manufacturing

Systems, Discrete Event Simulation, Manufacturing Applications, Industrial Application and Civilian Applications. These keywords brought to the identification of 26 core papers based on the number of citations ([4], [12], [8], [11], [9], [10], [20], [28], [29], [30], [33], [74], [75] , [48], [50], [47], [49], [58], [53], [59], [56], [68], [70], [68], [73] and [71]). These papers can be considered as introductory to the topic of distributed simulation in civilian domain. Starting from these articles the bibliographic search followed the path of the citations, i.e. works cited by the core papers and papers citing the core ones were considered. This search brought to the selection of 83 further articles. The overall 109 papers were published mainly in the following journals and conference proceedings: Advanced Simulation Technologies Conference, European Simulation Interoperability Workshop, European Simulation Symposium, Information Sciences, International Journal of Production Research, Journal of the Operational Society, Journal of Simulation, Workshop on Principles of Advanced and Distributed Simulation and Winter Simulation Conference.

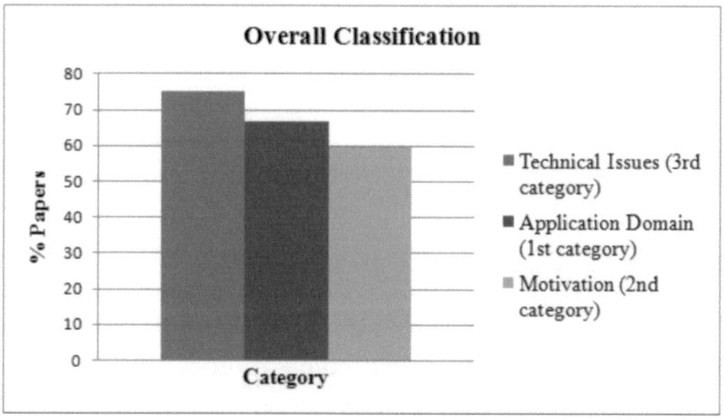

Figure 3. Overall Classification Criteria

2.2.2. *Domain of application*

More than 60% (Figure 3) of the analyzed papers propose an application in a specific field of the civilian domain (e.g. [72], [42]). As stated in [46], transportation and logistics are typical application areas of simulation and also the first areas where HLA has been tested by the civilian simulation community. Manufacturing and health care are acquiring increasing importance because of the growth of the extended enterprise and the increase in attention for bio-pharmaceutical supply chains respectively.

The main fields of application of DS (Figure 4) are Supply Chain Management (33% of the papers stating the domain of interest) (e.g. [64], [22], [42]), Manufacturing (29% of the papers) (e.g. [69], [77]), Health Care (e.g. [34]) and Production Scheduling & Maintenance (e.g. [72]), 17% of the articles are related to Health Care.

A further analysis was carried out by considering only the articles related to the manufacturing domain, aiming at evaluating whether the contributions addressed real industrial case applications or test cases applications. Only 22% of the articles address a real case, thus confirming the outcomes obtained by Boer [8] in the analysis of the adoption of distributed simulation in the manufacturing environment. Although solutions have been developed for the manufacturing domain, this technique is still far from being adopted as an evaluation tool by industrial companies because the end-users perceive HLA and distributed simulation as an additional trouble rather than a promising approach [10]. As a consequence, a lot of effort is put in the development of decision support systems that hide the complexity of a distributed environment to the end user [41].

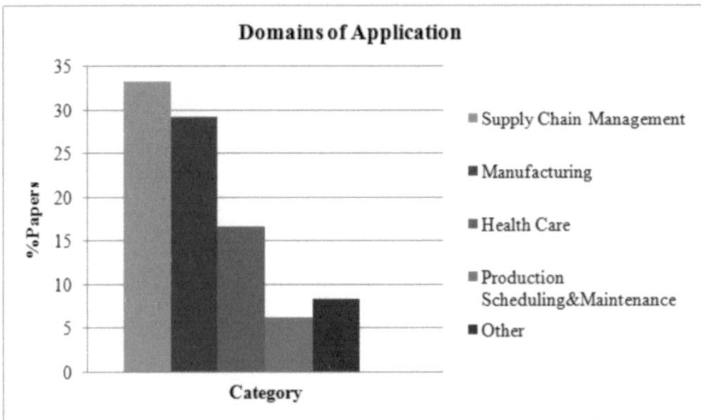

Figure 4. Distributed Simulation Main fields of application

2.2.3. *Motivations underlying the adoption of the distributed simulation*

As Boer stated in [8], if a problem can be solved by a monolithic simulation model created in a single COTS simulation package and a distributed approach is not explicitly required the simulation practitioner should certainly choose the monolithic solution in the selected CSP. Similarly, Strassburger [49] suggests that if a maintainable and reusable monolithic application can be built, then there is no point in building it in a distributed platform.

However, there are simulation projects where the distributed solution seems more advantageous and straightforward [38] because it enables to cope with:

1. Demand for *reusability* of the simulator output of the simulation project. Here the word reusability is adopted both in terms of the possibility to reuse simulators already developed and of building new simulators that can be readopted in the future.
2. *Lack of Shared information*. This is the case when no one modeler has enough information to develop the simulator. This condition holds when the whole system to be modeled is divided into subsystems owned by different actors that do not want to share data related to their subsystems.
3. *System complexity*. In this case no one modeler has enough knowledge to realize the whole simulation model.

All the papers stating a motivation for using DS mention the system complexity (e.g. [22], [72], [30], [32]), whereas 44% of the papers the demand for reuse [78]. The low percentage (around 5%) of papers using DS to cope with lack of shared information can be partially traced back to the lack of real industrial applications that still characterizes DS in civilian environment [76].

2.2.4. *Technical issue faced*

Over 70% of the articles deal with technical issues, thus showing that HLA and DS experts are putting a lot of effort in the enhancement and extensions of HLA-based DS to face civilian application problems. Indeed, the application of distributed simulation to civilian domain still presents several technical issues. In particular four main research areas can be identified:

1. *Integration of commercial discrete event simulators (CSP).* Several CSPs are put together and synchronized by means of the services offered by the HLA infrastructure.
2. *Interoperability reference models and entity transfer.* The papers in this category work in the standardization of the communication between federates within an HLA-compliant federation (Section 3.).
3. *Time management enhancement.* The issues related to the time synchronization of federates are faced.
4. *RTI-services extension.* In this case the services listed in Section 2.1. are enhanced for specific applications [82].

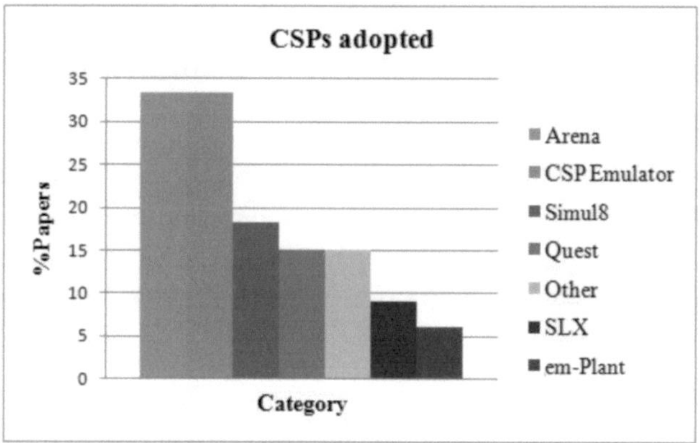

Figure 5. CSP adopted

The outcome of the review was that the integration of CSPs is the most addressed technical issue, (45% of the papers) nonetheless the integration of real CSPs (i.e. not general purpose programming languages) still represents a challenging topic. Figure 5 gives a picture of the main CSP solutions that have been adopted in the literature. In particular, the *y-axis* reports the percentage of articles that use one of the listed CSPs (e.g. [37], [21], [67]) within the papers that deal with the interoperation of simulators. It can be noticed that CSP Emulators (e.g. [68], [38]) are still one of the most used solutions because of the problems related to interoperating real CSPs. These problems are mainly caused by the lack of data and information mapping between simulators and the difficulty in interacting (e.g. send and receive information, share the internal event list) while the simulation is running.

The enhancement of the Run Time Infrastructure services is another key research topic ([2], [19]). In particular, the scientific articles deal with two open issues: (1) Time management (e.g. [39], [31]), (2) Data Distribution Management (e.g. [66], [73]). Time Management has received more attention (91% of the papers dealing with enhancement of RTI services) because it strongly influences the computational performance of the distributed simulation.

The following conclusions can be drawn from the literature analysis:

- There is a lack of distributed simulation applications in real manufacturing environments.
- The interoperability of CSPs still represents a technical challenging problem.
- The HLA architecture components (in particular RTI services) must be extended and adapted to civilian applications.

The issues faced to model complex systems give raise to problems in the distributed simulation realization that are strongly dependent on the specific application case [57] and the solutions to those needs can be implemented through an RTI in many different (incompatible) ways. Each way can be promising in its own context, but the lack of a standardized approach means it is difficult for end users and CSP vendors to choose a solution thus slowing down the spreading of the distributed simulation technique.

3. A standard based approach for distributed simulation

The main contribution in standardization of distributed modeling has to be credited to Simulation Interoperability Standard Organization (SISO) and in particular to the High Level Architecture Simulation Package Interoperability Forum (HLA-CSPIF). HLA-CSPIF and, then, COTS Simulation Package Interoperability Product Development Group (CSPI-PDG) were created in an attempt to produce a generalizable solution to the problem of integrating distributed heterogeneous CSPs.

As highlighted at the end of Section 2.2., a standardized approach is fundamental to increase the use of distributed simulation in civilian applications. This led to formalize the problem of the interaction between simulators in civilian applications and to standardize the way data are exchanged between federates within the federation.

The main results of the standardization effort are the Interoperability Reference Models (IRMs) and the Entity Transfer Specification (ETS), that will be presented in Section 3.1 and 3.2, respectively. Section 3.3 shows the distributed simulation communication protocol presented in [77], based on IRMs and the extended ETS proposed in [38].

3.1. Interoperability reference model

An interoperability problem type is meant to capture a general class of interoperability problems, whereas an IRM is meant to capture a specific problem within that class.

The creation of the IRMs has proved to be a powerful tool in the development of standards in the distributed simulation research community, as it is now possible to create solutions for specific integration problems.

An initial set of interoperability problems identified by the CSPI-PDG have been divided into a series of problem types that are represented by IRMs. The purpose of an IRM can be to [54]:

- Clearly identify the CSP/model interoperability capabilities of an existing distributed simulation.
- Clearly specify the CSP/model interoperability requirements of a proposed distributed simulation.

There are four types of IRM:

- Type A - Entity Transfer (Section 3.1.1.)
- Type B - Shared Resource (Section 3.1.2.)
- Type C - Shared Events (Section 3.1.3.)
- Type D - Shared Data Structure (Section 3.1.4)

The literature review showed that around 21% of the articles dealing with technical issues (Section 2.2.1.) taken into consideration deal with IRMs (e.g., [39], [56], [51], [63], [55] and [34]).

3.1.1. IRm type A: Entity transfer

IRM Type A Entity Transfer represents interoperability problems that can occur when transferring an entity from one simulation model to another. This IRM type is the most formalized at the present moment, since the need to transfer entities between simulators has been the most popular feature requested from the distributed simulation users so far.

Figure 6 shows an illustrative example of the problem of Entity Transfer where an entity *e1* leaves activity A1 in model M1 at time T1 and arrives at queue Q2 in model M2 at time T2. For example, if M1 is a car production line and M2 is a paint shop, then the entity transfer happens when a car leaves M1 at T1 and arrives in a buffer in M2 at T2 to wait for painting.

There are three subtypes of IRM Type A:

- IRM Type A.1 General Entity Transfer is defined as the transfer of entities from one model to another such that an entity *e1* leaves model M1 at T1 from a given place and arrives at model M2 at T2 at a given place and T1 ≤ T2 or T1 < T2. The place of departure and arrival will be a queue, workstation, etc.
- IRM Type A.2 Bounded Receiving Element. The IRM Type A.2 is defined as the relationship between an activity A in a model M1 and a bounded queue Q2 in a model M2 such that if an entity e is ready to leave activity A at T1 and attempts to arrive at the bounded queue Q2 at T2 then:
  - If the bounded queue Q2 is empty, the entity e can leave activity A at T1 and arrive at Q2 at T2
  - If the bounded queue Q2 is full, the entity e cannot leave activity A at T1; activity A may then block if appropriate and must not accept any more entities.
  - When the bounded queue Q2 becomes not full at T3, entity e must leave A at T3 and arrive at Q2 at T4, activity A becomes unblocked and may receive new entities at T3.

- T1 ≤ T2 and T3 ≤ T4.
- If activity A is blocked then the simulation of model M1 must continue.

- IRM Type A.3 Multiple Input Prioritization. As shown in Figure 7, the IRM Type A.3 Multiple Input Prioritization represents the case where a model element such as queue Q1 (or workstation) can receive entities from multiple places. Let us assume that there are two models M2 and M3 which are capable of sending entities to Q1 and that Q1 has a First-In-First-Out (FIFO) queuing discipline. If an entity *e1* is sent from M2 at T1 and arrives at Q1 at T2 and an entity *e2* is sent from M3 at T3 and arrives at Q1 at T4, then if T2 < T4 we would expect the order of entities in Q1 would be e1, e2. A problem arises when both entities arrive at the same time, i.e. when T2 = T4. Depending on implementation, the order of entities would either be *e1, e2* or *e2, e1*. In some modeling situations it is possible to specify the priority order if such a conflict arises, e.g. it can be specified that model M1 entities will always have a higher priority than model M2 (and therefore require the entity order *e1, e2* if T2 = T4). Furthermore, it is possible that this priority ordering is dynamic or specialized.

Note that the IRM sub-types are intended to be cumulative, i.e. a distributed simulation that correctly transfers entities from one model to a bounded buffer in another model should be compliant with both IRM Type A.1 General Entity Transfer and IRM Type A.2 Bounded Receiving Element.

The largest part of the papers analyzed in the literature review deal with the basic IRM that is the general entity transfer (85% of the papers dealing with IRMs), since most of the applications are related to Supply Chain Management and queues can often be modeled as infinite capacity as they represent inventory, production or distribution centers.

The situation is slightly different if the manufacturing domain is considered. Indeed, IRM Type A.2 (70% of the articles dealing with IRMs), is largely adopted when a production system is modeled, because the decoupling buffers between workstations must be usually represented as finite capacity queues.

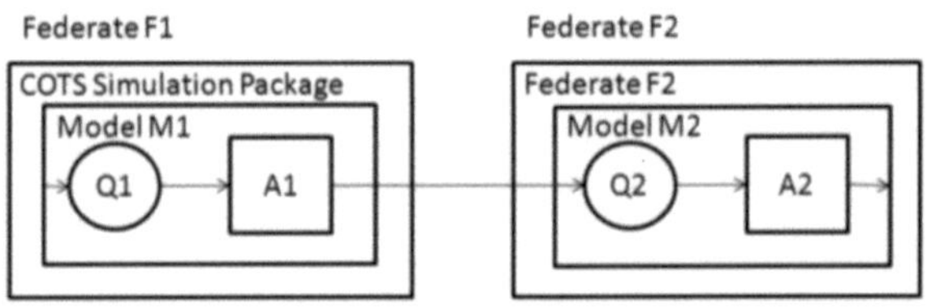

Figure 6. Typr A.1 IRM

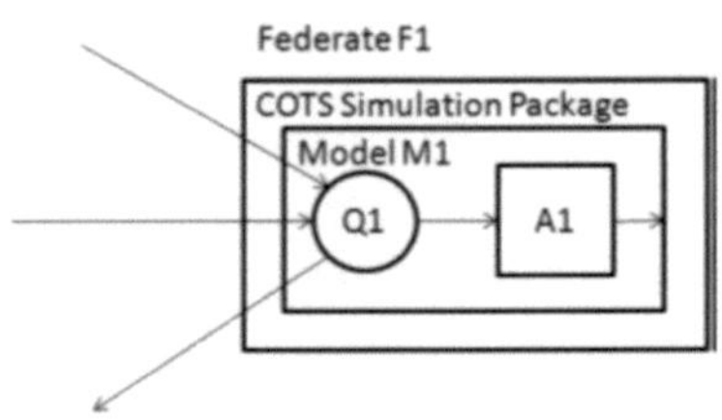

Figure 7. Type A.3 IRM

3.1.2. IRM type B: Shared resource

IRM Type B deals with the problem of sharing resources across two or more models in a distributed simulation. A modeler can specify if an activity requires a resource (such as machine operators, conveyor, pallets, etc.) of a particular type to begin. If an activity does require a resource, when an entity is ready to start that activity, it must therefore be determined if there is a resource available. If it is available then the resource is secured by the activity and held until the activity ends. A resource shared by two or more models leads to a problem of maintaining the consistency change the deleted part with: related to the status of the resource..

Currently there is only one IRM Type B subtype. The IRM Type B.1 General Shared Resources is defined as the maintenance of consistency of all copies of a shared resource such that:

- if a model M1 wishes to change its copy of the resource at time T1 then the value of all other copies of the same resource present in other models will be guaranteed to be the same at T1.
- if two or more models wish to change their copies of the resource at the same time T1, then all copies will be guaranteed to be the same at T1.

3.1.3. Type C: Shared event

IRM Type C deals with the problem of sharing events (such as an emergency signal, explosion, etc.) across two or more models in a distributed simulation.

There is currently one IRM Type C sub-type. The IRM Type C.1 General Shared Event is defined as the guaranteed execution of all local copies of a shared event E such that:

- if a model M1 wishes to schedule a shared event E at T1, then its local copies (i.e. the events scheduled within each simulator) will be guaranteed to be executed at the same time
- if two or more models wish to schedule shared events E1, E2, etc. at T1, then all local copies of all shared events will be guaranteed to be executed at the same time T1.

3.1.4. Type D: Shared data structures

IRM Type D Shared Data Structure deals with the sharing of variables and data structures across simulation models that are semantically different to resources (e.g. while referring to the supply chain environment, this is the case with bill of material information management or shared inventory). There is currently one IRM Type D sub-type.

3.2. Entity transfer specification

CSPI-PDG proposed the Entity Transfer Specification (ETS) Protocol ([51], [52], [62]) which refers to the architecture shown in Figure 8.

Each federate consists of a COTS simulation package (CSP), a model that is executed by the CSP, and the middleware that is a sort of adaptor interfacing the CSP with the Run Time

Infrastructure (RTI) (Figure 8). The relationship between CSP, the middleware and the RTI consists of two communication flows: (1) middleware-RTI, (2) CSP-middleware. The middleware translates the simulation information into a common format so that the RTI can share it with the federation. In addition, the middleware receives and sends information from/to the CSP. The CSP communicates with its middleware by means of Simulation Messages (Section 3.3.1.) [77]. The presence of Simulation Messages is the main difference between the reference architecture in Figure 8 and the architecture proposed by Taylor et al [51].

ETS defines the communication between the sending model and the receiving model (*ModelA* and *ModelB* in Figure 8, respectively) at RTI level. In particular the way the middleware of each federate and the RTI exchange information is formalized by means of a special hierarchy of interaction classes. An interaction class is defined as a template for a set of characteristics (parameters) that are shared by a group of interactions (refer to IEEE HLA standard, 2000). The middleware of the sending model instantiates a specific interaction class and sends it to the RTI whenever an entity has to be transferred.

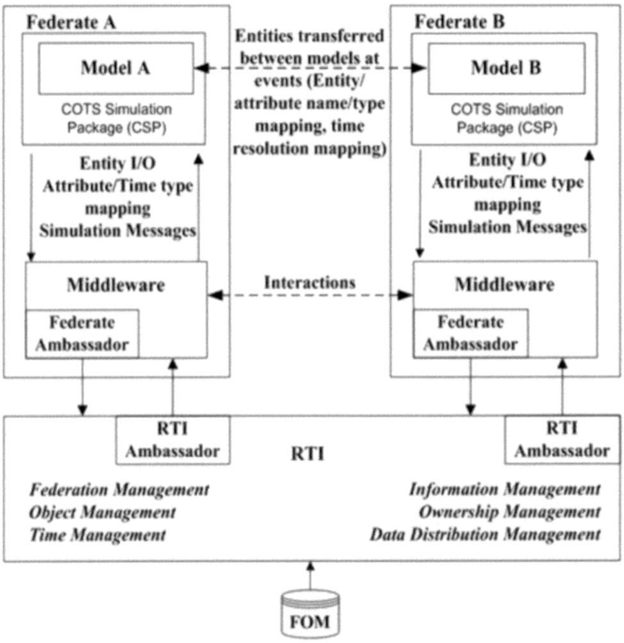

Figure 8. ETS refrence Architecture

Two main issues arise when the simulation information is translated for the RTI:

- A common time definition and resolution is necessary. For example, the time should be defined as being the time when an entity exits a source model and then instantaneously arrives at the destination model (i.e. the definition of time implies zero transit time) [62]. Alternatively, it should be defined including the notion of travel time and the entity would arrive at destination with a delay equal to the transfer time.

- The representation of an entity depends on how the simulation model is designed and implemented in a CSP. Indeed, the names that the modelers use to represent the same entity might be different. A similar problem can arise for the definition of simple datatypes. For example, some CSPs use 32-bit real numbers while others use 64-bit [62].

Straburger [50] highlighted some relevant drawbacks in the ETS standard proposal:

- It is not possible to differentiate multiple connections between any two models.
- ETS suggested interaction hierarchy does not work: a federate subscribing to the superclass will never receive the values transmitted in the interaction parameters.
- The specification of user defined attributes is placed into a complex datatype, this introduces new room for interoperability challenges as all participating federates have to be able to interpret all of the attributes.
- There are some possibilities for misinterpretation in the definition of Entity and EntityType introducing changes in FOMs whenever a new entity type is talked about.

Furthermore, the ETS was not designed to manage the Type A.2. IRM and the interaction class hierarchy refers to the entity transfer without taking into account any information on the state of the receiving buffer (e.g. Q2 in Figure 6).

One of the most recent contributions in ETS was presented by Pedrielli et al. [77] and consists in the proposal of a new class hierarchy. In particular, different subclasses of the transferEntity class were defined to enable the differentiation of multiple connections between models and the Type A.2. IRM management. After developing the interaction class hierarchy, following the HLA standard, the Simulation Object Model (SOM) and Federation Object Model (FOM) were developed to include the novel interactions and their parameters. In particular, extensions were proposed to the Interaction Class Table (part of the OMT, Section 2.1) to include the novel interaction classes and define them as publish and/or subscribe. The Parameter Table (part of the OMT, Section 2.1) was modified to include the proposed parameters for the interactions and the Datatype table was also modified.

The resulting class hierarchy consists of the following classes [38]:

- *transferEntity*, as already defined in the ETS protocol. This superclass allows the federate subscribing to all the instances of entity transfer. The instantiation of this class is related to visualization and monitoring tasks.
- *transferEntityFromFedSourceEx* is a novel subclass defined for every exit point, where FedSourceEx stands for the name or abbreviation of a specific exit point in the sending model. This class is useful to group the instances of the transferEntity that are related to the source federate, so that the FedSourceEx can subscribe to all these instances without explicitly naming them.
- *transferEntityFromFedSourceExToFedDestEn* is a novel subclass defined for each pair of exit point (Ex) of the source federate (FedSource) and entry point (En) of the receiving federate (FedDest). This class is instantiated both when a sending model needs to transfer a part to a specific entry point in the receiving model, and when a receiving model needs to share information about a buffer state or about the receipt of a part from

a specific exit point in a sending model. The models both publish and subscribe to this subclass that was designed to create a private communication channel between the sending and the receiving model. Therefore, if an entry point in the receiving model is connected with multiple federates/exit points, then the receiving federate has to inform about the state of the entry point by means of multiple interactions, each dedicated to a specific federate/exit point. This communication strategy is not the most efficient in a generic case, but it offers the possibility to deliver customized information and adopt different priorities for the various federates/exit points. This becomes fundamental in real industrial applications where information sharing among different subsystems is seen as a threat, thus rising the need to design a protocol that creates a one to one communication between each pair of exit/entry point inside the corresponding sending/receiving model.

The ETS Interaction class table was modified to represent the *transferEntityFromFedSourceEx* and *transferEntityFromFedSourceExToFedDestEn* subclasses. The Parameter Table was modified to include the parameters of the novel interaction class *transferEntity FromFedSourceExToFedDestEn*. The introduced parameters are presented below. The similarities with the parameters included in the ETS Parameter Table are highlighted where present.

- *Entity*. It is a parameter of complex datatype containing the *EntityName* that is used to communicate the type of the entity, and the *EntityNumber* that is used to communicate the number of entities to be transferred. The *EntityName* and *EntityNumber* play the role of the *EntityName* and *EntitySize* defined in ETS, respectively [51], [62].
- *ReceivedEntity*. It refers to the entity received by the receiving federate and has the same type of the parameter Entity.
- *Buffer_Availability*. It was designed to enable the communication about the buffer availability.
- *SourcePriority*. This parameter was designed to communicate the priority assigned to the entity source, so that the infrastructure can be further extended to manage Type A.3 IRM (Section 3.1)
- *EntityTransferTime*. It defines the simulation time when the entity is transferred to the destination point, i.e. the arrival time. Herein the entity leaves the source node and reaches the destination node at the same time, since it is assumed that the transferred entity instantaneously arrives at destination.

The resulting tables are shown in Tables 1, 2 and 3.

HLAinteractionRoot(N)	TransferEntity (N/S)	TransferEntityFrom FromFedSourceExA (N/S)	TransferEntity FromFedSourceExAToFedDestEnC(PS)
			TransferEntity FromFedSourceExBToFedDestEnC(PS)

Table 1. Table 1. Interaction Class Table

Interaction	Parameter	DataType	Transportation	Order
TransferEntityFromFedSourceExAtoFedDestEnC (P/S)	Entity	EntityType	HLAreliable	TimeStamp
	ReceivedEntity	EntityType	HLAreliable	TimeStamp
	Buffer_Availability	HLAInteger32BE	HLAreliable	TimeStamp
	SourcePriority	HLAInteger32BE	HLAreliable	TimeStamp
	EntityTransferTime	HLAFloat32BE	HLAreliable	TimeStamp

Table 2. Parameter Table

Record Name	Field		Encoding
	Name	Type	HLAfixedRecord
EntityType	EntityName	HLAASCIIString	
	EntityNumber	HLAInteger32BE	

Table 3. Fixed Record Datatype table

3.3. Communication within the HLA-based integration infrastructure

Pedrielli et al. [77] proposed a communication protocol (see Section 3.3.2) based on messages to manage the communication between a CSP and its middleware (or adapter). The communication protocol was conceived for the distributed simulation of network of Discrete Event Manufacturing Systems characterized by the transfer of parts in the presence of buffers with finite capacity, with the objective to minimize the use of zero-lookahead [62] for the synchronization of federates.

Before illustrating the communication protocol, Section 3.3.1. presents the concept and functioning of Simulation Messages created to support the communication between a CSP and the middleware. The communication protocol between federates is then explained in Section 3.3.2., whereas Section 3.3.3. defines the hypotheses needed to minimize the zero lookahead when applying the proposed protocol.

3.3.1. Simulation messages

The function of the simulation messages depends on the role played by the federate. The sending federate uses the message for communications concerning the need of sending an entity to another model (outgoing communication) and/or information on the availability of the target receiving federate (incoming communication). The receiving federate uses the message for communications concerning the buffer state and/or the acceptance of an entity (outgoing communication) and/or the receipt of an entity from other models (incoming communication). Simulation Messages are implemented as a class that is characterized by the following attributes:

- time referring to the simulation time when the message is sent to the middleware from the CSP. This attribute is used by the middleware to determine the TimeStamp of the interaction that will be sent to the RTI.

- BoundedBuffer containing the information about the availability of the bounded buffer in the receiving model.
- TransferEntityEvent representing the entity transfer event scheduled in the sending model event list and contains the information about the entity to be transferred and the scheduled time for the event.
- ExternalArrivalEvent representing the external arrival event that is scheduled in the receiving model. It contains the information about the entity to be received and the scheduled time for the event.
- ReceivedEntity representing the information about the entity that was eventually accepted by the receiving model.

3.3.2. Communication protocol

Herein, the behavior of the sending federate will be analyzed at first, then the receiving federate will be taken under consideration. Finally an example will be described to clarify how the protocol works.

Sending Federate. The CSP of the sending federate sends a message to its middleware whenever a *TransferEntityEvent* is scheduled, i.e. the departure event of an entity from the last workstation of the sending model is added to the simulation event list. Then, the middleware uses the attributes time and *TransferEntityEvent* to inform the RTI about the need of passing an entity, while the simulation keeps on running (the *TransferEntityEvent* time corresponds to the *EntityTransferTime* presented in Section 3.2.).

The request to advance to *EntityTransferTime* is sent by the middleware to the RTI as soon as all local events scheduled for that time instant have been simulated.

After the time has advanced, the middleware can inform the CSP of the sending model about the state of the receiving buffer in the receiving model. If the receiving buffer is not full, then the workstation can simulate the *TransferEntityEvent*, otherwise it becomes blocked. From the blocking instant until when the middleware informs the sending model that the receiving buffer is not full, the model keeps on sending requests for time advance at the lookahead value.

Receiving Federate. The CSP of the receiving federate sends a message to its middleware whenever a change in the buffer availability occurs. This message contains the updated value of the attribute *boundedBuffer* representing the availability of the buffer, i.e. the number of available slots. Then, the middleware communicates this information to the RTI via interactions. In particular the information on the availability of the buffer represents a field of the timestamped interaction *transferEntityFromFedSourceExToFedDestEn* (Section 3.2.).

If the change in the buffer availability is due to the arrival of an entity from another model, then the update of the information does not imply zero lookahead and the communication is characterized by defining the entity that has been accepted (i.e. the *ReceivedEntity* attribute). If the buffer state change is not related to an external arrival, then the update of the buffer information may imply a zero lookahead whenever it is not possible to determine an advisable a-priori lookahead for the federation (Section 3.3.3) [62]. After being informed by the middleware that another federate needs to transfer an entity, the receiving model actually simulates the arrival of the entity only if the buffer is not full, otherwise the arrival is not simulated and the workstation in the sending model becomes blocked.

Example. The application of the Simulation Messages can be better appreciated by presenting an example (see Figure 9) that is characterized as follows: (1) the reference production system is represented in Figure 10, (2) the buffer Q2a at time t accommodates a number of parts that is greater than zero and less than the buffer capacity and an entity enters workstation W1a, (3) a departure event from workstation W1a is scheduled for time t' = t + p, where p represents the processing time of the leaving entity at station W1a, (4) during the time interval (t; t'), no event happening in the federate M2 (local event) influences the state of the buffer Q2a. Since W1a is the last machine in model M1, the departure event is also a *TransferEntityEvent*. Therefore, the CSP sends a message to its middleware containing time (t) and the *TransferEntityEvent* attributes. After receiving the message, the middleware of the sending model informs the RTI via interaction.

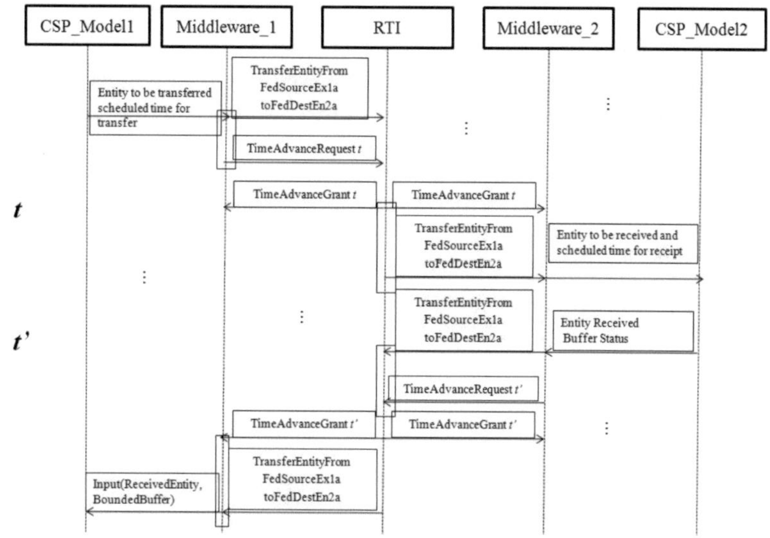

Figure 9. Communication Protocol

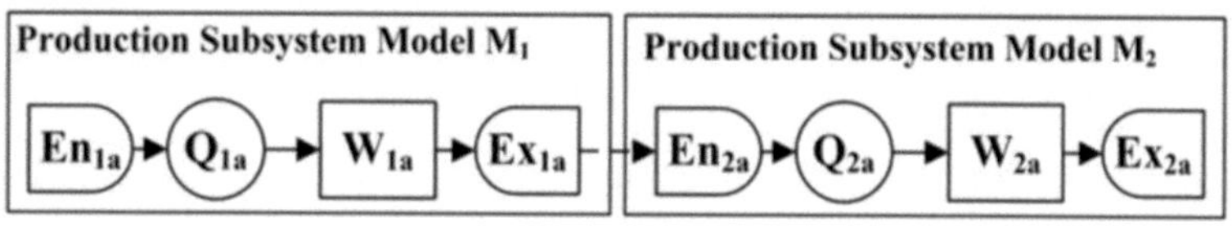

Figure 10. Reference Production System

Once the RTI time advances to time t, the middleware of the receiving model receives the information about the need of the sending model to transfer an entity at time t'. Then, the middleware sends to the receiving model a simulation message containing the *ExternalArrivalEvent*. The receiving model simulates the external arrival as soon as the simulation time advances to t' and all local events for that time have been simulated (since the buffer Q2a is not full according to the example settings). A message is sent to the middleware of the receiving model containing the updated level of Q2a (attribute *BoundedBuffer*) together with the information concerning the recently accommodated part (attribute *ReceivedEntity*).

Afterwards, the middleware sends two interactions to the RTI: one is with a TimeStamp equal to t′ and contains the updated state of the buffer Q2a and the receipt of the entity, the other contains the request of time advance to time t′. Once the RTI reaches time t′, the middleware of the sending model receives the information regarding the state of Q2a and the received entity by means of the RTI. Since the entity has been delivered to the receiving model, the station W1a is not blocked by the middleware.

3.3.3. Formal characterization of the communication protocol

This section defines which hypotheses are needed to minimize the occurrence of zero lookahead if the communication protocol afore presented is adopted.

Let represent an external event scheduled in the i-th federate j-th exit (entry) point at simulation time t, where t can be, in general, smaller or equal to t′ that represents the simulation time when the event is supposed to be simulated. An event scheduled into the event list of a simulator is defined as external if one of the three following conditions holds:

- The realization of the event depends on the state of a federate that is, in general, different from the one that scheduled the event. One example of external event is when the sending federate (model M1) wants to transfer a part to the receiving federate (model M2), the possibility for the leaving event to be simulated depends on the state of the queue of the receiving federate.
- The simulation of the event leads to changes into the state of other federates in the federation. This is the case when the downstream machine to the first buffer in the receiving model takes a part from the buffer thus changing its availability, this information must be delivered to sending models that are willing to transfer an entity, the state of the sending federate(s) will change depending on the information delivered (W1a can be idle or blocked).
- The event is not scheduled by the simulator that will simulate it, but is put into the simulation event list by the middleware associated with the simulator. This is the case of the External Arrival Event (Section 3.3.1.).

Herein three types of external events are taken into consideration:

- *Entity transfer event*, this event happens when a sending federate wants to transfer a part to a receiving federate.
- *Buffer_availability* change event, this is a departure event from the workstation downstream the buffer representing the entry point of the receiving model.
- *External Arrival event*, this event is scheduled by the middleware inside the simulation event list of the receiving federate every time a part has to be transferred.

If t < t′ it means that the simulation message can be sent by the sending (receiving) model and received by the target federate before the event contained in the message has to be executed. When this happens it is possible to minimize the use of the zero lookahead for the communication between federates.

The federate sending the message can communicate with $t < t'$ under the following conditions:

- The Entity transfer event is scheduled when the part enters the machine in the sending model. In this case the event is put into the event list a number of time units before it must be simulated that is at least equal to the processing time of the workstation under analysis. In the case the event is scheduled when the part leaves the workstation, then the condition holds if there exists a transfer time between the sending and the receiving model that is larger than zero and no events affect the arrival of the part once the transfer has started. The conditions aforementioned are not unrealistic when a manufacturing plant is simulated: both in the case the event is scheduled before or after the processing activity, the time between the departure from the exit point and the arrival to the entry point is in general not negligible. Nonetheless, in both the aforementioned cases, it is required that no other external events are scheduled by the same exit point during the interval $(t; t')$. This can happen when, after a leaving event has been scheduled, a failure affects the machine. In this case the information related to the part to be transferred has already been delivered and cannot be updated. As a consequence an external arrival event will be scheduled in the receiving model although the sending model will not be able to deliver the part because of the machine failure. A solution to this issue is part of present research.
- It is possible to communicate in advance the Buffer availability change event if the workstation processing the part schedules the leave event in advance to its realization and no other events are scheduled by the same workstation during the interval $(t; t')$. However, the zero lookahead cannot be avoided by the sending federate which cannot be aware of the downstream buffer changes and then it will send update request at the lookahead value.
- The zero lookahead can be avoided if the middleware of the receiving model can schedule the External Arrival event in advance and then inform the target federate(s) on the availability of the buffer in advance. This condition can be satisfied based on the entity transfer event characteristics.

In the case one or more of the conditions aforementioned do not hold than the communication protocol shown in the Section 3.3.2. implies the use of zero lookahead. If the hypothesis that no additional external events must be scheduled by the same exit (entry) point in a federate (sending or receiving) within the time interval $(t; t')$ is relaxed, then the middleware should be able to arrange incoming events in a queue and wait before delivering the information to the simulator until when the most updated information has been received. However it is quite straightforward to show that, in the worst case, the middleware should wait until when the simulation time reaches t', and therefore all the time advance requests would be performed at the zero lookahead. This relaxation is under analysis.

4. Distributed simulation in industry: A case study

This section presents an application of the architecture and communication protocol proposed in Section 3.3. The aim is to evaluate whether the use of distributed simulation can help to better analyze the dynamics of complex manufacturing systems, whereas the comparison between the HLA-based distributed simulation and a monolithic simulation in terms of computational efficiency is out of scope.

Herein the attention is focused on the industrial field represented by sheet metal production. In this industrial field, the production systems are characterized by the presence of at least two subsystems interacting with each other: the Roll Milling System and the Roll Shop. The Roll Milling System produces sheet metal using milling rolls that are subject to wearing out process. The rolls must be replaced when worn out to avoid defects in the laminates. Then the Roll Shop performs the grinding process to recondition the worn out rolls.

The following types of rolls have been considered in the case study:

- Intermediate Rolls (IMR) representing back-up rolls that are not in contact with the laminate. Depending on the size of the roll, the IMR roll will be referred to as IMR_1 (the bigger roll type) and IMR_2.
- Work Roll (WR) representing the rolls directly in contact with the laminate. Also in this case there are two subtypes that will be referred to as WR_1 (the bigger roll type) and WR_2.

If the attention is focused on the rolls, then the resulting production system is a closed loop: the Roll Milling System sends batches of worn out rolls to the Roll Shop following a given policy and receives reconditioned rolls back. Both the Roll Milling System and the Roll Shop have finite capacity buffers, therefore it is necessary to check whether the buffer in the system receiving the rolls has enough free slots. The deadlock in the closed loop is avoided because the number of rolls circulating in the system is less than the number of available slots (taking into account also the machines) and it is constant.

The two subsystems forming a closed loop are strongly related and their reciprocal influence should be considered to properly evaluate the performance of the whole factory by means of a comprehensive simulation model. However, both the Roll Shop designer and the Roll Milling System owner usually develop their own detailed simulator to evaluate the performance of their subsystem, because of the lack of shared information between the owner of the Roll Milling System and the Roll Shop designer. Indeed, the owner of the Roll Milling System usually provides the Roll Shop designer only with aggregated data about the yearly average demand of worn out rolls to be reconditioned. Moreover, the Roll Milling System works according to specific roll changing policies that are not shared with the Roll Shop designer even if they play a key role in the dynamics of the whole factory. For instance, when a roll is worn out, also the other rolls are checked and if their remaining duration is under a predefined threshold, then they are sent to the Roll Shop together with the completely worn out rolls. The presence of roll changing policies determines a relation between different roll types, since a roll can be sent to the Roll Shop depending on the behavior of other roll types.

Even if separate simulators are developed, the Roll Shop designer still has to evaluate the performance of the whole system while taking into account the influence of the Roll Milling System related to (1) the arrival rate of worn out rolls from the Roll Milling System that is estimated from the yearly aggregate demand of reconditioned rolls and (2) the acceptance of the reconditioned rolls sent by the Roll Shop (closed loop model).

In addition to this the Roll Shop designer has to guarantee that the Roll Milling System the Roll Shop is being designed for, never waits for reconditioned rolls interrupting the production of sheet metal.

Hence, even if simulation models are available, usually the Roll Shop designer over-dimensions the number of rolls that have to populate the whole system to avoid any waiting time at the Roll Milling System. For this reason we focused our first analysis on the effect of the number of rolls over the performance of the whole system (Roll Milling System and Roll Shop).

Sections 4.1 and 4.2 will give the main details characterizing the simulation models, whereas Section 4.3 will present (Section 4.3.1 and Section 4.3.2) and compare (Section 4.3.3) two approaches for the system analysis.

4.1. The Roll Shop simulator

In this section the simulator of the Roll Shop developed for the case of interest will be explained in detail.

The Roll Shop simulator has been developed in C++ language using the object oriented paradigm. The C++ based simulator emulates a COTS, following the approach showed in Wang et al. [67], [68]. Figure 11 gives a pictorial representation of the simulation model for the Roll Shop under analysis.

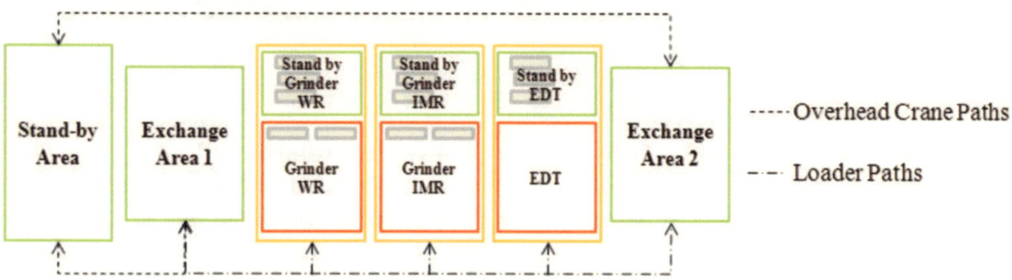

Figure 11. The Roll Shop System representation

The Roll Shop is composed by the following elements (Figure 11).

- *Buffer areas* where the rolls are kept while waiting to be transferred to the Roll Shop or the Milling system. The buffer areas can be:

- *Stand-by Area,* represents the entry/exit point of the Roll Shop and only the overhead crane can access it. The batches of rolls coming from the Roll Milling System and the batches of grinded rolls to send back to the Roll Milling System are placed here.
- *Exchange Area 1,* represents the interface between the part of the system managed by the overhead-crane and the grinding system served by the loader
- *Exchange Area 2,* represents the interface between the exit of the grinding system and the exit from the roll shop system managed by the overhead-crane.

- *Workstations* where the rolls are reconditioned;
  - *Grinder Machine Work* (Grinder WR), i.e. grinding machine dedicated to *work roll* type.
  - *Grinder Machine Intermediate* (Grinder IMR), i.e. grinding machine dedicated to *intermediate roll* type.
  - *Electro-Discharge Texturing Machine* (EDT), i.e. machine executing a surface finishing process on the rolls.
- Two types of conveyors:
  - *Loader,* i.e. an automatic conveyor that transfers rolls to the grinding machines
  - *Overhead crane,* i.e. a semi-automatic handling system to transfer rolls from the arrival point in the roll shop (Stand by area) to the exchange areas of the system

All the workstations, but the EDT, have two buffer positions (grey rectangles in Figure 11) within the working area.

The main parameters needed to configure the simulator are:

- *Size* of the roll batches
- *Type* of rolls (e.g. WR_1 and WR_2, IMR_1 and IMR_2 as described in Section 4)
- *Process Sequence* for every roll, i.e. the process plan and the assignment of operations to the production resources in the Roll Shop. The process sequence depends on the roll type.
- *Processing time* of each operation. Those processing time have been considered deterministic for the experiments presented in this section (i.e. no failures affect the workstations).
- *Transfer time, i.e.* the time to move the roll within the Roll Shop. This is a deterministic quantity as a function of the path.
- *Number of workstations* of each type. We have dedicated machines, in particular we have one grinding machine dedicated to WR type (i.e. WR_1 and WR_2) and one grinding machine dedicated to IMR type roll (i.e. IMR_1 and IMR_2). We have one EDT machine (processing only WR type rolls). In case the WR type roll finds the dedicated grinding machine occupied and the IMR machine is idle, then it can be processed also on the IMR machine. However the time required for the process increases.

Table 4 summarizes the output statistics that can be gathered from the Roll Shop simulator. The minimum, maximum average values are supplied for every statistic, and the variance is computed as well.

Component	Statistics	Unit of Measurement
Roll	Number of rolls in the Roll Shop system for every roll type	-
	System Time for every roll type	[min/roll]
	Grinding time for every roll type	[min/roll]
	Transfer time for every roll type	[min/roll]
Machine	Utilization	[%]
	Processing Time	[min/roll]
	Number of processed rolls	-
	Number of rolls in the buffer area	-
Conveyor	Transfer time	[min/transfer]
	Idle time	[min]
	Utilization	[%]
Buffer	Number of rolls in the buffer	-
	Waiting time in the buffer	[min/roll]

Table 4. Roll Shop Statistics

4.2. The Roll Milling System simulator

In this section the simulator of the Roll Milling System developed for the case of interest will be explained in detail.

The Roll Milling System simulator has been developed in C++ language. The C++ based simulator emulates a COTS, following the approach showed by Wang et al. [67], [68].

A generic milling system can be represented as shown in Figure 12, whereas the simulation model realized for the case presented is graphically represented in Figure 13.

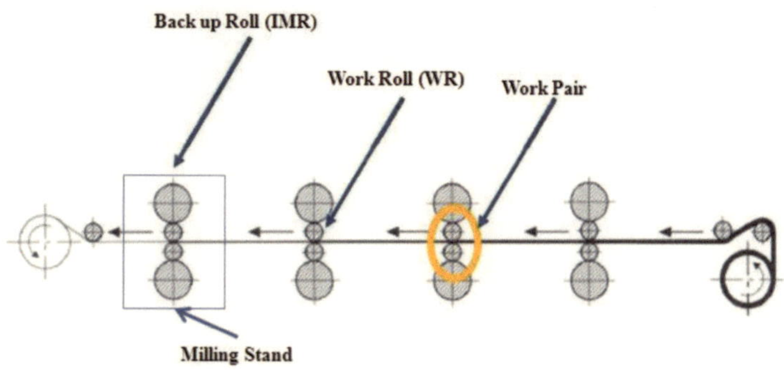

Figure 12. Roll Milling System [87]

Figure 13. Milling System Simulation Model

The Roll Milling System considered for the industrial case is composed of 5 stands (refer to Figure 12 for the definition of *stand*) each characterized by a milling station and a buffer for rolls (Figure 13). It is important to highlight that more rolls are needed with respect to those in use to process the metal sheet in order to minimize the waiting time of the milling system when the rolls are changed.

Once the rolls worn out, the Roll Milling System interrupts the process and the rolls must be replaced. The rolls are then replaced with the rolls of the same type available at the rolls buffer (Figure 13) close to the station. In the case the rolls required are not available the Roll Milling System stops producing. The worn out rolls are sent to the Roll Shop System as soon as a batch of rolls is ready (the size of the batch is usually fixed and represents a parameter of the simulation model). The batches are then transferred to the Roll Shop by means of a special conveyor, the *Transfer Car*.

The interval between roll changes (*interchange time*) is the interval between two consecutive sending of the same roll to the Roll Shop. This interval is fundamental to the correct sizing of the Roll Shop Plant (i.e. the number of grinding machines for every type, the size of the buffer areas) and of the number of rolls, for every type, populating the system.

This interval is mainly related to the life duration and the roll changing policies adopted within the system. For the industrial case considered, these policies can be brought back to two main criteria:

1. If an IMR roll has to be changed, since this requires high setup time, also the WR rolls from the same station are sent to the Roll Shop even if they have not reached their end on life.
2. If more batches have almost reached their life duration, they are sent together to grinding process to avoid multiple sending.

The main parameters to configure the simulation model are:

- Number of stands
- Capacity of the buffers at every stand
- Number of rolls in the system
- Size of roll batches and types of rolls
- Life duration for each roll type

The Roll Milling System simulator supplies the following output statistics (Table 5):

Component	Statistics	Unit of Measurement
Roll	Number of rolls in the Roll Milling system for every roll type	-
	Interchange Time	[min]
Station	Utilization	[%]
	Waiting Time	[min]
	Busy Time	[min]
	Number of rolls in the buffer area	-
Buffer	Number of rolls in the buffer	-
	Waiting time in the buffer	[min/roll]
Service Level	Busy Time/Simulation Time	[%]

Table 5. Roll Milling System Simulator Statistics

The Service Level (SL) is the typical key performance indicator (KPI) for analyzing the Roll Milling System. It is defined as the time the Roll Milling System produces sheet metal over the time it is operative (the total simulation time in the case of the computer experiment). It must be highlighted that the system cannot produce if all the required rolls are not present at each station. For this reason every station will have the same "Busy Time", i.e. the same time period during which it produces. The service level of a system can be increased managing the plant in a way such that we always have an available batch of rolls to change the worn out ones that have to be sent to the Roll Shop.

It is then clear that the Service Level would be reduced if the Roll Milling System had to wait too long for reconditioned rolls coming from the Roll Shop.

4.3. Sheet metal production system analysis: Approach A, approach B

The Roll Shop designer may choose two possible approaches to estimate the effects of the Roll Shop design choices over the performance of the Roll Milling System:

- *Approach A.* The Roll Milling System is represented by a simplified model inside the detailed simulation model of the Roll Shop (Section 4.1). This simplified model roughly reproduces the Roll Milling System by generating the arrival of worn out rolls and accepting the reconditioned ones.
- *Approach B.* The performance of the whole factory is evaluated by adopting the HLA-based Infrastructure integrating the simulators of the Roll Milling System and of the Roll Shop.

4.3.1. Approach A

The simulator of the whole system is realized introducing within the detailed simulation model of the Roll Shop a simplified model of the Roll Milling System. Also this simulator is developed in C++ language.

More specifically, the Roll Milling System is modeled as an oracle sending (receiving) batches of worn out (reconditioned) rolls to the Roll Shop based on the information on the wearing out time of every roll type.

It must be stressed that the simulator of Approach A cannot be considered as a proper monolithic simulator of the whole factory, since the Roll Milling System is only poorly modeled.

The input parameters needed to initialize the oracle are:

- Number of rolls present in the system, when the simulation starts, for every type. In this case the number of rolls represents the total number of rolls in the Roll Milling System. The only initial condition we can set using this simulation model is that all the rolls at the simulation start are at the beginning of their life and are all in the Roll Milling System, whereas the Roll Shop is empty.
- Life duration of every roll type.
- Size of the batch of rolls for every roll type (the rolls are moved in batches as explained in Section 4.1 and Section 4.2).

Table 6 defines the life duration of the rolls (for every type) given as input for Approach A..

Roll Type	WR_1	WR_2	IMR_1	IMR_2
Batch Size [#Rolls/batch]	8	2	8	2
Duration [min/batch]	438	288	3228	1452

Table 6. Rolls parameters

Table 7 reports the results in terms of average intervals between rolls change, estimated running the simulation model of the Roll Milling System (Section 4.2) as standalone. The life duration given as input to the Roll Milling System simulator was the same given in Table 6. Although the life duration used is the same the resulting intervals between rolls change are different because of the effect of the roll changing policies which are not taken into account in the simplified model of the Roll Milling System (Section 4.2).

Time to change rolls batch [min/batch]	Detailed Model
WR_1	432
WR_2	288
IMR_1	3024.04
IMR_2	1440

Table 7. Rolls interarrival time estimated running the MS simulation model

In particular the intervals between rolls change result decreased because the WR_2 type, characterized by the shorter life duration, draws the change of all other roll types. This result represents a first motivation towards the distributed approach. Indeed it shows that the aggregated information related to the interchange time is not enough to represent the dynamics of the Roll Milling System. A possible idea to increase the accuracy of Approach A could be to replace data in Table 6 with the estimated information in Table 7, thus taking into account, at least on average, the behavior of the Roll Milling System.

However, the missing feature of this approach is that in any case, even updating the life duration, we will not be able to reproduce the *dynamics* over time of the Roll Milling System which is what really affects the estimation of the performance of the whole system more than the average behavior captured by data in Table 7.

In addition, the only statistics of the Roll Milling System that can be gathered if Approach A is adopted are:

- Average Number of Rolls at every stand
- Average Waiting Time for grinded rolls
- Service Level. In particular, the utilization time (Section 4.2) is estimated as the difference between the total simulation time and the computed sum of time intervals during which the number of rolls for at least one type are equal to 0. If this condition is verified then the Roll Milling System cannot produce and has to wait for reconditioned rolls. As defined in Section 4.2, the ratio between this time and the total simulation time gives the estimate of the service level.

Summarizing, Approach A supplies an approximate estimate of the whole system performance:

- The real behavior of the Roll Milling System cannot be precisely modeled since it is reduced to a black box sending and receiving rolls (e.g. the roll changing policies are not modeled).
- The performance of the Roll Milling System cannot be evaluated in detail (e.g. mean starvation time for every station, mean level of roll buffers, etc).

4.3.2. Approach B

In Approach B, the detailed models of the two subsystems are directly adopted. Indeed the two simulators described in Section 4.1 and 4.2 are linked together thanks to the HLA-based developed infrastructure (Figure 15).

The HLA-based architecture was implemented as follows:

- MAK-RTI 3.3.2 (www.mak.com) was used as the RTI component implementation.
- The middleware was developed in C++ language following the specifications defined in Section 3.3 and was named *SimulationMiddleware*.

The *FederateAmbassador* and *RTIAmbassador* were provided by MAK-RTI as C++ classes and were linked to the *SimulationMiddleware*. Further extensions were needed to implement the proposed modification to ETS (Section 3.2) and the Simulation Messages (Section 3.3.1). The former required a modification to *FederateAmbassador* class, whereas the latter led to the development of a new C++ class. The *SimulationMiddleware* was implemented to manage the information contained in Simulation Messages.

The interaction tables (Section 3.2) developed for this case are shown in Tables 10,11,12 and 13.

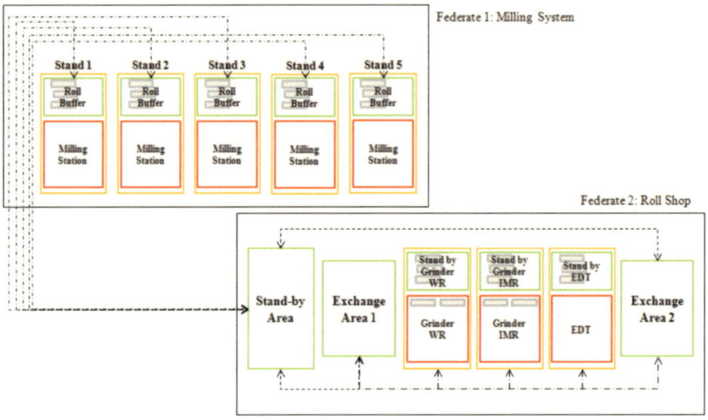

Figure 14. Distributed Simulation of Roll Shop and Roll Milling System

4.3.3. Comparison between approach A and approach B

The two approaches have been compared by designing a set of experiments characterized as follows:

- Three experimental conditions were designed with reference to the total number of rolls circulating in the whole system. These three conditions were defined as Low, Medium, High level.
- The simulation run length was set to six months (4 weeks of transitory period). The roll changing policy adopted for the Approach B simulator has been kept fixed throughout the experimentation.

The results of the experiments are shown in Table 8. Approach A and Approach B are compared in terms of the estimated Service Level (refer to Section 4.2 for the definition). The results show that the difference between the two approaches is larger for the High and Medium level conditions.

When the level of rolls is Low the roll changing policy does not affect the overall performance of the production system because the Roll Milling System is frequently starved and therefore the estimations are similar (consider also that the Low level condition has no industrial meaning, but was considered to study the service level response). In case of Medium and High level conditions the workload of the rolls in the Roll Shop can be strongly influenced by the roll changing policy, thus generating a higher difference in the estimation between the two approaches.

Approach B generates more accurate estimates of the whole system performance because the Roll Milling System is represented with high level of detail and the roll changing policies are modeled. In addition to this if Approach B is used, detailed information related to the Roll Milling System performance are available. Table 9 shows an example of output for the average statistics related to the Roll Milling System from the simulation of the High level condition in Table 8.

Experimental Conditions	*Approach A*	*Approach B*	*Percentage difference*
High Level	0.995	0.872	12.3
Medium Level	0.946	0.682	27.7
Low Level	0.308	0.273	3.5

Table 8. Service Level Results

Output Statistic	**Value**
Busy Time	5.2[months]
Waiting Time	0.8[months]
Utilization	87.2[%]
Number of Rolls	Stand 1: 1.177 WR 1.470 IMR
	Stand 2: 1.177 WR 1.470 IMR
	Stand 3: 1.177 WR 1.470 IMR
	Stand 4: 1.177 WR 1.470 IMR
	Stand 5: 3.401 WR 1.740 IMR
Service Level	87.2[%]

Table 9. Roll Milling System simulator. Output Statistics

The number of rolls in the system together with the roll changing policy have a strong impact on the workload conditions of the Roll Shop. This aspect can only be taken into account under Approach B and the results show the dramatic difference in performance estimation due to this additional information that characterizes the model.

Approach A is overestimating the performance of the system, thus decreasing its effectiveness as supporting tool for decision making.

Based on the analysis carried out so far, it was decided to design further experiments to analyze the behavior of the whole system with different starting workload conditions, i.e.

the number of rolls that are present in the Roll Milling System when the simulation starts. These experiments can be useful to analyze the ramp-up period and select the roll changing policy that avoids the arising of critical workload conditions. These additional experiments can be carried out only adopting *Approach B*, since the starting workload conditions cannot be modeled with *Approach A* (Section 4.3.1). Indeed, the simplified model generates rolls for the Roll Shop independently from the starting workload conditions. Therefore, the simplified model would generate roll arrivals even if all the rolls are already located in the Roll Shop, thus incorrectly increasing the number of rolls in the whole system.

The second set of experiments was designed as follows:

- Two *types of roll* circulate in the factory (*WR* and *IMR*). The roll of type *IMR* has a longer roll life than *WR*
- For each type of roll three levels of the *Starting Workload* (i.e. number of rolls) in the Roll Milling System are considered
- Three simulation run lengths are considered, i.e. 1 week, 2 weeks and 4 weeks
- The roll changing policy is fixed for all experiments
- total number of rolls is equal to the *High* level of the previous experimentation and is fixed for all the experiments.

Fig. 15 shows the main effects plot for the *Service Level* evaluated by simulating the 27 resulting experimental conditions with *Approach B*. The plot suggests a significant influence of the factor *Starting Workload for WR*. This roll type assumes a key role because of its short roll life (Section 4.3.1). If the *Starting Workload For WR* is *Low*, the Roll Shop can hardly follow the frequent roll requests of *WR* from the Roll Milling System and low values of *SL* are observed. This phenomenon occurs in all conditions of the simulation lengths, however it mitigates when the simulation length increases. Indeed the *SL* tends to a stationary value that is independent from the starting conditions. Nonetheless this analysis can be useful for the Roll Milling System owner that can individuate critical conditions, thus designing roll changing policies that avoid the occurrence of these situations during the ramp-up period.

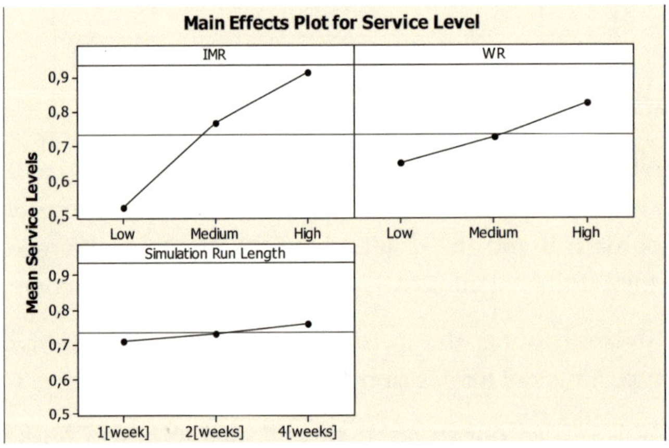

Figure 15. Main Effects Plot of Service Lovel, Approach B

HLAinteraction Root(N)	Transfer Entity (N/S)	TransferEntityFromFedSource Milling(N/S)	TransferEntityFromFedSourceExMillingtoFedDestEnRollShop(P/S)
	Entity (N/S)	TransferEntityFromFedSource RollShop(N/S)	

Table 10. Interaction Class Table

Interaction	Parameter	DataType	Transportation	Order
TransferEntityFromFedSourceExMillingtoFedDestEnRollShop(P/S)	RollEntity	RollType	HLAreliable	TimeStamp
	ReceivedRollEntity	RollType	HLAreliable	TimeStamp
	RollShopBuffer	HLAInteger32BE	HLAreliable	TimeStamp
	SourcePriority	HLAInteger32BE	HLAreliable	TimeStamp
	EntityTransferTime	HLAFloat32BE	HLAreliable	TimeStamp

Table 11. Parameter Table for Roll Shop SOM

Interaction	Parameter	DataType	Transportation	Order
TransferEntityFromFedSourceExRollMillingtoFedDestEnRollShop (P/S)	RollEntity	RollType	HLAreliable	TimeStamp
	ReceivedRollEntity	RollType	HLAreliable	TimeStamp
	MillingBuffer	HLAInteger32BE	HLAreliable	TimeStamp
	SourcePriority	HLAInteger32BE	HLAreliable	TimeStamp
	EntityTransferTime	HLAFloat32BE	HLAreliable	TimeStamp

Table 12. Parameter Table for Milling System SOM

Record Name	Field		Encoding
	Name	Type	HLAfixedRecord
RollType	Roll	HLAASCIIString	
	BatchSize	HLAInteger32BE	

Table 13. Fixed Record Datatype Table (SOM) for Roll Shop and Milling Systems

5. Conclusions

This chapter has presented an overview of distributed simulation and the contemporary innovations in the use of distributed modeling to support the analysis of complex systems. The attention has been focused on CSP-based distributed simulation in civilian applications and especially in manufacturing domain. The literature review showed the need of a general standard solution to the distributed simulation of systems within the civilian domain to increase the use of distributed techniques for the analysis of complex systems. The Interoperability Reference Model standard released by SISO CSPI-PDG has been analyzed. Furthermore, the latest advancements in ETS standard proposal and Communication Protocol between federates within HLA-based distributed environment have been shown. In the end the industrial application of an HLA-based infrastructure proved the benefits of the distributed approach to effectively analyze the behavior of complex industrial systems.

The distribute simulation is acquiring more and more interest also because the need to interoperate several simulators leads to the need to improve the methodologies and the tools developed so far for the simulation of Discrete Event Systems. In other words the issues arising when trying to make several simulators interoperate are those issues the simulation community has been dealing with in the last years.

Further effort is needed in the formalization of the IRMs. In particular the presence of shared resources and the modeling of the control policies characterizing the system represent challenging issues not yet solved.

The communication protocols need to be enhanced and the zero-lookahead issue represents one of the main bottlenecks against the increase of efficiency of distributed simulations. Research effort is necessary to come up with new algorithms enabling the avoidance of zero-lookahead. In this area the research on protocols that do not force to send interaction at every time unit to communicate the state of the federates, but enable the interaction depending on the system state (Adaptive Communication Protocols) look promising.

The need of a shared data model ([26], [7]) and of a common definition of the objects which are input and output of the simulation and a common simulation language, are all scientific and technical challenging topics that make research in distributed simulation always up to date.

In particular the definition of a common reference model to describe information generated by each simulator while it is running will be a key factor for the success of the distributed simulation technique. A fundamental contribution in this field was given by the Core Manufacturing Simulation Data CMSD [7], but the interoperability between simulators is still far from being reached. The data modeling research topic is wider than what just stated and covers several areas and simulation is just one of those. For example proposals to standardize the information modeling for manufacturing systems have been done in [83-84].

The European project Virtual Factory Framework VFF ([38] [85-86]) represents one of the latest proposals from the research community in terms of framework supporting the interoperability between digital tools. Future research will evaluate if the VFF approach can be exploited by distributed simulation applications.

Author details

Giulia Pedrielli and Tullio Tolio
Politecnico di Milano, Dipartimento di Ingegneria Meccanica, Milano (MI), Italy

Walter Terkaj and Marco Sacco
Istituto Tecnologie Industriali e Automazione (ITIA), Consiglio Nazionale delle Ricerche (CNR), Milano (MI) Italy

Acknowledgement

The research reported in this chapter has received funding from the European Union Seventh Framework Programme (FP7/2007-2013) under grant agreement No: NMP2 2010-228595, Virtual Factory Framework (VFF). Sections of this chapter are based on the paper: Pedrielli, G., Sacco, M., Terkaj, W., Tolio, T., Simulation of complex manufacturing systems via HLA-based infrastructure. *Journal Of Simulation, to be published.* Authors would like to acknowledge Professor Taylor S.J.E and Professor Starssburger S. for their ongoing support and their work the in developing current range of standards for distributed simulation. Authors acknowledge Tenova Pomini Company for providing the support to build the industrial case.

6. References

[1] Ieee standard for modeling and simulation (m amp;s) high level architecture (hla) - framework and rules. IEEE Std. 1516-2000, pages i-22, 2000.

[2] Khaldoon Al-Zoubi and Gabriel A. Wainer. Performing distributed simulation with restful web services approach.

[3] James G. Anderson. Simulation in the health services and biomedicine, pages 275{293. Kluwer Academic Publishers, Norwell, MA, USA, 2003.

[4] J. Banks, J.C. Hugan, P. Lendermann, C. McLean, E.H. Page, C.D. Pegden, O. Ulgen, and J.R. Wilson. The future of the simulation industry. In Simulation Conference, 2003. Proceedings of the 2003 Winter, volume 2, pages 2033-2043 vol.2, dec. 2003.

[5] J. Banks and B.L. Nelson. Discrete-event system simulation. Prentice Hall, 2010.

[6] Lee A. Belfore, II. Simulation in environmental and ecological systems, pages 295-314. Kluwer Academic Publishers, Norwell, MA, USA, 2003.

[7] S. Bergmann, S. Stelzer, and S Strassburger. Initialization of simulation models using cmsd. In Simulation Conference (WSC), Proceedings of the 2011 Winter, WSC '11, pages 594-602. IEEE Press, 2011.

[8] C.A. Boer. Distributed Simulation in Industry. PhD thesis, Erasmus University Rotterdam, Rotterdam, The Netherlands, October 2005.

[9] C.A. Boer, A. de Bruin, and A. Verbraeck. Distributed simulation in industry - a survey part 1 - the cots vendors. volume 0, pages 1053-1060, Los Alamitos, CA, USA, 2006. IEEE Computer Society.

[10] C.A. Boer, A. de Bruin, and A. Verbraeck. Distributed simulation in industry - a survey part 3 - the hla standard in industry. In Simulation Conference, 2008. WSC 2008. Winter, pages 1094-1102, dec. 2008.

[11] Csaba Attila Boer, Arie de Bruin, and Alexander Verbraeck. Distributed simulation in industry - a survey: part 2 - experts on distributed simulation. In Proceedings of the 38th conference on Winter simulation, WSC '06, pages 1061-1068. Winter Simulation Conference, 2006.

[12] Csaba Attila Boer and Alexander Verbraeck. Distributed simulation and manufacturing: distributed simulation with cots simulation packages. In Proceedings of the 35th conference on Winter simulation: driving innovation, WSC '03, pages 829-837. Winter Simulation Conference, 2003.

[13] Vesna Bosilj-Vuksic, Mojca Indihar Stemberger, Jurij Jaklic, and Andrej Kovacic. Assessment of e-business transformation using simulation modeling. Simulation.

[14] Agostino G. Bruzzone. Preface to modeling and simulation methodologies for logistics and manufacturing optimization. Simulation, 80(3):119-120, 2004.

[15] Judith S. Dahmann, Frederick Kuhl, and Richard Weatherly. Standards for simulation: As simple as possible but not simpler the high level architecture for simulation. SIMULATION, 71(6):378- 387, 1998.

[16] Wilhelm Dangelmaier and Bengt Mueck. Simulation in business administration and management, pages 391-406. Kluwer Academic Publishers, Norwell, MA, USA, 2003.

[17] Paul K. Davis. Military applications of simulation, pages 407-435. Kluwer Academic Publishers, Norwell, MA, USA, 2003.

[18] T. Eldabi and R.J. Paul. A proposed approach for modeling healthcare systems for understanding. In Simulation Conference, 2001. Proceedings of the Winter, volume 2, pages 1412 -1420 vol.2, 2001.

[19] Richard Fujimoto, Michael Hunter, Jason Sirichoke, Mahesh Palekar, Hoe Kim, and Wonho Suh. Ad hoc distributed simulations. In Proceedings of the 21st International Workshop on Principles of Advanced and Distributed Simulation, PADS '07, pages 15-24, Washington, DC, USA, 2007. IEEE Computer Society.

[20] R.M. Fujimoto. Parallel and distributed simulation systems. Wiley series on parallel and distributed computing. Wiley, 2000.

[21] Boon Ping Gan, Peter Lendermann, Malcolm Yoke Hean Low, Stephen J. Turner, Xiaoguang Wang, and Simon J. E. Taylor. Interoperating autosched ap using the high level architecture. In Proceedings of the 37th conference on Winter simulation, WSC '05, pages 394-401. Winter Simulation Conference, 2005.

[22] Boon Ping Gan, Peter Lendermann, Malcolm Yoke Hean Low, Stephen J. Turner, Xiaoguang Wang, and Simon J. E. Taylor. Architecture and performance of an hla-based

distributed decision support system for a semiconductor supply chain. SimTech technical reports, 7(4):220-226, 2007.

[23] Sumit Ghosh and Tony Lee. Modeling and Asynchronous Distributed Simulation Analyzing Complex Systems. Wiley-IEEE Press, 1st edition, 2000.

[24] Strong D.R. Richards N. Goel N.C. Goel, S. A simulation-based method for the process to allow continuous tracking of quality, cost, and time. Simulation, 78(5):330-337, 2001.

[25] Hironori Hibino, Yoshiyuki Yura, Yoshiro Fukuda, Keiji Mitsuyuki, and Kiyoshi Kaneda. Manufacturing modeling architectures: manufacturing adapter of distributed simulation systems using hla. In Proceedings of the 34th conference on Winter simulation: exploring new frontiers, WSC '02, pages 1099-1107. Winter Simulation Conference, 2002.

[26] Marcus Johansson, Bjorn Johansson, Anders Skoogh, Swee Leong, Frank Riddick, Y. Tina Lee, Guodong Shao, and Par Klingstam. A test implementation of the core manufacturing simulation data specification. In Proceedings of the 39th conference on Winter simulation: 40 years! The best is yet to come, WSC '07, pages 1673-1681, Piscataway, NJ, USA, 2007. IEEE Press.

[27] Frederick Kuhl, Richard Weatherly, and Judith Dahmann. Creating computer simulation systems: an introduction to the high level architecture. Prentice Hall PTR, Upper Saddle River, NJ, USA, 1999.

[28] P. Lendermann. About the need for distributed simulation technology for the resolution of realworld manufacturing and logistics problems. In Simulation Conference, 2006. WSC 06. Proceedings of the Winter, pages 1119 -1128, dec. 2006.

[29] P. Lendermann, M.U. Heinicke, L.F. McGinnis, C. McLean, S. Strassburger, and S.J.E. Taylor. Panel: distributed simulation in industry - a real-world necessity or ivory tower fancy? In Simulation Conference, 2007 Winter, pages 1053-1062, dec. 2007.

[30] Richard J. Linn, Chin-Sheng Chen, and Jorge A. Lozan. Manufacturing supply chain applications 2: development of distributed simulation model for the transporter entity in a supply chain process. In Proceedings of the 34th conference on Winter simulation: exploring new frontiers, WSC '02, pages 1319-1326. Winter Simulation Conference, 2002.

[31] A. W. Malik. An optimistic parallel simulation for cloud computing environments. SCS M&S Magazine, 6:1-9, 2010.

[32] Charles McLean and Swee Leong. The expanding role of simulation in future manufacturing. In Proceedings of the 33nd conference on Winter simulation, WSC '01, pages 1478-1486, Washington, DC, USA, 2001. IEEE Computer Society.

[33] Charles McLean, Swee Leong, Charley Harrell, Philomena M. Zimmerman, and Roberto F. Lu. Simulation standards: current status, needs, future directions, panel: simulation standards: current status, needs, and future directions. In Proceedings of the 35th conference on Winter simulation: driving innovation, WSC '03, pages 2019-2026. Winter Simulation Conference, 2003.

[34] Navonil Mustafee, Simon J.E. Taylor, Korina Katsaliaki, and Sally Brailsford. Facilitating the analysis of a uk national blood service supply chain using distributed simulation. SIMULATION, 85(2):113-128, 2009.

[35] Brian Unger, and David Jefferson. Distributed simulation, 1988 : proceedings of the SCS Multiconference on Distributed Simulation, 3-5 February, 1988, San Diego, California / edited by Brian Unger and David Jefierson. Society for Computer Simulation International, San Diego, Calif. 1988.

[36] Ernest H. Page and Roger Smith. Introduction to military training simulation: A guide for discrete event simulations, 1998.

[37] Jaebok Park, R. Moraga, L. Rabelo, J. Dawson, M.N. Marin, and J. Sepulveda. Addressing complexity using distributed simulation: a case study in spaceport modeling. In Simulation Conference, 2005 Proceedings of the Winter, page 9 pp., dec. 2005.

[38] G. Pedrielli, P. Scavardone, T. Tolio, M. Sacco, and W. Terkaj. Simulation of complex manufacturing systems via hla-based infrastructure. In Principles of Advanced and Distributed Simulation (PADS), 2011 IEEE Workshop on, pages 1 -9, june 2011.

[39] P. Peschlow and P. Martini. Eficient analysis of simultaneous events in distributed simulation. In Distributed Simulation and Real-Time Applications, 2007. DS-RT 2007. 11th IEEE International Symposium, pages 244-251, oct. 2007.

[40] A. R. Pritchett, M. M. van Paassen, F. P. Wieland, and E. N. Johnson. Aerospace vehicle and air traffic simulation, pages 365-389. Kluwer Academic Publishers, Norwell, MA, USA, 2003.

[41] M. Raab, S. Masik, and T. Schulze. Support system for distributed hla simulations in industrial applications. In Principles of Advanced and Distributed Simulation (PADS), 2011 IEEE Workshop on, pages 1 -7, june 2011.

[42] M. Rabe, F.W. Jkel, and H. Weinaug. Supply chain demonstrator based on federated models and hla application. 2006.

[43] Stewart Robinson. Distributed simulation and simulation practice. SIMULATION, 81(1):5-13, 2005.

[44] Marco Sacco, Giovanni Dal Maso, Ferdinando Milella, Paolo Pedrazzoli, Diego Rovere, and Walter Terkaj. Virtual Factory Manager, volume 6774 of Lecture Notes in Computer Science, pages 397- 406. Springer Berlin, Heidelberg, 2011.

[45] B. Sadoun. Simulation in city planning and engineering, pages 315{341. Kluwer Academic Publishers, Norwell, MA, USA, 2003.

[46] Thomas Schulze, Steffen Strassburger, and Ulrich Klein. Migration of hla into civil domains: Solutions and prototypes for transportation applications. SIMULATION, 73(5):296-303, 1999.

[47] S. Straburger. Overview about the high level architecture for modeling and simulation and recent developments. Simulation News Europe, 16(2):5-14, 2006.

[48] S. Straburger, G. Schmidgall, and S. Haasis. Distributed manufacturing simulation as an enabling technology for the digital factory. Journal of Advanced ManufacturingSystem, 2(1):111 -126, 2003.

[49] S. Strassburger. Distributed Simulation Based on the High Level Architecture in Civilian Application Domains. PhD thesis, Computer Science Faculty, University Otto von Guericke, Magdeburg, 2001.

[50] Steffen Strassburger. The road to cots-interoperability: from generic hla-interfaces towards plug and play capabilities. In Proceedings of the 38th conference on Winter simulation, WSC '06, pages 1111-1118. Winter Simulation Conference, 2006.

[51] Taylor, Strassburger, S.J. Turner, M.Y.H. Low, Xiaoguang Wang, and J. Ladbrook. Developing interoperability standards for distributed simulaton and cots simulation packages with the cspi pdg. In Simulation Conference, 2006. WSC 06. Proceedings of the Winter, pages 1101 -1110, dec. 2006.

[52] S J E Taylor and N Mustafee. An analysis of internal/external event ordering strategies for cots distributed simulation. pages 193-198. Proceedings of the 15th European Simulation Symposium (ESS2003), Delft, 2003.

[53] Simon J. E. Taylor, Navonil Mustafee, Steffen Strassburger, Stephen J. Turner, Malcolm Y. H. Low, and John Ladbrook. The siso cspi pdg standard for commercial off-the-shelf simulation package interoperability reference models. In Proceedings of the 39th conference on Winter simulation: 40 years! The best is yet to come, WSC '07, pages 594-602, Piscataway, NJ, USA, 2007. IEEE Press.

[54] Simon J. E. Taylor, Stephen J. Turner, and Steffen Strassburger. Guidelines for commercial-off-the-shelf simulation package interoperability. In Proceedings of the 40th Conference on Winter Simulation, WSC '08, pages 193-204. Winter Simulation Conference, 2008.

[55] Simon J.E. Taylor. A proposal for an entity transfer specification standard for cots simulation package interoperation. In Proceedings of the 2004 European Simulation Interoperability Workshop, 2004.

[56] Simon J.E. Taylor. Distributed Modeling, pages 9:1-9:19. Chapman & Hall/CRC, 2007.

[57] S.J.E. Taylor. Realising parallel and distributed simulation in industry: A roadmap. In Principles of Advanced and Distributed Simulation (PADS), 2011 IEEE Workshop on, page 1, june 2011.

[58] S.J.E. Taylor, A. Bruzzone, R. Fujimoto, Boon Ping Gan, S. Strassburger, and R.J. Paul. Distributed simulation and industry: potentials and pitfalls. In Simulation Conference, 2002. Proceedings of the Winter, volume 1, pages 688- 694 vol.1, dec. 2002.

[59] S.J.E Taylor, M. Ghorbani, N. Mustafee, S. J. Turner, T. Kiss, D. Farkas, S. Kite, and S. Strassburger. Distributed computing and modeling & simulation: speeding up simulations and creating large models. In Proceedings of the 2011 Winter Simulation Conference, pages 1-15, December 2011.

[60] S.J.E. Taylor, M. Ghorbani, N. Mustafee, S.J. Turner, T. Kiss, D. Farkas, S. Kite, and S. Strassburger. Distributed computing and modeling amp; simulation: Speeding up

simulations and creating large models. In Simulation Conference (WSC), Proceedings of the 2011 Winter, pages 161-175, dec. 2011.

[61] S.J.E. Taylor, Xiaoguang Wang, S.J. Turner, and M.Y.H. Low. Integrating heterogeneous distributed cots discrete-event simulation packages: an emerging standards-based approach. Systems, Man and Cybernetics, Part A: Systems and Humans, IEEE Transactions on, 36(1):109- 122, jan. 2006.

[62] S.J.E. Taylor, Xiaoguang Wang, S.J. Turner, and M.Y.H. Low. Integrating heterogeneous distributed cots discrete-event simulation packages: an emerging standards-based approach. Systems, Man and Cybernetics, Part A: Systems and Humans, IEEE Transactions on, 36(1):109- 122, jan 2006.

[63] Sergio Terzi and Sergio Cavalieri. Simulation in the supply chain context: a survey. Computers in Industry, 53(1):3-16, 2004.

[64] J. Vancza, P. Egri, and L. Monostori. A coordination mechanism for rolling horizon planning in supply networks. CIRP Annals - Manufacturing Technology, 57(1):455- 458, 2008.

[65] Gabriel A. Wainer, Olivier Khaldoon, Al-Zoub Dalle, David R.C. Hill Hill, Saurabh Mittal, Jos L. Risco Martn, Hessam Sarjoughian, Luc Touraille, Mamadou K. Traor, and Zeigler Bernard P. Standardizing DEVS model representation. 2010.

[66] Gang Wang, Chun Jin, and Peng Gao. Adapting arena into hla: Approach and experiment. In Automation and Logistics, 2007 IEEE International Conference on, pages 1709-1713, aug. 2007.

[67] Xiaoguang Wang, Stephen John Turner, and Simon J. E. Taylor. Cots simulation package (csp) interoperability -a solution to synchronous entity passing. In Proceedings of the 20th Workshop on Principles of Advanced and Distributed Simulation, PADS '06, pages 201-210, Washington, DC, USA, 2006. IEEE Computer Society.

[68] Xiaoguang Wang, Stephen John Turner, Simon J. E. Taylor, Malcolm Yoke Hean Low, and Boon Ping Gan. A cots simulation package emulator (cspe) for investigating cots simulation package interoperability. In Proceedings of the 37th conference on Winter simulation, WSC '05, pages 402-411. Winter Simulation Conference, 2005.

[69] Xiaoguang Wang, Sthephen John Turner, Malcolm Yoke Hean Low, and Boon Ping Gan. A generic architecture for the integration of cots packages with the hla. In Proceedings of the 2004 Operational Research Society Simulation Workshop, Special Interest Group for Simulation, pages 225-233. Association for Computing Machinery's, 2005.

[70] Gregory Zacharewicz, Claudia Frydman, and Norbert Giambiasi. G-devs/hla environment for distributed simulations of workows. Simulation, 84:197-213, May 2008.

[71] zer Uygun, Ercan ztemel, and Cemalettin Kubat. Scenario based distributed manufacturing simulation using hla technologies. Information Sciences, 179(10):1533-1541, 2009. <ce:title>Including Special Issue on Artificial Imune Systems</ce:title>.

[72] Y. Zhang and L. M. Zhang. The Viewable Distributed Simulation Linkage Development Tool Based on Factory Mechanism. Applied Mechanics and Materials, 58:1813-1818, June 2011.

[73] Cosby, L.N. SIMNET: An Insider's Perspective. Ida documenT D-1661, Institute for Defense Analyses 1801 N. Beauregard Street, Alexandria, Virginia 22311-1772. pp: 1-19. March 1995

[74] SISO CSPI-PDG www.sisostds.org.

[75] SISO COTS Simulation Package Interoperability Product Development Group, (2010). Standard for Commercial - off - the - shelf Simulation Package Interoperability Referenve Models. SISO-STD-006-2010.

[76] Kubat, C., Uygun O. (2007). HLA Based Distributed Simulation Model for Integrated Maintenance and Production Scheduling System in Textile Industry. *P.T. Pham, E.E. Eldukhri, A. Soroka (Eds.), Proceedings of 3rd I*PROMS Virtual International Conference, 2–13 July 2007*: 413–418.

[77] Pedrielli, G., Sacco, M, Terkaj, W., Tolio, T. (2012). Simulation of complex manufacturing systems via HLA-based infrastructure. *Journal Of Simulation*. To be published.

[78] Kewley, R., Cook, J., Goerger, N., Henderson, D., Teague, E., (2008). "Federated simulations for systems of systems integration," *Simulation Conference, 2008. WSC 2008. Winter*, vol., no., pp.1121-1129, 7-10 Dec. 2008.

[79] Bruccoleri M, Capello C, Costa A, Nucci F, Terkaj W, Valente A (2009) Testing. In: Tolio T (ed) Design of Flexible Production Systems. Springer: 239-293. ISBN 978-3-540-85413-5.

[80] http://www.pitch.se/

[81] MAK RTI, www.mak.com

[82] Ke Pan; Turner, S.J.; Wentong Cai; Zengxiang Li; , "Implementation of Data Distribution Management services in a Service Oriented HLA RTI," *Simulation Conference (WSC), Proceedings of the 2009 Winter*, vol., no., pp.1027-1038, 13-16 Dec. 2009 doi: 10.1109/WSC.2009.5429557

[83] Colledani M, Terkaj W, Tolio T, Tomasella M (2008) Development of a Conceptual Reference Framework to manage manufacturing knowledge related to Products, Processes and Production Systems. In Bernard A, Tichkiewitch S (eds) Methods and Tools for Effective Knowledge Life-Cycle-Management. Springer: 259-284. ISBN 978-3-540-78430-2.

[84] Colledani M, Terkaj W, Tolio T (2009) Product-Process-System Information Formalization. In: Tolio T (ed) Design of Flexible Production Systems. Springer: 63-86. ISBN 978-3-540-85413-5.

[85] Pedrazzoli, P, Sacco, M, Jönsson, A, Boër, C (2007) Virtual Factory Framework: Key Enabler For Future Manufacturing. In Cunha, PF, Maropoulos, PG (eds) Digital Enterprise Technology, Springer US, pp 83-90

[86] Sacco M, Pedrazzoli P, Terkaj W (2010) VFF: Virtual Factory Framework. Proceedings of 16th International Conference on Concurrent Enterprising, Lugano, Switzerland, 21-23 June 2010.

[87] Kalpakjian Serope; Schmid Steven R. Book title: Tecnologia Meccanica, Editor: Pearon Education Year: 2008 The Figure 12 picture was inspired by the book

Chapter 2

The Speedup of Discrete Event Simulations by Utilizing CPU Caching

Wennai Wang and Yi Yang

Additional information is available at the end of the chapter

http://dx.doi.org/10.5772/50397

1. Introduction

Discrete event simulation (DES) has been widely used for both theoretical and application researches in various fields. The low-cost numerical experiments by DES can be carried out repeatedly to investigate the collective behavior or dynamics of a complex system which usually consists of a huge number of elements or is too expensive to be established realistically [3]. As for engineering applications, new algorithms, measures, or even standards, often require a great deal of DES experiments before actual deploying, especially in the field of communication networks. However, the feasibility of DES method relies not only on the correctness of computational model of the target system but also the spend in the time of computation. An experiment that costs over days of computer computation will limit the application area of DES considerably.

For a DES system designed for communication network simulation, which is implemented by the event-driven method, computation tasks waiting for processing are usually represented by their corresponding events. These events need to be maintained in-sequence by a systematic scheduler. The causality that a scheduler must preserve is usually guaranteed by sorting and dispatching according to the time of event. An event is to be suspended unless its time value is smaller than or equal to the present time. When a great number of tasks or events are in pending, the cost of event scheduling becomes the top contributor to the computational time. For a large scale communication network simulation, for example, scheduling can consume over 40% of the total computational time [12]. To accelerate scheduling, several practical algorithms have been proposed and adopted for some widely used simulators such as NS2 [9] and OMNet++ [14]. These algorithms can be categorized, according to the data structure used, into linear list, partitioning list, heap and tree. Among them, the partitioning list has attracted much attention.

The partitioning list algorithm proposed by R. Brown is called Calendar Queue (CQ) [4], where a data structure, named bucket, is used to partition events into a sequence of sub-lists.

CQ can reduce the time for event searching and decrease the complexity down to O(1). Since then, some improved algorithms, such as Dynamic CQ (DCQ) [1], SNOOPy CQ [13], and sluggish CQ [15], have been proposed in order to improve the adaptability of CQ to the event distribution in the time domain. However, the way of event enqueue and dequeue remains unchanged. For these algorithms, the complexity of O(1) is only valid for bucket searching and it doesn't take into account event locating within a bucket. In addition, the overhead for bucket managing inevitably results in some negative effects on the performance of computation. K. Chung, J. Sang and V. Rego compared some earlier-day scheduling algorithms and found that, for a token-ring network simulation, both CQ and DCQ are no better than those based on heap or tree structure [6].

In the past decades, researchers have put their interesting into parallel and distributed approaches [7] to speedup simulation by a cluster of computers or processors. Parallel and distributed event scheduling need to cope with challenges such as time synchronization and task balance and remain a gap to extensive adoption. An alternative way to speedup DES simulation, we think, is to exploit the potentials offered by the modern processors. As an instance of attempts, recently H. Park and P.A. Fishwick proposed a graphics processing units (GPU) based algorithm which shows 10-fold speedup [11]. However, until now the caching mechanism of processor has not been considered in existing event scheduling algorithms. Herein we provide a cache aware algorithm and verify its improvement on the performance by extending the conventional NS2.

The motivation to utilize caching of processor or CPU is straightforward. Both cache based method and cache aware method have been applied successfully in some heavy data-retrieving algorithms, including IP routing table lookup [5] and Radix tree implementation [2], where a huge amount of data are frequently accessed. This situation happens for a large scale DES as well, and CPU caching is benefit to speed up event scheduling.

The chapter is organized as follows. Section 2 gives a analysis of event driven mechanism of the NS2 simulator, an estimation on the number of event of the typical application, and a description of the conventional CQ algorithm. A cache aware algorithm is presented in Section 3, followed by a complexity analysis on enqueue and dequeue operations. In section 4, experiments to verify CPU cache awareness are provided, aiming at the evaluation of performance and its relationship with the size of event queue. Section 5 summarizes the chapter.

2. NS2 and Calendar Queue algorithm

For the typical event-driven DES system, simulation events waiting for processing are buffered in a queue and sorted according to their simulation time or timestamp. A simple and natural choice is to introduce a linear list to manage the queue of event. The number and distribution of events in the time domain hence dominate the performance of queue management. Such performance depends on not only simulation complexity, but also the implementation of a simulator. In order to make the issue tractable, the following analyses are developed on the widely used network simulator NS2 [9].

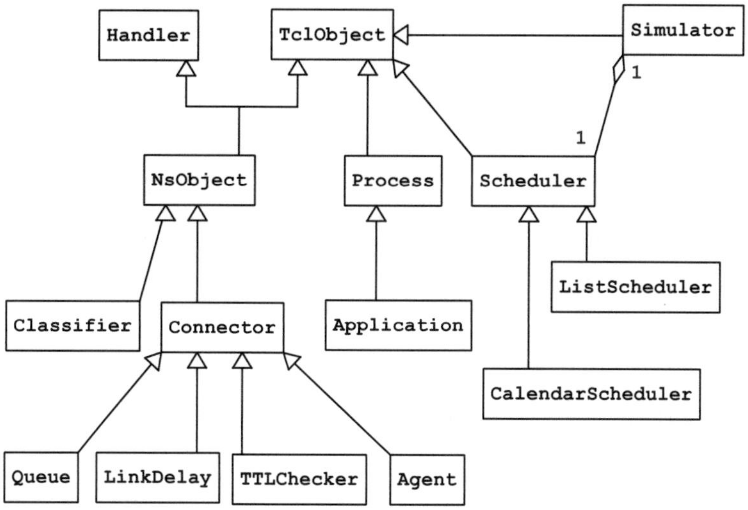

Figure 1. The hierarchical structure of main classes of NS2 in UML schema

2.1. Event handling mechanism

Aiming at network simulating at packet level, NS2 has been developed as a platform consisting of a comprehensive network elements by the object-oriented programming method. Four classes of fundamental objects, named `Node`, `Link`, `Agent`, and `Application`, are modeled for packets transporting, generating and terminating. While, functionalities such as configuration helping, routes computing, experiment managing and so on, are put into a global container class and named after `Simulator`.

Unlike `Agent` and `Application`, both `Node` and `Link` are compound classes which consist of some other elemental objects. For example, a simplest `Node` contains two routing objects, one for addressing/routing at network layer and the other for multiplexing/demultiplexing at transport layer, both derived from the same parent class `Classifier`. The physical link is modeled by `Link` which consists in series of three objects: `Queue`, `LinkDelay`, and `TTLChecker`. The elemental classes including `Agent`, `Queue`, `LinkDelay`, and `TTLChecker` are all derived from the parent class `Connector`. Together with `Classifier`, `Connector` is derived from `NsObject` and `Handler` in turn, as depicted in Fig.1.

In the class `NsObject`, two abstract functions named `recv()` and `send()` are defined for simulating packet receiving and sending, respectively. The class `Handler` encapsulates a function named `handle()` for specific event handling. These functions are overridden in the derived classes for different purposes. For instance, the implementation of `recv()` in `Classifier`, ie. `Classifier::recv()`, is to forward the received packet to the next object predefined by `Simulator` according to routing logics. Details of the implementation mechanism of NS2 can be referred to [10].

During network simulating, a packet handling causes usually one or more elemental objects to change their state. In most cases, the change results in at least one new event which relates to another function `Handler::handle()` of the next specified object. This event-driven invocation is managed systematically by a global sole object of `Scheduler`, which is instantiated and kept by another global object of `Simulator`. The derived classes based on

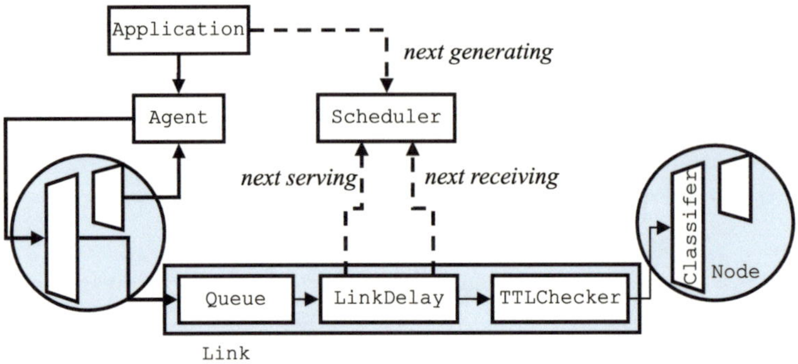

Figure 2. The configuration node and link of NS2 and typical events written in italic

the `Scheduler` include `ListScheduler`, which implements the linear list algorithm, and `CalendarScheduler`, which implements CQ and DCQ.

The event generation and consumption can be illustrated by tracing a packet transportation along a simulation link. As it can be imaged, the end of packet transferring at a output port of node will trigger a next serving event which will be sent back to the output queue, i.e. `Queue`, in the future time of simulation. While time delay due to propagation through the `LinkDelay` will create a packet arriving event which will be forwarded the input interface, i.e. `TTLChecker`, of the next node later. These two kinds of events lead to invocations of the class `Queue` and `TTLChecker` are buffered into the event queue of `Scheduler`, as showed in Fig.2.

Packet generating is controlled by the object `Application`, which has been developed and divided into two types which represent the stochastic generator and application simulator, respectively. The former creates an event that will trigger packet generating of `Application` recursively. The latter generates packet according to the mechanism of the simulated application. The following discussion will focus on the former for simplicity.

2.2. Population of standing events

As mentioned above, there are 3 types of events in NS2, including packet generating, timer and "at-event". Packet is used to model packet's transmission, timer to build protocol state-machine and packet's generator, and "at-event"to control computation. `Application` and its derivations are designed to generate a flow of packets, where one or more timer(s) is/are used to trigger the generation in a recursive manner. `Queue` and `LinkDelay` are designed for packet forwarding and transmitting through a link connecting a pair of neighbor nodes, respectively. Two timers are generated when a `LinkDelay` handles a received packet, one for triggering packet receiving at the next node later on, the other for calling `Queue` back when the `LinkDelay` is available for transmitting next packet buffered in the `Queue`. Hopping of a packet along a link, hence, induce two consequential events.

Let h_k denotes the number of hops or links over an end-to-end path indexed by k. The number, represented by g_k, of packets are generated by the corresponding `Application` during One Way Delay (OWD) of the path. The total number of `Application`'s instances, n, is assumed as the same as the number of paths. Then, in the context of NS2, one packet-typed event induces $2h_k$ timer-typed events if the packet does not drop during forwarding and transmitting. Therefore, the number N of pending events is as follows,

$$N = \sum_{k=1}^{n} g_k \times (2h_k + 1), \tag{1}$$

where, $k \in [1..n]$, is also the index of `Applications` of n concurrent traffic flows. For a network with 100 nodes and a full mesh typed traffic pattern, n equals 9900.

For a typical traffic with bandwidth demand 1 Mbps and packet size 1000 bytes, the packet generation rate r is 125 packet/s. Assuming the propagation delay along each link is fixed as 2 ms and each path consists of 6 hops in average, we have $h_k = 6$ and OWD is greater than 12 ms. Then,

$$g_k = r \times OWD = 125(packet/s) \times 12(ms) = 1.5. \tag{2}$$

It is easy to figure out that the number of events is approximately,

$$N = 9900 \times 1.5 \times 13 \approx 2 \times 10^5. \tag{3}$$

Here, for simplicity, we neglect the effects of packet transmitting and queuing at an output port. As one knows, transmitting delay is inverse proportion to the bandwidth of output link, and it contributes an increment to OWD. Queuing can bring about packet drops and introduce a decrement to g_k during network congestion. However, as it is the result of overloading, network congestion implies much more pending events. Therefore, the above estimated N can be seen taken roughly as the low bound for event scheduling.

If N events are buffered in single one linear list, the average times of memory accessing for sorted insertion is about $N/2$ (10^5). Such heavy volume of accessing can lead to much too high time overhead. For networks with burst pattern traffics and higher traffic demands, the speed of event scheduling becomes a critical factor for fast simulation.

2.3. The Calendar Queue scheduling

The default event scheduler of NS2 is based on Calendar Queue (CQ) algorithm, which works similar to a desktop calendar [4]. In CQ, a bucket is used to stand for the day of year and store a sub-list of events. Events happening on the same day, despite the deference of year, are stored in the same bucket as shown in Fig.3.

For simplicity, 5 events, E_0 to E_4, are illustrated in Fig.3, whose timestamps are defined as 0, 1, 1, 3 and 16 in second. Given that the depth or size of bucket, T_B, is 2 seconds in time and one year consists of 3 buckets, the length of year, T_y, is 6 seconds. Therefore, events E_0 to E_2 are located in bucket $B(0)$, E_3 in $B(1)$, and E_4 in $B(2)$ of the third year.

The bucket location or index is determined by the following arithmetic computation,

$$n_B = \lfloor (t_e \bmod T_y)/T_B \rfloor, \tag{4}$$

where, t_e is the timestamp of an event. E_0, E_1 and E_2 are inserted in the bucket $B(0)$ since computations according to Eq.(4) result in the same value 0. Again, the computation of the time, 16, of E_4 gives a value 2, indexing the bucket $B(2)$.

The computation of Eq.(4) is independent on the number of events in the queue, the complexity is therefore of O(1) [4]. However, event enqueue in a single bucket works as the

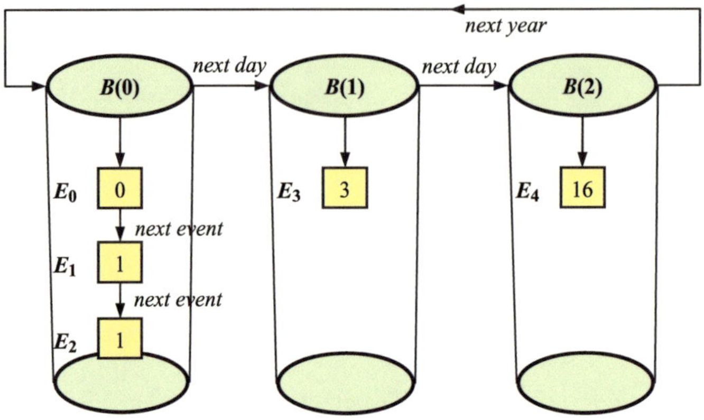

Figure 3. The structural relationship between event and bucket in CQ

same way as a linear list. In the case as showed in Fig.3, the insertion of E_2 will require two extra steps of comparing. The final complexity is dominated by the sorted insertion in the bucket unless the number of bucket is greater than the total number of events and the distribution of event in time is uniform.

Actually, bucket plays as a container and its size determines events partitioning. The fixed structure of bucket becomes an obstacle for performance improvement. It has been shown that a skewed nonuniform distribution of events in the time domain can degrade the performance of CQ [12]. Since then, several improved scheduling algorithms [1, 13, 15] have been proposed to solve the problem of adaptability to the distribution.

In addition to the structure of bucket, there are two issues that CQ and the related improved algorithms can not cope with readily. One is concurrent events insertion and the other is the earliest event fetching. The former can be seen from the insertion of E_2 after E_1 as shown in Fig.3. Although they have equal timestamp, logically E_2 occurs later than E_1 and one more comparison is needed to insert E_2. If the number of concurrent events is huge, say 9900 as cited in Eq.(3), a large number of comparisons are needed. The latter can be illustrated via E_4's fetching. After E_3 departing, a CQ scheduler will carry out 6 times of bucket access across two years, then reach E_4. This is more complex than a linear list, in which the earliest event is always located at the head.

As is seen, CQ and the related improved algorithms do not take the modern structure of processor into considerations, especially high speed CPU caches. It has been demonstrated that a cache aware algorithm can speedup greatly an application that involves heavy data-retrieving [2, 5]. In the following section, we provide a fast cache aware scheduling algorithm to accelerate the simulation of large scale communication networks.

3. The cache aware scheduling

3.1. Data structure for event partitioning

Similar to CQ, the algorithm with cache awareness belongs to the category of partitioning list. Two lists work in a correlated manner, one for DES events and named event queue (*Qe*), and the other for indexing the sub-list of DES events and named digest queue (*Qd*). *Qe* is organized the same as a linear list, while *Qd* is implemented in an array structure acts as a

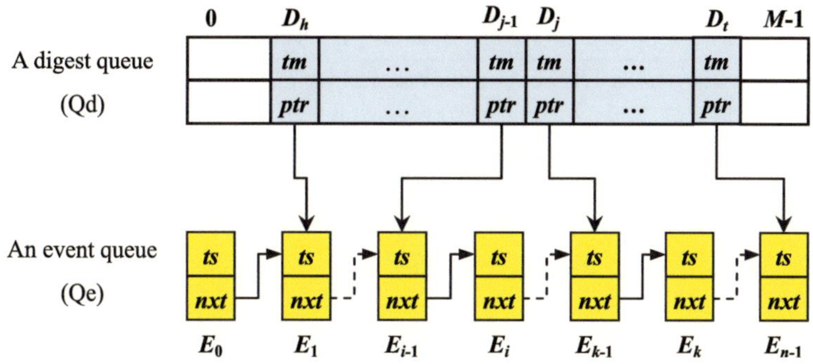

Figure 4. Event digests and their relationship with DES events

ring-typed buffer. The element of *Qd*, called digest, is used to index the tail of a sub-list of *Qe*, as depicted in Fig.4.

A digest D_j contains a time delimiter *tm* and an event pointer *ptr* to the corresponding DES event of a sub-list. In Fig.2, D_0 is the digest of the sub-list (E_0, E_1), and D_j is the digest of the sub-list (E_i, ..., E_{k-1}). The time delimiter of digest is defined as follows,

$$tm = \lfloor g \times ts \rfloor \tag{5}$$

where the coefficient g is used to control the size of sub-list, and *ts* is the timestamp of the corresponding event. If $g = 1$, in unit of timestamp, a sub-list consists of only those events with the same timestamp. For $g > 1$, events happen within g interval are indexed by a digest pointing to the latest of them. In effect, the configurable coefficient g is analog to bucket size of CQ. The difference is that two successive digests need not have their *tm* contiguous. In other words, $D_{j+1} \rightarrow tm$ - $D_j \rightarrow tm$ is allowed to be greater than $1 \times g$. This makes our sub-list more adaptive to event distribution in the time domain.

The value of *ptr* of a digest is the address of corresponding DES event. The function of this address is two-fold, one for heading of the next sub-list, the other for tailing of the current sub-list. The reason why the *ptr* points to the tail of a sublist is to avoid repeating comparisons for concurrent events with the same time-stamp. This situation happens more frequently in case simulation parameters, ex. bandwidth or link delay, are configured with the same value.

3.2. Enqueue and dequeue operations

As described in Algorithm 1, inserting a new DES event, or ENQUEUE, is a little more complex operation than a linear list. There are 6 significant steps in ENQUEUE operation, including,

- to calculate the time maker, x, of the new DES event, according to Eq.(4);
- to find the target sub-list by comparing x with each digest of *Qe*;
- to sort and insert the new event into the sub-list by `InsertList()`;
- to replace the digest if the new event is inserted at the tail, otherwise;
- to update the digest if digest queue is full, otherwise;
- to create a digest and insert it into digest ring buffer by `InsertDigQueue()`.

Algorithm 1: ENQUEUE operation over a non-empty digest queue

```
input : A new event new, a DES event list headed by H, and a digest ring headed by h
        and tailed by t.
output: Updated event list and digest ring.

x ⟵ ⌊g × new → ts⌋;
list ⟵ H;
for j ⟵ h to t do /*To find the target sub-list*/
    if D[j] → tm > x then
        break;
    end
end
if j != h then
    j ⟵ j − 1;
    list ⟵ D[j] → ptr;
end
InsertList (list, new);
if D[j] → tm == x then /*To check the time maker of the digest*/
    if list → ts <= new → ts then /*To replace the end of sub-list*/
        (D[j] → ptr) ⟵ new;
        return;
    end
else if t + 1 ==h then /*To update the digest*/
    (D[j] → ptr) ⟵ new;
    (D[j] → tm) ⟵ x;
else /*To create a digest and insert it at (j+1)-th of the digest ring */
    InsertDigQueue (new, x, j + 1);
end
```

Since an array structure is used for the digest queue, the conventional ring-buffer access method can be adopted to implement `InsertDigQueue()`. The function `InsertList()` is, however, the same as that for a linear list.

The event departure or DEQUEUE operation is simply as a linear list, as shown in Algorithm 2. The function `FetchList()` is to fetch the head of DES event list, and the following block of codes to update the variable h is to remove the first of digest queue. The extra processing on the head is used to keep the correctness of digesting.

Algorithm 2: DEQUEUE operation when digest queue is not empty

```
input : An event queue Qe, and a digest ring headed by h.
output: The earliest event evt.

evt ⟵ FetchList(Qe);

if D[h] → ptr == evt then
    h ⟵ h + 1;
end
```

3.3. Cache awareness and computational complexity

The difference between a cache aware algorithm and CQ is the way to partition events into sub-lists. For the cache aware algorithm, an array of digest is designed to index sub-lists and works as a ring buffer. In the ENQUEUE operation, both sub-list searching and digest inserting (`InsertDigQueue()`) execute at first over the array.

Generally speaking, a fixed array of data is with great possibility allocated by the memory management of an OS to be continuously distributed in the memory space. This locality is feasible for fast accessing by a processor with caches. Caches are fast memories in which a block of data around the request are loaded from the main memory. The caching operation is benefit to the future requests if they locate in the loaded block. The ratio, β, of access latency of main memory to cache, is usually greater than 10. Therefore, an optimum data structure and its accessing can be designed to utilize the benefit. Two types of approach have been used in designing, one is to access cache directly by instructions based on the hardware structure, the other is to design a deliberate data structure and access them as locally as possible. The former promises better performance but less applicable for different hardware structures, while the latter is cache awareness and has a better compatibility for general purposes.

Buckets of CQ/DCQ embedded in NS2 are allocated by an array and can assure locality. But this locality can not make use of the benefit of caching, because the bucket determination for event searching is computed directly and has no relationship with buckets' allocation.

For the cache aware algorithm, the target sub-list is searched via the digest queue Qd. If whole of Qd can be loaded into caches, the searching can speed up β times. Therefore, the complexity of sub-list searching is equivalent to $O(\frac{m}{2\beta})$. For an average distribution of event in time, the size of each sub-list bing $\frac{n}{m}$, the complexity of `InsertList()` is then $O(\frac{n}{2m})$. This leads to the complexity of $O(\frac{m}{2\beta}) + O(\frac{n}{2m})$ for an ENQUEUE operation. The optimum condition is as follows,

$$m = \sqrt{\beta n}. \tag{6}$$

Consequently, the lowest complexity of ENQUEUE is $O(\sqrt{\frac{n}{\beta}})$, twice as that of CQ configured with $m = \sqrt{\beta n}$ buckets. However, for the case of a sub-list consists of concurrent events with the same timestamp, the cache aware algorithm has an advantage over CQ since that the tail of sub-list is indexed. Sublist searching of the algorithm is of O(1) while that of CQ goes up of $O(\sqrt{\frac{n}{\beta}})$.

As for DEQUEUE operation, the cache aware algorithm is equivalent to remove the head of a list. The complexity is O(1) and it is independent on the distribution of event in time. As a conclusion, the algorithm is better than CQ.

4. Implementation and performance evaluations

4.1. Description of implementation

The cache aware algorithm has been implemented within an extended class `CacheScheduler` which is derived from the existing `ListScheduler`. Two functions, `insert()` and `deque()`, are overridden, and some helper functions appended. Modifications are based on the NS with version 2.33 and should be compatible with the most of other versions because no change is required except a config modification for `Simulator` is required to select `CacheScheduler` rather than `CalendarScheduler` in default.

Two fixed array are defined in the class `CacheScheduler`, one named `key_` with type of `unsigned int` for digest's time, the other named `event_` with type of `Event *` for digest's pointer. Two variable members, `head_` and `tail_`, are defined to index the ring-typed buffer. The coefficient g in Eq.(5) is represented by the third variable member `pricision_`, and the size of digest by the last `size_`.

The overridden function `deque()` is defined in c++ as following,

```
Event* CacheScheduler::deque() {
     Event *e = queue_;
     if (e)} {
          queue_ = e->next_;
          if (event_[head_] == e) {
               event_[head_] = 0;
               key_[head_] = 0;
               head_ = ++head_ % size_;
          }
     }
     return (e);
}
```

where, the variable member `queue_` points to the head of DES event list. The condition `(event_[head_] == e)` is for checking whether it should remove the head of digest queue or not. The c++ codes of the function `insert()` is showed as following,

```
Event* CacheScheduler::insert(Event *e) {
     Event **p;
     unsigned int idx, key;
     double t = e->time_;

     key = t * pricision_;
     idx = findDigest(t, key, p);

     for( ;* p != 0; p = &(*p)->next_ )
          if ( t < (*p)->time_ ) break;

     e->next_ = *p;
     *p = e;

     insertDigest(t, key, idx, *p);
}
```

where, the functions `findDigest()` and `insertDigest()` operate over the array `key_` and `event_`. The function `findDigest()` results the pointer `p` of sublist of DES event after which the new should be inserted, and the index `idx` of the sublist in the digest queue. The c++ codes of `findDigest()` is defined as,

```
01    unsigned int CacheScheduler::findDigest(double t, \\
02                       unsigned int key, Event **& p) {
03        unsigned int idx = head_;
04
05        for (; idx != tail_; idx++, idx %= size_)
06            if (key_[idx] >= key) break;
07
08        if (idx == head_) { // is it at head
09            p = &queue_;
10            return idx;
11        }
12
13        if (idx == tail_ || event_[idx]->time_ > t) {
14            // go to the tail of previous sub-list
15            idx = idx + size_ - 1;
16            idx %= size_;
17        }
18
19        p = (Event**)event_[idx];
20        return idx;
21    }
```

Codes in the above from Line 05 to 06 are to find out the sublist that the event timestamped with *key* should be contained. Codes from Line 08 to 10 are to handle the special case of the first sublist, and codes from Line 13 to 17 are introduced to compensate tail pointing mechanism used in sublist digesting, considering that the head of a sublist is equivalent to the tail of its previous one.

The insertion function `insertDigest()` is little more complex as listed in the following,

```
void CacheScheduler::insertDigest(double t, unsigned int key, \\
        unsigned int idx, Event *e) {
    unsigned int tmp = (tail_+1) % size_; // target of tail moving

    if (tmp == head_) {               // buffer is full
        ...
    } else if (head_ == tail_) {      // buffer is empty
        ...
    } else if (key_[idx] == key) { // replace only
        if (event_[idx]->time_ <= t)
            event_[idx] = e;
    } else if (!e->next_) {           // append at tail
        key_[tail_] = key;
        event_[tail_] = e;
```

```
15            tail_ = tmp;
16        } else {                          // in the middle
17            idx = ++idx % size_;
18            if (key_[idx] > key) {        // insert a new element
19                if (tail_ > idx) {        // right moving
20                    for (tmp = tail_; tmp > idx; tmp--) {
21                        key_[tmp] = key_[tmp-1];
22                        event_[tmp] = event_[tmp-1];
23                    }
24                    tail_ = ++tail_ % size_;
25                } else {                  // left moving
26                    head_ --;
27                    idx --;
28                    for (tmp = head_; tmp < idx; tmp++) {
29                        key_[tmp] = key_[tmp+1];
30                        event_[tmp] = event_[tmp+1];
31                    }
32                }
33            }                             // end of moving
34            key_[tmp] = key;
35            event_[tmp] = e;
36        }
37    }
```

There are 5 conditional branches in the function `insertDigest()`, the 1st (omitted at Line 06) and 2nd (omitted at Line 08) handle the buffer of digest with full and empty, respectively. The 3rd case is that the new digest has the same digest time as an existing one, os replacing is required. The 4th is identified in order to avoid the complex operations as defined in the 5th case. The last case involves element movings over an array and can lead to much more memory accesses. Such processing is, however, executing on a memory area that can be allocated continually or locally. The time overhead of `insertDigest()` can be hence reduced by the benefit of CPU caching, as discussed in the section 3.

The variables `precision_` and `size_` dominate the dynamics of cache aware scheduling. The bigger the `precision_` is, the longer the sub-list of DES event tends to be. The optimal value depends on the population of standing events and distribution in the time domain. However, `size_` can be determined according to the size of CPU caches.

4.2. Experiment environment and results

For simplicity in performance evaluation, simulation experiments are carried out over a random network with 100 nodes, each node connects to 6 others being selected randomly. Simulation configurations are coded in a Tools Command Language (TCL) script. Every link of the network is configured with fixed bandwidth 155 Mbps and fixed propagation delay 2 ms. A Constant Bit Rate (CBR) generator with demand bandwidth 10 Mbps and packet size 1000 bytes is assigned for each traffic flow and kept active during simulation time from 0.01 to 2.0 seconds. The number of flows varies from 99, i.e. one node is chosen to generate packets to the rest, to 9900, i.e. a full mesh-typed flow pattern is arranged. Before putting into computations, the simulated network is examined and replaced by a regenerated topology until it is fully connected. In order to make the experiment more generalized, the simulated network topology is built randomly. The number of network nodes and the pattern of traffics are adjustable.

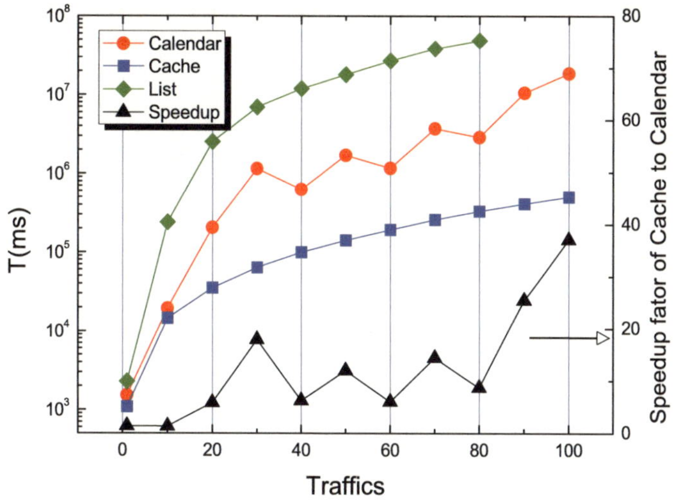

Figure 5. Computational time and speedup factor over CQ VS traffics (in unit of 99 flows)

Num. of traffic flows	List (ms)	Calendar (ms)	Cache (ms)	Speedup factor
1×99	2,273	1,517	1,086	1.40
10×99	238,797	19,245	14,455	1.33
20×99	2,523,570	203,784	34,991	5.82
30×99	6,916,930	1,144,140	63,792	17.94
40×99	11,862,000	621,804	99,360	6.26
50×99	17,934,800	1,692,130	140,996	12.00
60×99	26,835,100	1,159,060	192,093	6.03
70×99	38,388,600	3,712,680	257,185	14.44
80×99	48,637,600	2,880,920	330,402	8.72
90×99	-	10,459,600	410,934	25.45
100×99	-	18,573,400	501,229	37.06

Table 1. Computational times of three scheduling algorithms and speedups of the proposed (Cache) to CQ

Table 1 and Fig.5 show the computational time spending for simulations T versus the number of traffic flows, for CQ (Calendar), the cache aware (Cache) and the linear list (List) schedulers. Experiments are carried out on a personal computer with a Intel(R) Pentium(R) 4 typed CPU with 2.93 GHz in frequency and 1024 kB in cache size. The computational time is evaluated by invoking TCL predefined command `clock` at 0.0 and 2.0 seconds in the simulation time. It can be seen from Fig.5 that the cache aware algorithm is always faster than CQ and the maximum speedup factor reaches 37.

Fig.6 shows the computational time varying with the size of digest queue, for the case configured with a cache aware scheduler and 30 sources, i.e. $99 \times 30 = 2970$ flows. Since a ring-buffer management is used in the cache aware algorithm, the actual capacity of the queue is one smaller than its literal size. The condition with the queue sized 1 means to disable the digest queue, and the cache aware algorithm is degraded and equivalent to the linear list. The condition with the queue sized 2 allows only one digest which always points to the tail of DES event list. Experiment results on the size of digest queue are also listed in Tab.2.

size	1	2	3	4	8	16	32	64
T(ms)	4,052,043	4,131,210	1,929,621	281,398	64,113	63,186	64,140	63,109

Table 2. Computational time (T) varies with the size of digest queue

From Fig.6 and Tab.2, it can be concluded that a cache aware algorithm makes use of the benefit of CPU caches when the size of digest queue is greater than 16. It is can be seen also that the speedup efficiency relies on the size of cache-line rather than the size and topology of the simulated network. The detailed analysis is given in the next section.

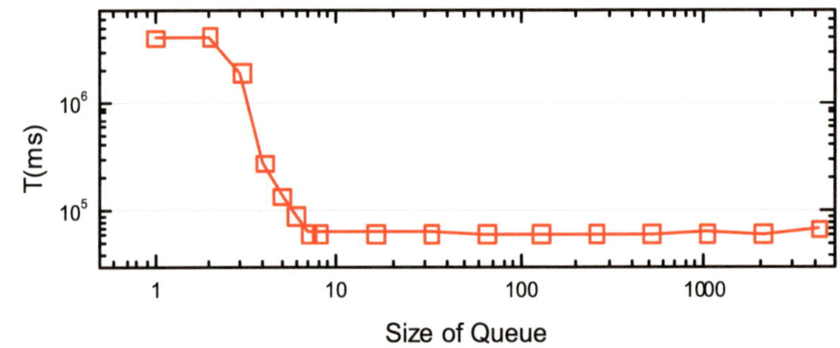

Figure 6. Computation time VS digest queue size

4.3. Effectiveness of CPU caching

The result of the experiment indicates that the cache aware algorithm can speedup DES event scheduling for large scale networks. Continuously allocated digest queue in memory is benefit to fully use the feature of caching. Meanwhile, the digest queue acts as a classifier to partition DES event list into sub-lists with a shorter length, and hence reduce the searching time of ENQUEUE operations.

The digest in the cache aware algorithm is managed by two variables, `key_` and `Event_`, each 4 bytes in length. Hence, a digest queue with size 16 occupies 128 bytes in the main memory. This is exactly equivalent to 128-byte sized L2 cache line of the processor [8] used in experiments. The dropping approaching the size 16 shown in Fig.6 coincides with the CPU L2 caching capability. Therefore, the algorithm is cache-line awareness for the CPU chip employed in our experiments. This means that computation time reduction remains nearly constant when the size of digest queue increases over that of cache line, i.e., 8 elements or 64 bytes, roughly 10 as showed in experiments. In this condition, missing in single a cache line causes a regular main memory access so that the contribution of CPU caching is saturated.

The algorithm provided in this chapter is not the best that can fully utilize the capability of CPU resources since that the design of digest queue and operations have no knowledge of CPU's microstructure. However, a further improvement that depends on the specific CPU products will bring a serious issue in compatibility. The trade-off between performance and compatibility needs extensive investigations and relates to the application field of discrete event simulations.

5. Conclusion

Discrete event simulation method has been employed in various research fields for exploring a complex or large system numerically. The applicability of this kind of simulation method relies in large on the computation speed. In this chapter, fast event scheduling approaches for simulations of large scale networks is discussed. The typical simulation procedures are described according to NS2 platform, followed by a brief analysis of the conventional Calendar Queue algorithm. Based on the list partitioning method, a digest queue on the fixed array structure is introduced to partition and index the sub-list of DES events. The double-list structure can utilize the benefit of caching mechanism of modern CPU chips.

Details of enqueue and dequeue algorithm are given and the complexity analysis is presented. Also, developments based on the open-source NS2 software are showed for the algorithm implementation. In order to verify the benefit of cache awareness to speedup simulation, we report computational experiments over an on-shelf personal computer. It is shown that the performance of a cache aware algorithm is considerably better than the conventional Calendar Queue. Experiment results show that the cache aware algorithm makes simulation faster by up to a factor of 37. The improvement in computation efficiency is applicable for any ordinary network topology and traffic pattern since the randomized topologies and patterns are employed in our experiments.

For simplicity, the algorithm's design and implementation are focused on the network simulation with all traffics assumed over UDP/IP protocol stacks. As for the simulation involves in TCP connection, events used for protocol machine controlling, such as those for time-out processing, bring numbers of canceling operations into event scheduling. The event cancelation in the queue based on the ring-typed buffer should result in more computational complex than that of convectional algorithms. A better solution, we think, is to put these "at-events" being significant for the local network node into a separate object from the global event scheduler. This separation is not only benefit in speedup to the scheduler but also to parallel enabler.

On the other hand, the advancement of multi-core architecture of CPU deserves to be verified whether the proposed algorithm can utilize caches of multi-core chip as well. Moreover, it's valuable to study multi-core technology to achieve parallel speedup in the meantime.

Author details

Wennai Wang and Yi Yang
Key Lab of Broadband Wireless Communication and Sensor Network Technology, Nanjing University of Posts and Telecommunications, China

6. References

[1] Ahn, J. & Seunghyun, O. [1999]. Dynamic calendar queue, *Annual Simulation Symposium*, pp. 20–25.

[2] Askitis, N. & Sinha, R. [2007]. Hat-trie: a cache-conscious trie-based data structure for strings, *Proc. of the thirtieth Australasian conference on Computer science - Volume 62*, Australian Computer Society, Inc., Darlinghurst, Australia, pp. 97–105.

[3] Banks, J. [1999]. Introduction to simulation, *Proceedings of the 31st conference on Winter simulation: Simulation—a bridge to the future - Volume 1*, WSC '99, ACM, New York, NY, USA, pp. 7–13.
URL: *http://doi.acm.org/10.1145/324138.324142*

[4] Brown, R. [1988]. Calendar queues: A fast O(1) priority queue implementation for the simulation event set problem, *Communications of the ACM* 31(10): 1220–1227.

[5] Chiueh, T. & Pradhan, P. [1999]. High performance ip routing table lookup using cpu caching, *INFOCOM*, pp. 1421–1428.

[6] Chung, K., Sang, J. & Rego, V. [1993]. A performance comparison of event calendar algorithms: an empirical approach, *Softw. Pract. Exper.* 23: 1107–1138.

[7] Fujimoto, R. [1999]. Parallel and distributed simulation., *Winter Simulation Conference'99*, pp. 122–131.

[8] Hinton, G., Sager, D., Upton, M., Boggs, D., Carmean, D., Kyker, A. & Roussel, P. [2001]. The microarchitecture of the pentium 4 processor, *Intel Technology Journal* 5(1): 1–13.

[9] Issariyakul, T. & Hossain, E. [2008]. *Introduction to Network Simulator NS2*, 1 edn, Springer Publishing Company, Incorporated.

[10] Fall, K. & Varadhan, K. [2009]. The ns manual.
URL: *http://www.isi.edu/nsnam/ns/ns-documentation.html*

[11] Park, H. & Fishwick, P. A. [2011]. An analysis of queuing network simulation using gpu-based hardware acceleration, *ACM Trans. Model. Comput. Simul.* 21(18): 1–22.

[12] Siangsukone, T., Aswakul, C. & Wuttisittikulkij, L. [2003]. Study of optimised bucket widths in calendar queue for discrete event simulator, *Proc. of Thailand's Electrical Engineering Conference (EECON-26)*, Phetchaburi, pp. 6–7.

[13] Tan, K. L. & Thng, L. [2000]. Snoopy calendar queue, *Winter Simulation Conference*, pp. 487–495.

[14] Varga, A. & Hornig, R. [2008]. An overview of the omnet++ simulation environment, *Simutools '08: Proceedings of the 1st international conference on Simulation tools and techniques for communications, networks and systems & workshops*, ICST, Brussels, Belgium, pp. 1–10.

[15] Yan, G. & Eidenbenz, S. [2006]. Sluggish calendar queues for network simulation, *Proc. of the 14th IEEE International Symposium on Modeling, Analysis, and Simulation of Computer and Telecommunication Systems (MASCOTS'06)*, Monterey, CA, USA, pp. 127–136.

Chapter 3

Sensitivity Analysis in Discrete-Event Simulation Using Design of Experiments

José Arnaldo Barra Montevechi,
Rafael de Carvalho Miranda and Jonathan Daniel Friend

Additional information is available at the end of the chapter

http://dx.doi.org/10.5772/50196

1. Introduction

The use of discrete-event simulation as an aid in decision-making has grown over recent decades [1, 2, 3, 4]. It is already used as one of the most utilized research techniques for many sectors due to its versatility, flexibility and analysis potential [5, 6].

However, one of simulation's greatest disadvantages is that, on its own, it does not serve as an optimization technique [7]. This forces simulation practitioners to simulate multiple system configurations and choose the one which presents the best system performance. Computational development has helped alter this scenario due to the increasing availability of faster computers and ever improving search and heuristic optimization techniques.

Simulation optimization can be defined as the process of testing different combinations of values for controllable values, aiming to find the combination of values which offers the most desirable output result for simulation models [8].

In support of this claim, [1, 9, 10, 11] assert that using optimization along with simulation has been continuously increasing due to the emergence of simulation packages which possess integrated optimization routines.

The overarching idea of including these routines is to search for improved definitions for the system parameters in relation to its performance. However, according to [10], at the end of optimization, the user has no way of knowing if an optimal point was truly reached.

Despite the fact that simulation has been around for more than half a century, until quite recently, the scientific community was reluctant to use optimization tools in simulation. The first time the subject emerged in two renowned simulation books, [12] and [13], was at the close of the 20th century [9]. This resistance has begun to diminish with the convent of meta-heuristic research, along with strides being made in statistic analysis [14].

According to [15], verification of system performance for a determined set of system parameters with reasonable precision using simulation, demands a considerable amount of computational potential. In order to find the optimal or near-optimal solution, one needs to verify a large number of parameter values, thus, optimization via simulation is normally exhaustive from a computational standpoint.

Having highlighted the computational strains, [8] states that despite the evolution of optimization software, a common criticism made about such commercial packages is that, when more than one variable is manipulated at a time, the software becomes very slow.

Considering that not all decision variables are of equal importance in respect to the response variable that one desires to optimize [16, 17], a sensitivity analysis may be carried out on the simulation model in order to select the variables which will compose the optimization search space in order to limit the number of variables and, in turn, make the search faster.

Thus, in order to proceed to the variable selection, screening can be done in order to separate the most important variables from those which may be eliminated from consideration [16, 17]. The same author presents some examples of experimental design utilized in screening experiments:

- 2^n factorial design;
- 2^{n-p} fractional factorial design;
- Supersaturated designs;
- Groups screening designs.

The current chapter presents an application of Design of Experiments (DOE), specifically fractional factorial design, in order to select the significant input variables in a simulation model, and thus accelerate the optimization process. For information about experimental design, the reader can consult [1, 4, 18, 19].

Fractional factorial design is a DOE technique in which only a fraction of the total number of experiments is executed, thus realizing fewer experiments than full factorial design. Throughout this chapter, it is shown that the use of such a design serves to reduce the search space in the optimization phase of simulation studies.

In this chapter, real examples of how to conduct sensitivity analysis with factorial design are given. In order to reach this goal, two study objects are presented, comparing the optimization carried out without previous investigation of input variable significance, with the optimization carried out in reduced search space. Finally, a comparison is made of the results of the optimization, with and without the sensitivity analysis.

2. Simulation optimization

A simulation model generally includes *n* input variables (x_1, x_2,...,x_n) and *m* output variables (y_1, y_2, ..., y_m) (Figure 1). The optimization of this simulation method implies finding the optimal configuration of input variables; that is, the values of x_1, x_2, …, x_n which optimize the response variable(s) [20].

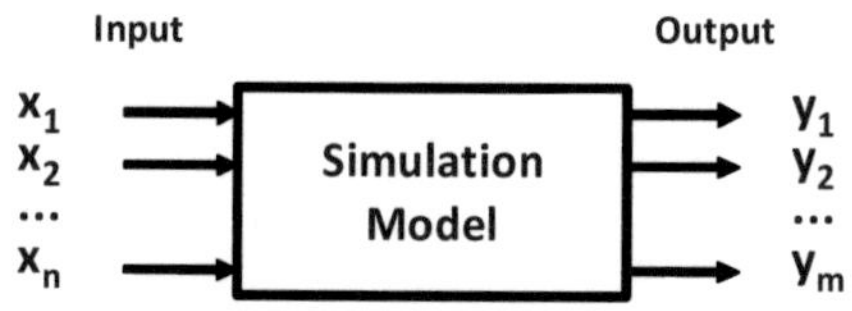

Figure 1. Simulation Model [20]

Optimization helps respond to the following questions: What are the optimal adjustments to the input variables (x) which maximize (or minimize) a given simulation model output? The objective is to find an optimal value which maximizes or minimizes a determined performance indicator [11].

According to [21], simulation optimization is one of the most important technologies to come about in recent years. These authors recall that previous methodologies demanded carrying out complex changes to the simulation model, thus consuming time and computational potential and, in many cases, not even being economically viable for real cases due to the large number of decision variables.

A traditional simulation optimization problem (minimization of a single objective) is given in Eq. 1 [22]:

$$\min f(\theta) \tag{1}$$

$$s.t\ \theta \in \Theta$$

Where $f\ (\theta) = E[\psi(\theta,\omega)]$ is the system's expected performance, estimated for $\hat{f}(\theta)$, which is obtained using the simulation model samples $\psi_j(\theta,\omega)$, observed according to the discrete or continuous input parameters, restricted by θ within a viability set $\Theta \subset \mathfrak{R}^d$.

According to [23], the optimization method which serves for the problem presented in Eq. (1) depends on whether the simulated variables are discrete or continuous. There are many methods for resolving this problem in the literature, like the one presented in Eq. (1), and unfortunately depending on the model being optimized, some methods cannot guarantee that an optimal solution is found [24].

Table 1 shows the main optimization software packages which are both on the market and cited in academic literature, as well as the simulation packages with which they are sold. The optimization techniques utilized in each software package is also shown.

As shown in Table 1, different optimization software packages utilize different search methods, such as: Evolutionary Algorithms [25], Genetic Algorithms [26], Scatter Search [27], Taboo Search [28], Neural Networks [29] and Simulated Annealing [30].

According to [31] and [32], the simulation optimization's greatest limitation is the number of variables being manipulated, as the software's performance is considerably reduced in models with a great number of variables. Thus, [33] asserts that convergence time is the most significant restriction in reaching computational efficiency for optimization algorithms.

Optimization Software	Simulation Package	Optimization Technique
AutoStat®	AutoMod®, AutoSched®	Evolutionary and Genetic Algorithms
OptQuest®	Arena®	Scatter Search, Taboo and Neural Networks
Optimiz®	Simul8®	Neural Networks
Optimizer®	Witness®	Simulated Annealing e Taboo Search
SimRunner®	ProModel®	Evolutionary and Genetic Algorithms

Table 1. Optimization software packages [4, 7, 9]

In order to ease this process, the use of fractional factorial design can be used to conduct sensitivity analysis on a simulation model in order to select the input variables which truly impact the response variable and enable the elimination of variables which are not statistically significant. In terms of the simulation, sensitivity analysis may be interpreted as a systematic investigation of the model's outputs, in accordance with the model's input variables [19].

By using DOE techniques, it is possible to reduce the number of experiments executed, determine which independent variables affect the dependent variable, and identify the amplitude or intensity of this effect. For optimization purposes, identification of the most significant variables is important, as the greater the number of variables in the search space, the longer the optimization process will take.

Thus, by using sensitivity analysis in simulation optimization problems, one can work with those input variables which actually have a significant effect over the determined response variable, thus reducing the number of experiments necessary and the computational potential involved in this process.

3. Experimentation strategies

An experiment can be defined as a test or series of tests in which purposeful changes are made to input variables, with the objective of observing and identifying the form in which the system responses are affected, in function of the changes carried out on the input variables [18].

According to [34], there are two types of process variables (Figure 2): controllable variables (x_1, x_2, ..., x_p), and non-controllable variables (z_1, z_2, ..., z_q), which are many times called "sound". The same author states that the experiment's objectives can be:

- Determine the variables which have the most influence over the response (y);
- Determine the values of x (significant variables) in order that the response is close to the nominal demand;
- Determine the values of x (significant variables) in order that the variability in y is small;

- Determine the values of x (significant variables) in order that the effect of the non-controllable variable effects are minimized.

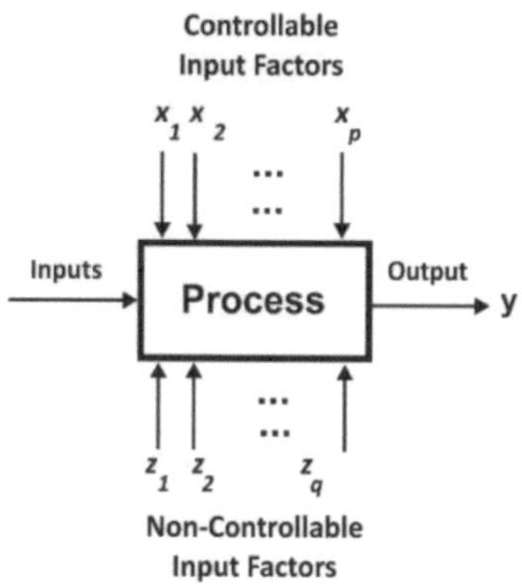

Figure 2. General process model [34]

The experimentation strategy is the method of designing and conducting experiments [18]. According to this author, there are many methods which can be used for the realization of experiments. Some examples are listed below:

Best-guess: This strategy is based on the specialists' technical or theoretical knowledge, which alters the value of one or two variables for the test in function of the previous result. This procedure presents at least two disadvantages: The first disadvantage occurs when the initial configuration does not produce the desired result and then the analyst must search for another input variable configuration. These attempts may continue indefinitely and certainly take a long time without guaranteeing success. The second disadvantage is that, supposing an acceptable initial configuration, the analyst will be tempted to stop testing, even though there is no guarantee that the best results has been obtained.

One factor at a time: This strategy involves selecting the starting configuration for each input variable and then successively varying each variable within a given range, while simultaneously maintaining the other variables constant. The greatest disadvantage of this strategy is its inability to detect interaction between variables; nonetheless, many analysts disregard this fact and it is often used [18].

Factorial Design: According to [18], when an experiment involves the study of two or more factors, the most effective strategy is factorial design. In using this strategy, factors are altered at the same time, instead of one at a time. That is, in each complete attempt or experimental replica, all possible combinations are investigated [35]. This strategy is more efficient than the one previously mentioned, as it allows for the effects of a single factor to be estimated across various factor levels, thus leading to valid conclusions within the experimental conditions, [18] and is the only way to discover interaction between factors [18, 35], avoiding incorrect conclusions when there is interaction between factors. The main problem with factorial design is the exponentially increasing number of combinations with each increase in the number of factors [19].

Response Surface Methodology (MSR): This method consists in a set of mathematical and statistical techniques that are used for modeling and analysis, in which the response of interest is influenced by multiple variables, and the objective is to optimize this response [35]. According to these authors, the relation between the independent and dependent response variables is unknown in most problems. [35] states that the first step of MSR is finding an accurate approximation for the true relation between the response (y) and the independent variables. In general, polynomials with a low degree are used to model a given region of the independent variables.

4. Simulated experiment design

According to [36], although classic experimental design methods were developed for real world experiments, they are perfectly applicable to simulated experiments. In fact, according to the same author, simulated experiment design presents many opportunities for improvements which are difficult or impossible to carry out using actual experiments.

[37] asserts that research related to experimental design are frequently found in specialized publications, but they are rarely read by simulation practitioners. According to these same authors, most simulation practitioners can get more from their analyses by using DOE theory developed specifically to experiment with computational models.

The benefits of DOE enable the possibility of improving simulation process performance by avoiding trial-and-error searches for solutions [38]. More specifically, the use of factorial design can minimize or even eliminate the disadvantages brought about by experimenting with simulated systems instead of the real system.

According to [36], in order to facilitate the understanding of simulation's role in experimental execution, it is necessary to imagine a response value (Y) or a dependent value variable can be represented in the following equation:

$$Y = f(x_1, x_2, ..., x_n) \tag{2}$$

Where:

- x_1, x_2, x_n represent the input variables, factors or independent variables;
- *f* represents the simulation model's transformation function.

[39] declares that simulation is a black box which transforms inputs variables into simulated outputs, which imitate the real system's perspective output. For each scenario, the analyst carries out one or more runs and registers the average output values.

In simulation models, the levels chosen for each factor must enable the effects to be programmed in the model. In order to exemplify this question, the following situation is proposed: a determined factor which is desired to be optimized corresponds to the possibility of using an experienced employee (upper level) or a new hire (lower level), thus verifying, what the impact would be on daily throughput. In simulation models, the modeler must be familiar with each variable to be affected by the change in levels. Thus, the modeler must decide which distribution to use for each variable time in the operation.

Experimentation using simulation presents some special advantages over using physical or industrial systems [4]:

- By using simulation, it is possible to control factors that, in reality, are uncontrollable, such as client arrival rate;
- By using simulation, it is possible to control the basic origin of variation, which is different from physical experiments, thus avoiding use of blocks.

Another experimental design characteristic is that commercial simulators come with random number generators and therefore, from an experimental point of view, the trouble of randomizing the experimental replicas is eliminated. Randomization is a problem with physical experimentation [36].

5. Design and analysis of experiments

According to [18], DOE can be defined as the process of designing experiments in order that the appropriate data are collected and analyzed by statistical methods, thus resulting in valid and objective conclusions. Any experimental problem must contain two elements: experimental design and statistical data analysis.

DOE techniques are seen with a broad range of application in many knowledge areas, thus showing itself as a set of tools of great importance for process and product development.

Those involved in the research should have a previous idea of the experiment's objective, which factors will be studied, how the experiment will be conducted and a comprehension of how the data will be analyzed [34].

According to [18], DOE should consider the following stages:

1. **Problem recognition and definition:** Completely develop all ideas about the problem and the objectives to be attained through the experiment, thus contributing to greater comprehension of the process and eventual problem solution;
2. **Choice of factors and working levels:** Choose the factors to undergo alterations, the intervals of these factors and the specific levels for each run to be carried out;
3. **Selection of the response variables:** Determine the response variables which really supply useful information about the performance of the process under study;
4. **Selection of the experimental design:** Consider the sample size (number of replications), selection of the correct order of runs for the experimental attempts, or the formation of blocks and other randomization restrictions involved;
5. **Realization of experiments:** Monitor the process to guarantee that everything is being completed according to the design – errors in this stage can destroy the experiment's validity;
6. **Statistical data analysis:** Analyze the data using statistical methods, given that results and conclusions are objective and not the outcome of opinions – residuals analysis and verification of model validity are important to this phase;

7. **Conclusions and recommendations:** Provide practical conclusions based on the results and recommend a plan of action. Accompanying sequences and confirmation tests must be conducted in order to validate the experiment's conclusions.

Stages 1 – 3 are commonly called the pre-experimental design and, for the experiment's success, it is important that these steps are carried out in the most appropriate manner possible [34].

5.1 DOE: Main concepts

There are three basic principles to DOE [18]:

- **Randomization:** Execution of experiments in a random order in order that the phenomenon's unknown effects are distributed among the factors, thus increasing the investigation's validity. According to the author, randomization is the base for the use of statistical methods in experimental design;
- **Replication:** Repetition of the same test multiple times, thus creating a variation in the response variable which is utilized to evaluate experimental error. With the use of each replication, it is possible to obtain an estimate of experimental error, allowing for the determination of whether the differences observed in the data are statistically different, as well as obtaining a more accurate estimate of an experimental factor's effect.
- **Blocking:** Design technique used to increase precision with the comparisons between the factors of interest. It is frequently utilized to reduce or eliminate variability transmitted by factors of sound. It should be utilized when it is not possible to maintain homogeneity of experimental conditions.

Now that the basic principles of DOE have been defined, the following list presents some of the fundamental terms which are used when dealing with DOE techniques:

- **Factor:** According to [37], factors are input parameters and the structural considerations which compose an experiment. Factors are altered during experimental conduction. According to [40], a factor may assume at least two values during an experiment, being quantitative or qualitative;
- **Levels:** The variations possible for each factor [41];
- **Main effect:** According to [36], the main effect for a factor may be defined as the average of the differences in the response variable, when the factor changes from an inferior to superior level;
- **Response variable:** The response variable is the performance measure for the DOE. The response variables describe how the system responds under a certain configuration of input factors [8];
- **Interaction:** There is interaction between the factors when the response difference between the levels of a given factor is not the same as for the rest of the factors.

Aside from these commonly utilized experimental design terms, two further important concepts should be presented: Analysis of variance (ANOVA) and residuals analysis.

According to [35], in order to test if the alteration in one of the levels or interaction is significant, a hypothesis test for the average can be used. In the case of DOE, this test can be conducted using ANOVA. The statistical test ANOVA is utilized to accept or reject hypotheses investigated with DOE. Its objective is to analyze the average variation of results and demonstrate which factors actually produce significant events over the system response variables [42].

However, according to [18], it is not advisable to trust solely in ANOVA since the validity of its suppositions may be unreliable. Problems with these results may be identified using residual analysis.

Residual analysis is an important procedure to guarantee that the models developed by means of experimentation adequately represent the responses of interest. [18] defines residuals as the difference between the predicted value and the observed experimental value; the same author also asserts that residues should be normal, random and non-correlated.

5.2. Full factorial design

Full factorial design with two levels or factorial 2^k is a type of design in which two levels are defined for each factor, an upper and lower level, and combinations of factors are tested [8]. 2^k factorial design is one of the most important types of factorial design, according to [35], and can be particularly useful in the initial phases of experimental work, especially when many factors are being investigated. Full factorial design offers the fewest executions for the k factors to be studied.

In full factorial design, the number of experiments is equal to the number of experimental levels, elevated to the number of factors. In the case of factorials with two levels, the number of experiments (N) in order to evaluate k factors is given by $N = 2^k$. These designs possess a simplified analysis and form the base of many other experimental designs [34].

In using this strategy, the factors are altered simultaneously and not just one at a time, which indicates that, for each run or complete replica, all possible combinations are investigated [35]. For example, if there are *a* levels for factor *A* and *b* levels for factor *B*, then each replica will contain *ab* combinations [18].

One aspect to be considered is that, as there are only two levels per factor, it must be supposed that the response is approximately linear within the range of levels chosen [35]. Another important aspect is that, for experiments with a great number of factors, full factorial design results in an extremely large number of combinations. In this situation, fractional factorial planning is used in order to select a subset of combinations within the full factorial design, aiming to identify the significant factors in system performance [8].

According to [39], many studies in operational research use full factorial design due to its simplicity and because the technique allows the analyst to identify interactions between factors as well as their main effects.

Factorial designs are more efficient than the one-at-a-time approach, as they allow for the factors' effects to be estimated via the other factors' levels, thus leading to valid conclusions about the experimental scope; they are also the only manner to discover interactions among the variables, thus avoiding erroneous conclusions when interactions between the factors are present [18].

5.3. Fractional factorial designs

When there is little interest in interaction behavior among the factors which compose the system, this can be disregarded [35]. Instead, fractional factorial design can be used.

For example, consider a factorial design of 2^5. In this planning, five degrees of freedom correspond to the main effects, 10 degrees of freedom correspond to second order interactions and 16 degrees of freedom correspond to the highest order of interactions. In initial system or project studies, there is little interest in the highest level of interactions [35].

If interactions can be disregarded, fractional factorial design involving fewer executions for a complete set of 2^k executions can be used in order to obtain information about the main effects and lower order interactions [35].

Thus, fractional factorial design provides a means by which to obtain estimates of main effects and, perhaps, second order interactions, with a fraction of the computational force required for full factorial design [4].

According to [18], the greatest application of fractional factorial designs is in screening experiments, where many factors are present in a system and the objective is to identify which factors indeed exercise a significant effect over the given response of interest. For the factors identified as significant through the use of fractional designs, the author recommends a more careful analysis with the use of other designs, such as full factorial design.

In fractional factorial design, a subset of 2^{k-p} is constructed from a set of all of the possible points for a 2^k design, and a simulation is executed for only the chosen points [4].

For this type of factorial design, the analyst must be attentive to its resolution. According to [35], the concept of resolution design is the form in which the fractional factorial designs are related in accordance with the associative standards which they produce. A design's resolution is represented by a Roman subscript number; for example, $2_{III}^{(3-1)}$represents a factorial design with resolution III, with half of the experiments used in full factorial design [18]. The designs with resolution of III, IV and V are particularly important; they are listed in detail below [35].

- **Design resolution III:** These are the designs in which the main effect is associated with another main effect, but these main effects are associated with second order interactions and second order interactions may be associated.
- **Design resolution IV:** These are the designs in which the main effect is associated with any other main effect or any other second order interaction, but second order interactions are associated with each other.

- **Design resolution V:** These are the designs in which no main effect or second order interaction is associated with any other main effect or second order interaction, but the second order interactions are associated with third order interactions.

6. Sensitivity analysis development stages

As a way of simplifying DOE application in sensitivity analysis of simulation models, the following sequence of steps is proposed.

The flowchart proposed in Figure 3 presents the necessary steps for conducting sensitivity analysis in discrete-event simulation models. Four stages are defined for the proposed method:

1. Simulation;
2. Fractional Factorial Design;
3. Full Factorial Design;
4. Optimization.

In the first step, the analyst should define the optimization objectives as well as verify if the simulation model is verified and validated. In doing so, the model will be apt to proceed to the following step, fractional factorial design. In this phase, the analyst should determine the model's input factors, their levels and select the response variables for analysis.

Once these initial steps have been completed, fractional factorial design can be applied. During execution of the experiments, the analyst should return to the simulation step and carry out the experiments in the simulation package. With the experiments done, the data should be analyzed using statistical means, determining the factors' significance level as well as its lower order interactions. At the end of this phase, the non-significant factors can be removed from analysis.

The third stage defined in the sensitivity analysis phase may be omitted by the analyst, depending on the degree of precision desired or for the cases in which the simulation models demand a lot of computational time in order to be processed. In this stage, a full factorial design is generated with experimental data, and only factors which show to be significant in the previous steps are tested. Depending on the necessity for executing more experiments in order to comply with full factorial design, the analyst will have to return to the simulation phase again to execute new experiments. In this stage, the residues should be analyzed in order to validate the results. Statistical analysis should be conducted once again in order to finalize this stage.

In the following stage, optimization simulation is utilized again. The significant factors after full factorial design application are utilized to configure the optimization tool, which is then executed. Many different configurations are tested for the input parameters until the optimizer converges on a solution. It is up to the analyst to evaluate the results and generate his or her conclusions and recommendations.

In order to demonstrate the utilization of this method in sensitivity analysis of discrete-event simulation models, two simulation models will be used as study objects in this chapter.

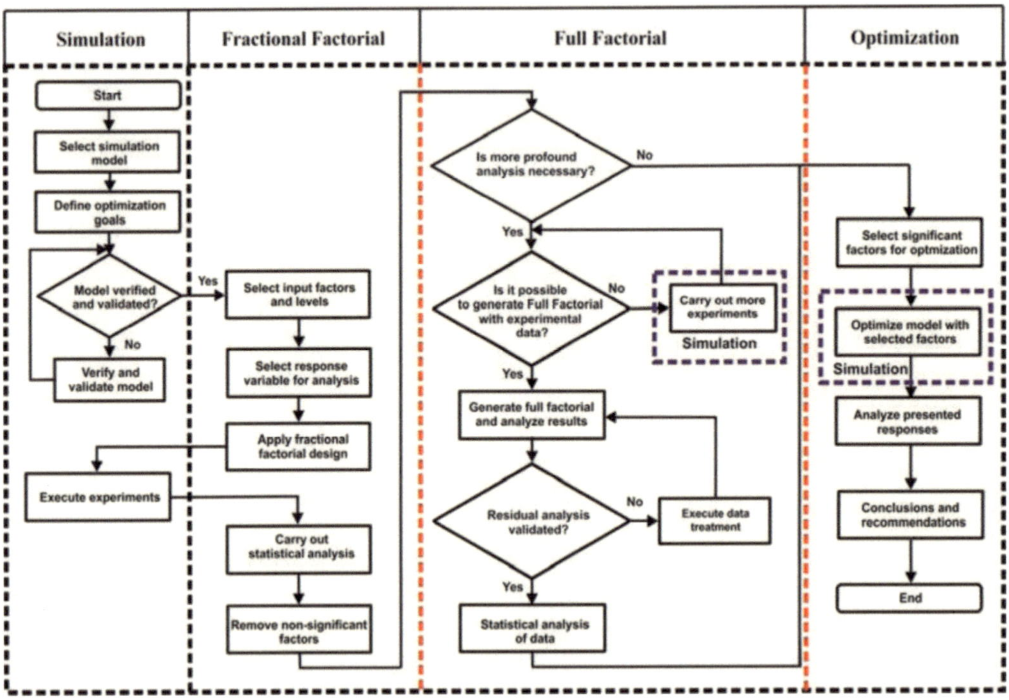

Figure 3. Sequence of steps in order to conduct sensitivity analysis

It should be highlighted here that, in spite of the proposed modeling being applied to great variety of discrete-event simulation models, this approach could be unviable for models which demand a greater amount of computational time to be processed. In these cases, other types of experimental design which involve a smaller number of experiments could be used, such as Plackett-Burman Design; however, according to [18], such designs should be used with great care, as they possess limitations which should be evaluated carefully. An example of this shortcoming is the inability of certain designs to analyze main effects.

7. Modeled systems

The simulation models presented in this chapter were implemented in the software ProModel® and optimized in the package's optimization software, SimRunner®. However, it should be highlighted that the results presented could have been obtained using other commercial simulation packages. Likewise, a commercial statistical software package was utilized to analyze the data.

7.1. Study object 1

The first simulation model represents a quality control station from a telecommunications components factory. The cell is responsible for testing a diverse range of products before shipping them to final clients. This cell receives approximately 75% of the products from the six production lines in the company.

The model in question was verified and validated, thus being ready for study. In order to verify the computational model and correct possible occurrences, some simulator resources such as counters, variables and signals were used, besides the conventional animation. Once the model was validated and verified, simulation was carried out. Statistical tests were utilized which compared the results obtained in the simulation model with data from the real system. The model was considered valid based on statistical tests which did not indicate a statistical difference between real and simulated data.

These conditions are indispensable for conducting sensitivity analysis. The utilization of a non-validated model would lead to erroneous conclusions and undesirable decision-making. For more information about validation and verification, readers are recommended to consult [3]. Figure 4 presents an image of the model implemented in the simulation software.

Figure 4. Representation of the real system implemented in the simulation software

The quality control station possesses the following characteristics:

- 7 inspection posts;
- 3 operators;
- 19 types of products to be tested;
- 31 types of operations possible to be carried out depending on the type of product.

For the case in question, discrete variables were defined, with little variation in the lower and higher levels. This fact is justified due to the fact that the majority of simulation optimization problems work with such conditions; however, the experimentation can be conducted using other variable types and a greater variation between the upper and lower limits. Other types of applications can be seen in [43].

For this study object, two levels were defined for each factor. For [18], when the experiment's objective is factor screening or process characterizations, it is common to utilize a small number of variables for each factor. According to the author, lower and higher levels are the most sufficient to obtain valid conclusions about the factors' significance. For example, even if the factor "Type 1 operators" exhibited the possibility of hiring 1 to 4 operators, for the purposes of the experimental matrix, only two levels would be considered: the lower level being 1 and the upper level being 4.

Variable	Factor	Lower level (-)	Upper level (+)
A	Type 1 operators	1	2
B	Type 2 operators	1	2
C	Type 3 operators	1	2
D	Type 1 inspection posts	1	2
E	Type 2 inspection posts	1	2
F	Type 3 inspection posts	1	2
G	Type 4 inspection posts	1	2
H	Type 5 inspection posts	1	2
J	Type 6 inspection posts	1	2
K	Type 7 inspection posts	1	2

Table 2. Experimental factors for the first study object

The optimum set of variables will be determined using three approaches. The first one performs several experiments to identify the main factors. After identifying the statistically significant simulation factors by using a two sample t hypothesis test (a usual procedure from any statistic package), the original fractional factorial design can -be converted to full factorial, eliminating the non-statistically significant terms. As these parameters are also important to the simulation arrangement, despite not being statistically significant, they can be kept constant in proper levels. Comparatively, a second approach can be established by using the main factors identified at the experiments DOE as input for the optimization via SimRunner. Finally, the third approach is performed using all ten factors in optimization via Simrunner.

7.2. Study object 2

The second study object represents an automotive components production cell. The objective in this study object is to find the best combination of input variables which maximizes cell throughput. As with the previous case, the model was verified and validated, being ready for sensitivity analysis and optimization. Figure 5 shows an image of the model implemented in the simulation software.

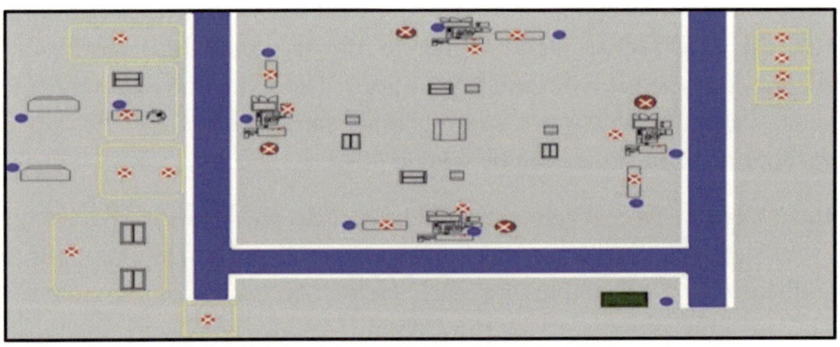

Figure 5. Representation of the real system implemented in the simulation software

The cell presents the following characteristics:

- 41 machines;
- 3 operators;
- 8 different types of products;
- 46 types of possible processes throughout the system.

Variable	Factor	Lower level (-)	Upper level (+)
A	Type 1 operators	1	2
B	Type 2 operators	1	2
C	Type 3 operators	1	2
D	Type 1 machines	1	2
E	Type 2 machines	1	2
F	Type 3 machines	1	2
G	Type 4 machines	1	2
H	Type 5 machines	1	2
J	Type 1 inspection posts	1	2
K	Type 2 inspection posts	1	2
L	Type 3 inspection posts	1	2
M	Type 4 inspection posts	1	2

Table 3. Experimental factors for the second study object

The optimum set of parameters is determined by three approaches similar to the first application.

8. Experimentation

8.1. Identification of significant factors

According to [4], in simulation experimental designs provide a way to decide which specific configurations to simulate before the runs are performed so that the desired information can be obtained with the fewest simulation runs. For instance, considering the second application where there are 12 factors, if a full factorial experiment were chosen, $2^{12} = 4096$ runs would be necessary. Therefore, a screening experiment must be considered. Screening or characterization experiments are experiments in which many factors are considered and the objective is to identify those factors (if any) that have large effects [18]. Typically, screening experiment involves using fractional factorial designs and is performed in the early stages of the project when many factors are likely considered to have little or no effect on the response [18]. According to this author, in this situation, it is usually best to keep the number of factors levels low.

8.2. Study object 1

For the first study object, ten experimental factors, each with two levels, were defined, as seen in Table 2. When considering full factorial design, a total number of $2^{10} = 1024$

experiments would be necessary. In order to reduce the acceptable number of experiments, fractional factorial design is used.

Table 4 presents four factorial designs for 10 factors and their resolutions. As the objective of this analysis was to identify the model's sensitivity to certain factors, resolution IV was chosen. Resolution IV indicates that no main effect is associated with any other main effect or second order interaction, but there is interaction between certain second order interactions [18].

Fraction	Resolution	Design	Executions
1/8	V	$2^{(10-3)}$	128
1/16	IV	$2^{(10-4)}$	64
1/32	IV	$2^{(10-5)}$	32
1/64	III	$2^{(10-6)}$	16

Table 4. Factorial designs for 10 factors and their resolutions

Experiment	A	B	C	D	E	F	G	H	J	K	WIP
1	-	-	-	-	-	-	+	+	+	+	99
2	+	-	-	-	-	-	+	-	-	-	95
3	-	+	-	-	-	-	-	+	-	-	101
4	+	+	-	-	-	-	-	-	+	+	104
5	-	-	+	-	-	-	-	-	+	-	94
6	+	-	+	-	-	-	-	+	-	+	98
7	-	+	+	-	-	-	+	-	-	+	100
8	+	+	+	-	-	-	+	+	+	-	99
9	-	-	-	+	-	-	-	-	-	+	93
10	+	-	-	+	-	-	-	+	+	-	95
11	-	+	-	+	-	-	+	-	+	-	97
12	+	+	-	+	-	-	+	+	-	+	98
13	-	-	+	+	-	-	+	+	-	-	101
14	+	-	+	+	-	-	+	-	+	+	101
15	-	+	+	+	-	-	-	+	+	+	99
16	+	+	+	+	-	-	-	-	-	-	98
17	-	-	-	-	+	-	+	+	-	-	101
18	+	-	-	-	+	-	+	-	+	+	95
19	-	+	-	-	+	-	-	+	+	+	100
20	+	+	-	-	+	-	-	-	-	-	98
21	-	-	+	-	+	-	-	-	-	+	94
22	+	-	+	-	+	-	-	+	+	-	95
23	-	+	+	-	+	-	+	-	+	-	93
24	+	+	+	-	+	-	+	+	-	+	99

25	-	-	-	+	+	-	-	-	+	-	93
26	+	-	-	+	+	-	-	+	-	+	98
27	-	+	-	+	+	-	+	-	-	+	99
28	+	+	-	+	+	-	+	+	+	-	98
29	-	-	+	+	+	-	+	+	+	+	95
30	+	-	+	+	+	-	+	-	-	-	101
31	-	+	+	+	+	-	-	+	-	-	98
32	+	+	+	+	+	-	-	-	+	+	100
33	-	-	-	-	-	+	-	-	+	+	99
34	+	-	-	-	-	+	-	+	-	-	98
35	-	+	-	-	-	+	+	-	-	-	97
36	+	+	-	-	-	+	+	+	+	+	99
37	-	-	+	-	-	+	+	+	+	-	98
38	+	-	+	-	-	+	+	-	-	+	100
39	-	+	+	-	-	+	-	+	-	+	98
40	+	+	+	-	-	+	-	-	+	-	99
41	-	-	-	+	-	+	+	+	-	+	98
42	+	-	-	+	-	+	+	-	+	-	97
43	-	+	-	+	-	+	-	+	+	-	100
44	+	+	-	+	-	+	-	-	-	+	96
45	-	-	+	+	-	+	-	-	-	-	99
46	+	-	+	+	-	+	-	+	+	+	100
47	-	+	+	+	-	+	+	-	+	+	98
48	+	+	+	+	-	+	+	+	-	-	103
49	-	-	-	-	+	+	-	-	-	-	99
50	+	-	-	-	+	+	-	+	+	+	96
51	-	+	-	-	+	+	+	-	+	+	101
52	+	+	-	-	+	+	+	+	-	-	100
53	-	-	+	-	+	+	+	+	-	+	99
54	+	-	+	-	+	+	+	-	+	-	100
55	-	+	+	-	+	+	-	+	+	-	98
56	+	+	+	-	+	+	-	-	-	+	102
57	-	-	-	+	+	+	+	+	+	-	96
58	+	-	-	+	+	+	+	-	-	+	97
59	-	+	-	+	+	+	-	+	-	+	95
60	+	+	-	+	+	+	-	-	+	-	99
61	-	-	+	+	+	+	-	-	+	+	97
62	+	-	+	+	+	+	-	+	-	-	97
63	-	+	+	+	+	+	+	-	-	-	99
64	+	+	+	+	+	+	+	+	+	+	98

Table 5. The $2_{IV}^{(10-4)}$ design matrix for principal fraction and results

Among the resolution IV designs presented in Table 4, the fractional factorial design $2_{IV}^{(10-4)}$ was chosen. This design, despite possessing a greater number of executions than the design $2_{IV}^{(10-5)}$, allows for the reduction of full factorial designs for six or less factors, without requiring new experiments; that is, the results of this design can be used in full factorial designs with six or less factors, without needing to conduct additional experiments. However, if preliminary studies show that there are a significant number of fewer variables (5 or less), the factorial design $2_{IV}^{(10-5)}$ could be chosen with no problems.

It is worth mentioning that factorials with a resolution less than IV should be omitted because, in these types of design, the main effects are associated with second level interactions, and second level interactions could possess interaction between each other, as well, thus making these designs undesirable.

Table 5 shows the design matrix for the principal fraction and the results obtained for the WIP. Wip represents the total number of pieces in quality control inspection; its result is shown by the variable introduced in the simulation model which subtracts the pieces which leave the system (inspected pieces) from the total number of entities which enter the system (pieces to be inspected). This value is then offered at the conclusion of the simulation in which the report is generated. In the table, the best results attained with the experimentation are shown. In Table 5, the symbols – and + indicate the lower and upper levels shown in Table 2, respectively.

As an example, the number of operator types 1, 2 and 3 and the number of inspection posts types 1, 2 and 3 (A B C D E F) were defined in the simulator as being equal to the lower level (1); for the inspection posts types 4, 5, 6 and 7 (G H J K), the upper level was defined. A replica utilizing this configuration was run in the simulation software, and work in process (WIP) statistics were stored for analysis. This process was repeated 63 other times until all of the experimental matrix's configurations were run.

The $2_{IV}^{(10-4)}$ fractional factorial design used in this research was not replicated. Therefore, it is not possible to assess the significance of the main and interaction effects using the conventional bilateral t-test or ANOVA. The standard analysis procedure for a non-replicated two-level design is a normal plot of the estimated factor's effects. However, these designs are so widely used in practice that many formal analysis procedures have been proposed to overcome the subjectivity of normal probability [18]. [44], for instance, recommend the use of Lenth's method, a graphical approach based on a Pareto Chart for the error term. If the error term has one or more degrees of freedom, the line on the graph is drawn at t, where t is the (1 - α/2) quartile of a t-distribution with a number of degrees of freedom equal to the number of effects/3. The vertical line in the Pareto Chart is the margin of error, defined as ME = t x PSE. Lenth's pseudo standard error (PSE) is based on sparseness of the effects principle, which assumes the variation in the smallest effects is due to the random error. To calculate PSE the following steps are necessary: (a) calculates the absolute value of the effects; (b) calculates S, which is 1.5 x median of the step (c); calculates the median of the effects that are less than 2.5 x S and (d) calculates PSE, which is 1.5 x median calculated in step (c).

With the aid of statistical software, it was possible to perform quantitative analysis of the stored data. Figure 6 presents the Pareto Chart for $2_{IV}^{(10-4)}$ fractional design with significance level of 5%.

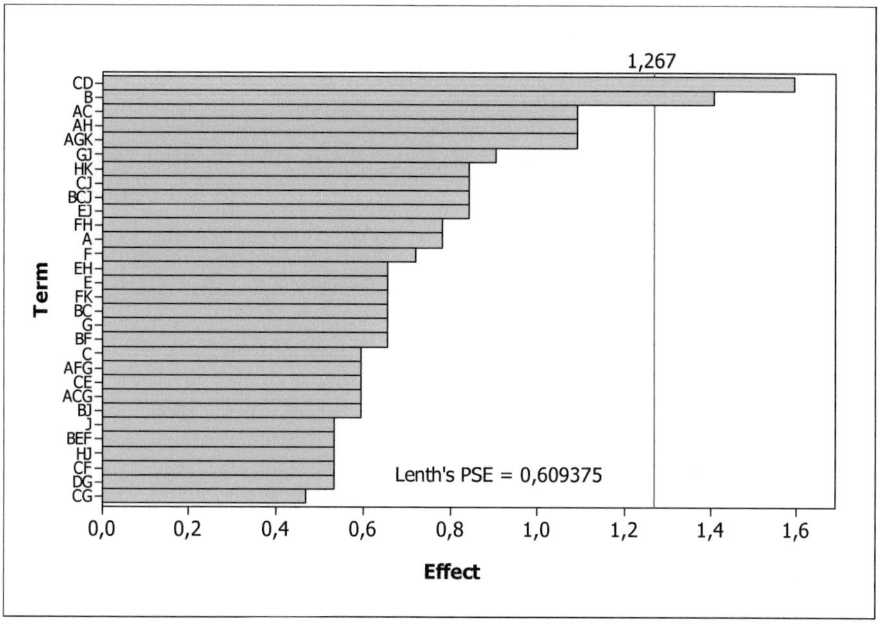

Figure 6. Pareto chart for $2_{IV}^{(10-4)}$ fractional design with a significance level of $\alpha = 5\%$

By analyzing the figure, it can be seen that factor B (number of type 2 operators) and interaction CD (number of type 3 and type 1 inspection posts) are significant. According to [18], if the experimenter can reasonably assume that certain high-order interactions are negligible, information on the main effects and low-order interactions may be obtained. Otherwise, when there are several variables, the system or process is likely to be driven primarily by some of the main effects and low-order interactions. For this reason, it is reasonable to admit that factors A, E, F, G, H, J and K are not significant, although they are still necessary for the simulation model and must be kept at the lower level (-).

Factors C and D may be considered significant, seeing as the interaction between the two factors are quite significant. In Figure 7, it can be seen that B and C exercise a positive effect over the WIP; shifting from the lower to upper level causes an increase in the WIP. Inversely, factor D exercises a negative effect; shifting from the lower to upper level causes WIP to fall. Analysis of interaction behavior in fractional factorial design is not recommended, since the effects possess the property of aliases. That is, according to [18], two or more factors are aliased when it is not possible to distinguish between the effects of overlapping factors. Only three main factors may be considered significant (B, C, D), and full factorial with these factors can be carried out with the data from the 64 experiments.

Factorial design's own structure helps explain why only factors B, C and D were chosen to compose the new factorial design. The main reason B is aliased with the triple interaction

AGH, which can be disregarded according to the chosen resolution for factorial design and by the sparsity of effects principle [18]. In turn, interaction CD is aliased with two triple interactions, AFH and BFG, which can be disregarded, just as in the last case. It can also be aliased with the double interaction in JK; however, as the main factors J and K are not significant, this interaction may also be discarded. The alias structure used in this analysis is available in many statistical packages.

Fractional factorial design $2_{IV}^{(10-4)}$ was converted into a full factorial design 2^3 with replicas. Residual analysis is also possible, since now there are replicas, seeing that the experimentation changed from fractional factorial design $2_{IV}^{(10-4)}$ to full factorial design 2^3 (8 experiments).

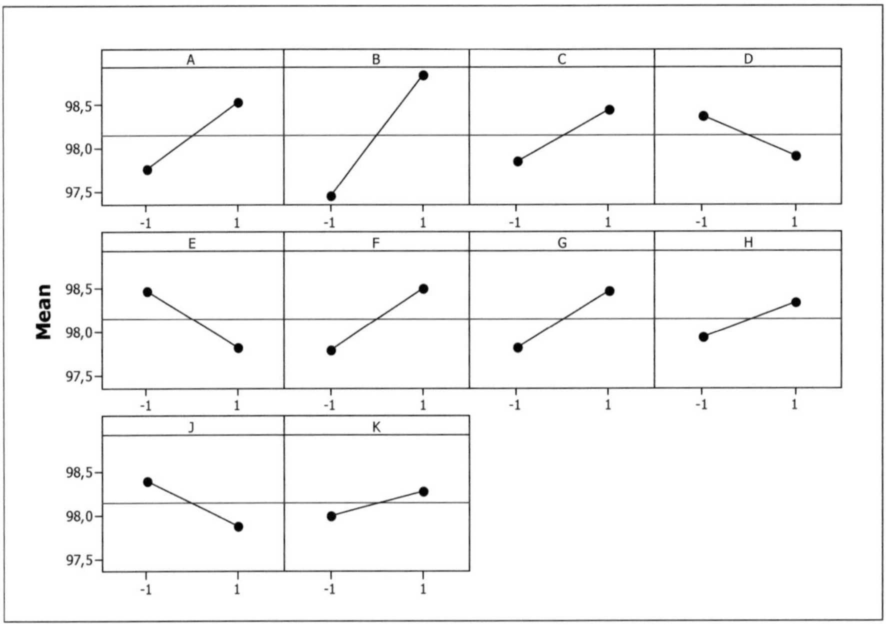

Figure 7. Main effects plot for WIP

According to [18], the residues need to be normal, random and not correlated in order to validate the experimental values obtained. Figure 8 shows the verification of the residues normality.

Evaluating the normality probability graph, one can see that the data are adjusted to a normal distribution, as is evidence by the way the points fall over the line in the graph as well as analysis of the P-value. One can see the data points follow the straight line, and the P-value for the normality test was less than 0.05, leading to the conclusion that the data are normally distributed. Figure 9 shows the verification of the residues independence. The standardized graphs versus the observed values do not present any random patterns of grouping or bias.

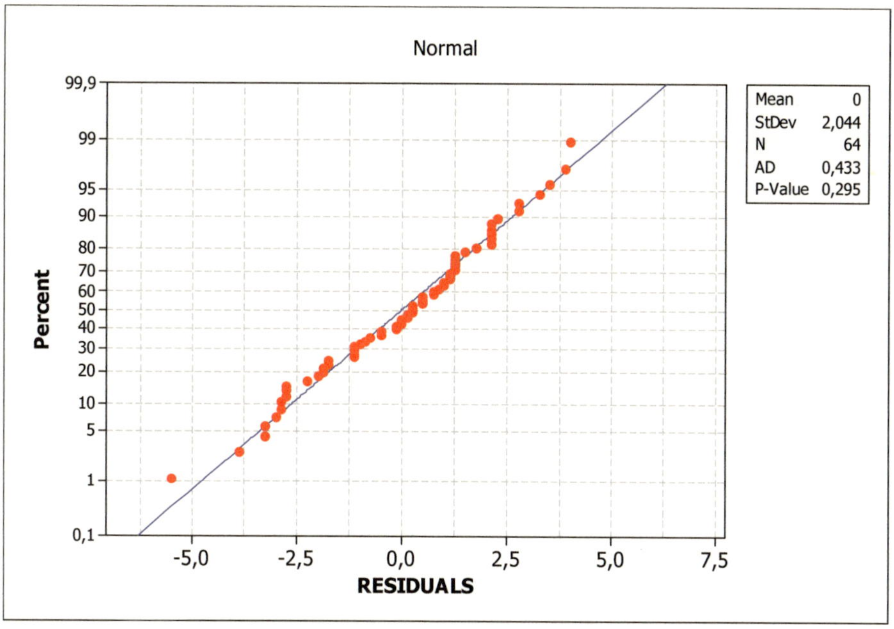

Figure 8. Verification of the residues normality

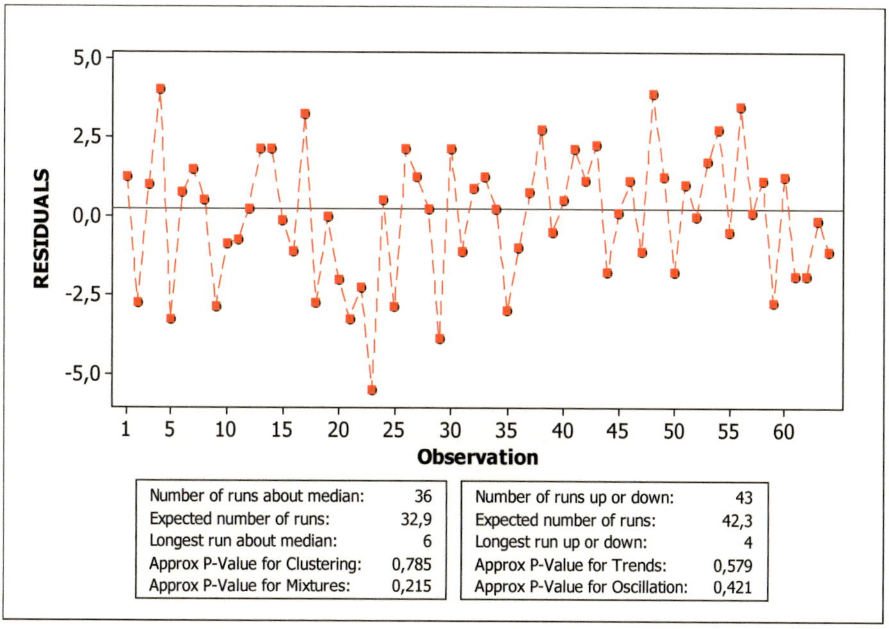

Figure 9. Verification of the residues independence

Once the residual validity was verified, the results could be analyzed using DOE. The analyses continued to be carried out via graphical analysis due to its ease of comprehension.

Figures 10 and 11 present the analysis for the new design. By analyzing figure 10, it can be verified that factor B (number of type 2 operators) and the interaction CD (number of type 3 operators and number of type 1 inspection posts) remained significant. In this new design, no other main factor or interaction demonstrated a significance level greater than 5%.

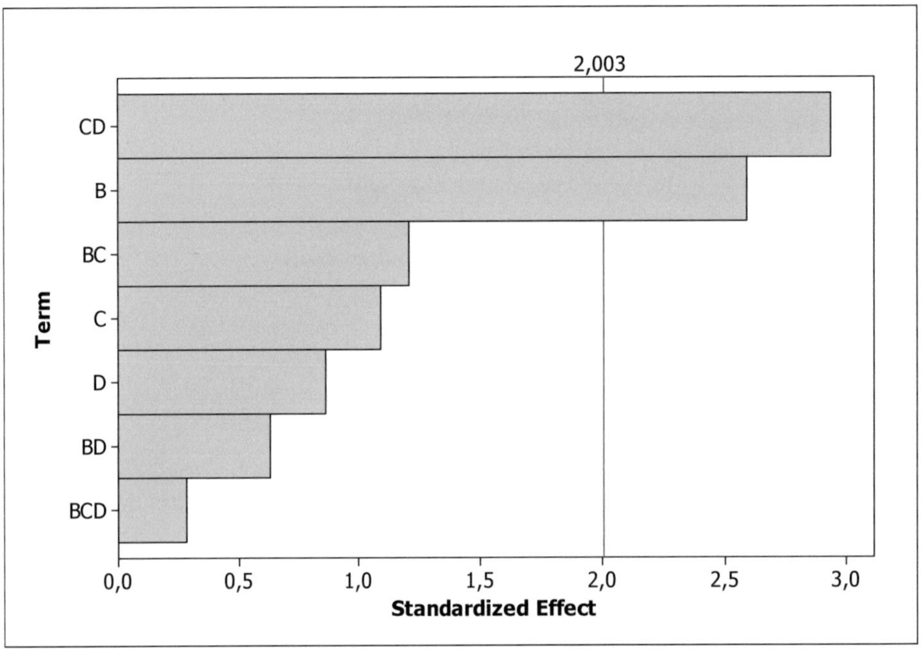

Figure 10. Pareto Chart for full factorial design with significance level $\alpha = 5\%$

Analysis of Figure 11 shows that factors B and C exercise a positive effect over the WIP; that is, they should be kept at the lower level in order to minimize the WIP count. Factor D should be kept at the upper level, since it exercises a negative effect on the WIP count. By observing Figure 11, it can be seen that the CD interaction has a strong effect on diminishing the WIP when the main effects C and D remain at their own respective lower and upper levels.

There are strong indications about an improved configuration for the input variables in order to minimize the WIP count. However, these suppositions will be tested using commercial optimization software. First, 10 input variables will be utilized; afterwards, only the three variables which showed to be significant according to the study in this section will be evaluated, and the seven other factors will be fixed in the lower level, seeing as they are not significant.

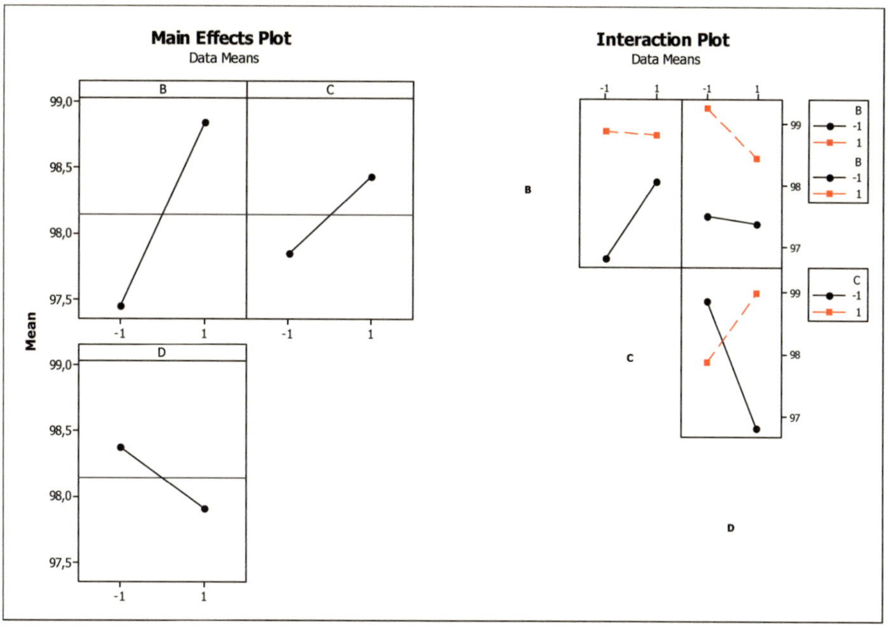

Figure 11. Factorial and interaction plots for 2^3 full factorial design

8.3. Study object 2

For the second study object, 12 experimental factors were defined, as presented in Table 3. Each factor possesses two levels. Unlike the previous case, for this study the objective is to maximize the manufacturing cell's throughput. Thus, the significance of the 12 factors will be analyzed. Considering full factorial design, 2^{12} = 4096 experiments would be necessary. Similar to the previous case, fractional factorial design was used to reduce the number of experiments.

Table 6 presents four factorial designs for 12 factors and their resolutions. As the analysis objective in this case is to identify the model's performance sensitivity to the factors, a resolution IV design was chosen.

Fraction	Resolution	Design	Executions
1/256	III	$2^{(12-8)}$	16
1/128	IV	$2^{(12-7)}$	32
1/64	IV	$2^{(12-6)}$	64
1/32	IV	$2^{(12-5)}$	128

Table 6. Factorial designs for 10 factors and their resolutions

Out of the resolution IV plans presented in Table 6, fractional factorial design $2_{IV}^{(12-6)}$ was chosen. Researchers opted for this design due to its location between the fractional factorial designs $2_{IV}^{(12-7)}$ and $2_{IV}^{(12-5)}$, thus enabling a reduction to full factorial design for six or less factors, without having to carry out new experiments. It should be noted here that if more than six factors are shown to be significant, another factorial design could be done while taking advantage of the data already acquired from the fractional factorial design $2_{IV}^{(12-6)}$ and realizing only the non-tested experiments.

Table 7 presents the experimental design matrix for the principal fraction and throughput. Throughput represents the number of pieces produced by the manufacturing cell. For this case, researchers needed to create a variable to store the number of pieces produced and present this value at the end of the simulation. The greatest value produced is highlighted.

Experiment	A	B	C	D	E	F	G	H	J	K	L	M	Throughput
1	-	-	-	-	-	-	-	-	+	+	+	+	369200
2	+	-	-	-	-	-	-	+	+	+	-	-	408200
3	-	+	-	-	-	-	-	+	-	-	-	+	392600
4	+	+	-	-	-	-	-	-	-	-	+	-	390000
5	-	-	+	-	-	-	-	+	-	-	+	-	392600
6	+	-	+	-	-	-	-	-	-	-	-	+	390000
7	-	+	+	-	-	-	-	-	+	+	-	-	400400
8	+	+	+	-	-	-	-	+	+	+	+	+	416000
9	-	-	-	+	-	-	+	-	-	-	+	+	403000
10	+	-	-	+	-	-	+	+	-	-	-	-	413400
11	-	+	-	+	-	-	+	+	+	+	-	+	429000
12	+	+	-	+	-	-	+	-	+	+	+	-	429000
13	-	-	+	+	-	-	+	+	+	+	+	-	413400
14	+	-	+	+	-	-	+	-	+	+	-	+	408200
15	-	+	+	+	-	-	+	-	-	-	-	-	421200
16	+	+	+	+	-	-	+	+	-	-	+	+	429000
17	-	-	-	-	+	-	+	-	-	+	-	-	390000
18	+	-	-	-	+	-	+	+	-	+	+	+	429000
19	-	+	-	-	+	-	+	+	+	-	+	-	426400
20	+	+	-	-	+	-	+	-	+	-	-	+	431600
21	-	-	+	-	+	-	+	+	+	-	-	+	416000
22	+	-	+	-	+	-	+	-	+	-	+	-	410800
23	-	+	+	-	+	-	+	-	-	+	+	+	410800
24	+	+	+	-	+	-	+	+	-	+	-	-	434200
25	-	-	-	+	+	-	-	-	+	-	-	-	392600
26	+	-	-	+	+	-	-	+	+	-	+	+	408200
27	-	+	-	+	+	-	-	+	-	+	+	-	400400
28	+	+	-	+	+	-	-	-	-	+	-	+	395200
29	-	-	+	+	+	-	-	+	-	+	-	+	405600
30	+	-	+	+	+	-	-	-	-	+	+	-	397800
31	-	+	+	+	+	-	-	-	+	-	+	+	395200
32	+	+	+	+	+	-	-	+	+	-	-	-	429000

33	-	-	-	-	-	+	+	-	+	-	-	-	400400
34	+	-	-	-	-	+	+	+	+	-	+	+	423800
35	-	+	-	-	-	+	+	+	-	+	+	-	421200
36	+	+	-	-	-	+	+	-	-	+	-	+	421200
37	-	-	+	-	-	+	+	+	-	+	-	+	400400
38	+	-	+	-	-	+	+	-	-	+	+	-	397800
39	-	+	+	-	-	+	+	-	+	-	+	+	405600
40	+	+	+	-	-	+	+	+	+	-	-	-	444600
41	-	-	-	+	-	+	-	-	-	+	-	-	371800
42	+	-	-	+	-	+	-	+	-	+	+	+	410800
43	-	+	-	+	-	+	-	+	+	-	+	-	403000
44	+	+	-	+	-	+	-	-	+	-	-	+	382200
45	-	-	+	+	-	+	-	+	+	-	-	+	384800
46	+	-	+	+	-	+	-	-	+	-	+	-	387400
47	-	+	+	+	-	+	-	-	-	+	+	+	395200
48	+	+	+	+	-	+	-	+	-	+	-	-	421200
49	-	-	-	-	+	+	-	-	-	-	+	+	397800
50	+	-	-	-	+	+	-	+	-	-	-	-	423800
51	-	+	-	-	+	+	-	+	+	+	-	+	382200
52	+	+	-	-	+	+	-	-	+	+	+	-	413400
53	-	-	+	-	+	+	-	+	+	+	+	-	395200
54	+	-	+	-	+	+	-	-	+	+	-	+	405600
55	-	+	+	-	+	+	-	-	-	-	-	-	392600
56	+	+	+	-	+	+	-	+	-	-	+	+	416000
57	-	-	-	+	+	+	+	-	+	+	+	+	395200
58	+	-	-	+	+	+	+	+	+	+	-	-	429000
59	-	+	-	+	+	+	+	+	-	-	-	+	429000
60	+	+	-	+	+	+	+	-	-	-	+	-	434200
61	-	-	+	+	+	+	+	+	-	-	+	-	410800
62	+	-	+	+	+	+	+	-	-	-	-	+	423800
63	-	+	+	+	+	+	+	-	+	+	-	-	418600
64	+	+	+	+	+	+	+	+	+	+	+	+	449800

Table 7. The $2_{IV}^{(12-6)}$ design matrix for principal fraction and results

Similar to the last case, fractional factorial design $2_{IV}^{(12-6)}$ was utilized without replicas. With the help of statistical software, the data were analyzed. Figure 12 shows the Pareto Chart for $2_{IV}^{(12-7)}$, fractional design with a significance level of 5%. By analyzing the first figure, it can be seen that factors G (number of type 4 machines), A (number of type 1 operators), H (number of type 5 machines), B (number of type 2 operators), E (number of type 2 machines) and the interaction BG (number of type two operators and number of type 4 machines) are significant according to the adopted significance level. It can be said that the factors C, D, F, J, K, L and M are not significant, although they are necessary for the simulation and their values may be fixed at the lower level (assuming a value of 1), since they do not exercise a significant effect over the model's throughput.

By analyzing Figure 13, it can be seen that the main factors A, B, E, G, and G exercise a positive effect over throughput; that is, by altering the lower level to the upper level, there is an increase in throughput.

Interaction behavior analysis in fractional factorial design is not recommended, seeing that aliasing between effects tends to emerge. Thus, full factorial design with the significant factors will be carried out using the data from the 64 experiments carried out. As was the previous case, the alias structure for factorial design $2_{IV}^{(12-6)}$ enables the explanation for why A, B, E, G and H were chosen to make up the full factorial design.

The main factor A is aliased with the two triple interactions BCH and HLM. Factor B is aliased with two other triple interactions, ACH and CLM. Factor E is aliased with the interactions DFG and FJK. Factor G is aliased with DEF and DKJ. Factor H is aliased with the interactions ABC and ALM. Finally, the interaction BG is aliased with four triple interactions, ADL, CEK, CFJ and DHM. All these interactions can be disregarded according to the chosen level of resolution for factorial design and the principle of sparsity of effects principle [18].

It can be concluded that, although the simulation model possesses 12 input variables which may be arranged in order to maximize total throughput, only 5 variables significantly contribute to increased throughput. In following, an optimization of this simulation model will be executed, using a commercial software package, first optimizing all 12 input variables, and then with only the 5 input variables which are statistically significant.

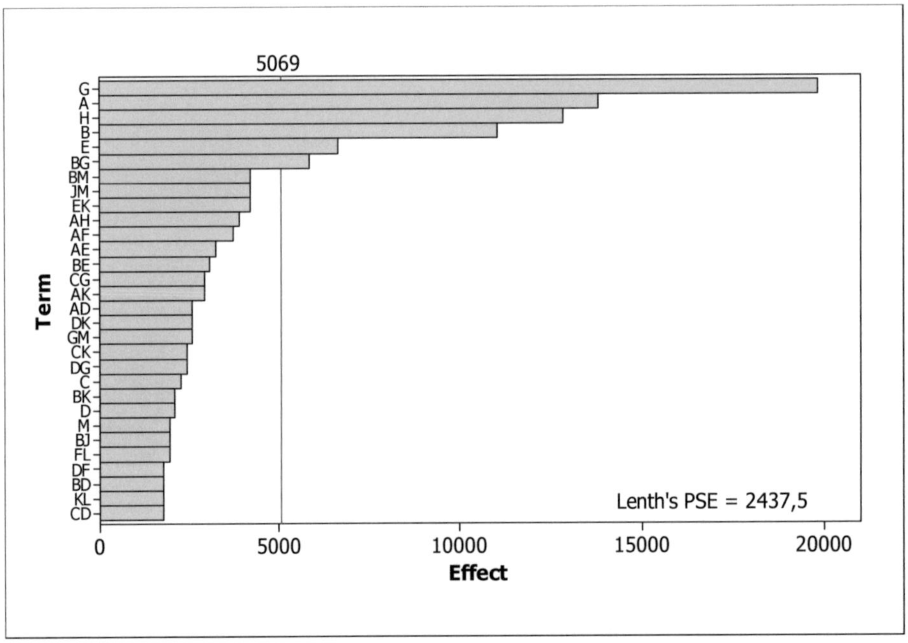

Figure 12. Pareto Chart for $2_{IV}^{(12-7)}$ fractional design with significance level of 5%

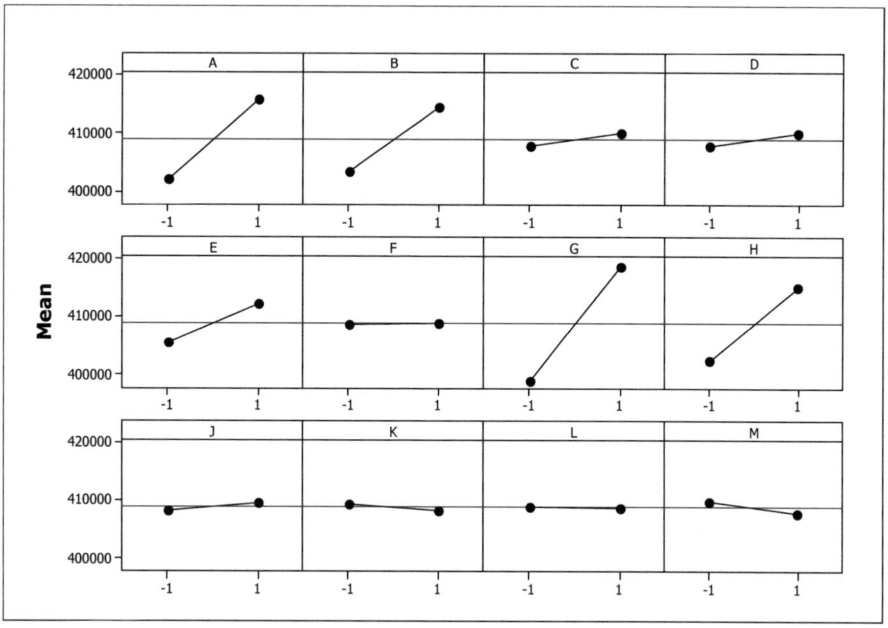

Figure 13. Main effects plot for throughput

Fractional factorial design $2_{IV}^{(12-6)}$ was converted into a full factorial design 2^5 with replicas. Before analyzing the new design's results, the validity of the results was tested, as was the case with the previous experiment. Once the validity of the new design's residues' was verified, it was then possible to statistically analyze the results with DOE.

With the new design, the main factors A, B, E, G and H, the interactions BG, AGH, ABEG and AH showed to be significant, according to the 5% significance level (Figure 14). All of the main factors presented positive effects on the throughput, according to Figure 15; that is, shifting from the lower (–) and upper (+) level, the production cell's throughput increases.

It can then be concluded that, although the simulation model possesses 12 input variables which can be arranged in order to maximize throughput, only five variables significantly contribute to increased production. In following, a comparison will be performed between the commercial optimization software; first, all 12 input variables will be optimized, and then only the five variables which are statistically significant will be optimized.

It is worth mentioning here another optimization approach which is commonly utilized in simulation optimization. By using full factorial design with replicas, it is possible to generate a metamodel for the response variable under analysis. With a mathematical model on hand, traditional optimization tools such as Microsoft Excel's Solver may be utilized in place of simulation optimization tools. An example of such a technique can be seen in [43].

Another approach which is commonly employed in the literature is Response Surface Methodology. As was cited in the previous strategy, a mathematical model, generally non-linear of second-order, is generated through the experimental data and then is optimized. The shortcoming of this strategy is that the model must possess a robust fit, which allows for a satisfactory representation of the response factor. If the model is not robust, experimental strategies should be employed in order to redefine the experimental region, which many times is not applicable for simulation optimization problems.

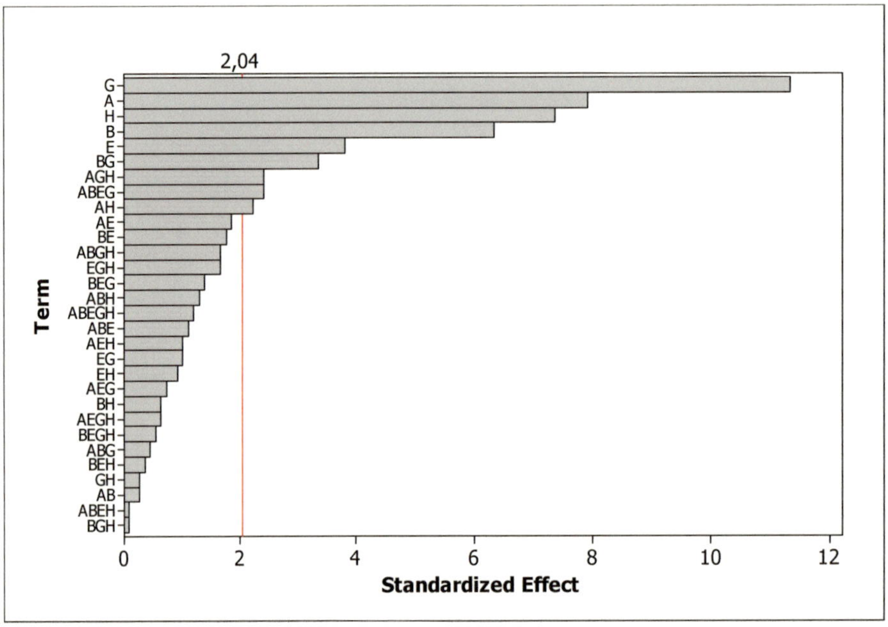

Figure 14. Pareto Chart for 2^5 full factorial design with significance level $\alpha = 5\%$

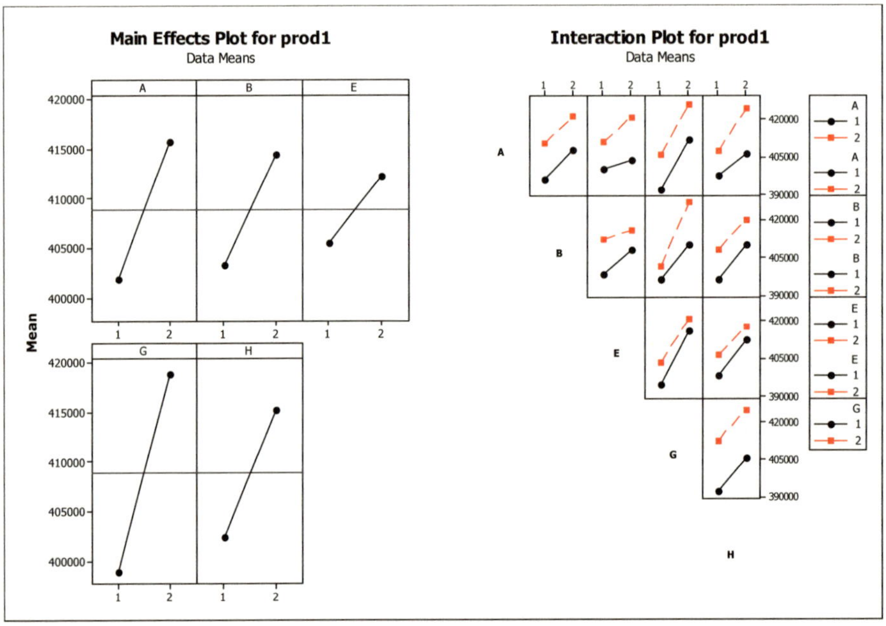

Figure 15. Factorial and interaction plots for 2^5 full factorial design

9. Simulation model optimization

Through the sensitivity analysis, each simulation model's significant variables may be identified. Considering only these results, the best combination of input variables can be inferred in order to optimize the simulation models; however, there is no way of guaranteeing this affirmation based in only a sensitivity analysis.

One way of confirming these results is through optimization. An example application of simulation optimization will be employed as a means of evaluating the efficiency of fractional factorial design in the execution of sensitivity analysis.

The adopted procedure is to optimize the study objects in two different ways. In the first case, all input variables will be optimized and, in the second case, only the factors selected in the sensitivity analysis will be optimized. Finally, the results attained will be compared in order to verify if the design techniques were advantageous to the process. The time involved in the process will not be the basis for comparison; thus it is evident that the number of experiments necessary will be reduced for the model to arrive at a solution.

The simulation software package SimRunner® from the ProModel Corporation will be utilized for the execution of experiments; however, there are other simulation optimization software packages that could have been chosen for this investigation. SimRunner® integrates resources to analyze and optimize simulation models through multivariable optimization. This type of optimization tests multiple factor combinations in search of the system input variable configuration which leads to the best objective function value [20].

SimRunner® is based in a genetic algorithm and possesses three optimization profiles: Aggressive, Moderate and Cautious. These profiles are directly related to the confidence in the solution and the time necessary to find this solution. The cautious profile was chosen for this study in order to consider the greatest possible number of solutions and in turn, guarantee a more comprehensive search and present better responses [45].

9.1. Optimization of the first study object

The optimization objective for the first simulation model was to find the best input variable combination in order to minimize the system's work in process count. As presented in Table 2, this model possesses 10 input variables, being varied at the lower level (1) and the upper level (2).

In the first optimization stage, 10 input model variables were selected and the optimizer was configured. The results found can be seen in Figure 16.

The optimizer converged with 296 experiments. The best result obtained was 92, which was attained during experiment 261, as seen in Figure 16. The values found for the factors are shown in Table 8.

The sensitivity analysis for the first study object identified three factors with significant effects which can be utilized for simulation (Table 9). The other variables were maintained at their original values, defined as the lower level (*).

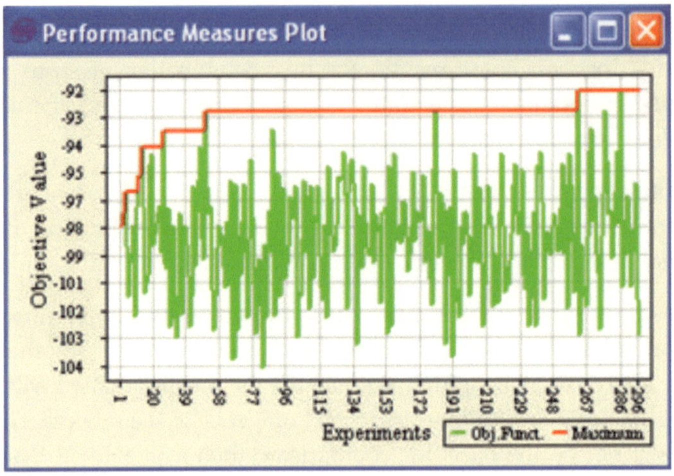

Figure 16. Performance measures plot for optimization using all factors

Factor	Variable	Value
A	Type 1 operators	2
B	Type 2 operators	2
C	Type 3 operators	1
D	Type 1 inspection posts	2
E	Type 2 inspection posts	1
F	Type 3 inspection posts	1
G	Type 4 inspection posts	1
H	Type 5 inspection posts	2
J	Type 6 inspection posts	1
K	Type 7 inspection posts	1

Table 8. The best solution for optimization using all factors

Factor	Variables	Value Range
B	Type 2 operators	1 - 2
C	Type 3 operators	1 - 2
D	Type 1 inspection posts	1 - 2

Table 9. Significant factors for the first study object

The results found can be seen in Figure 17.

Simrunner® converged after 8 experiments. The best result was 93, which was obtained in the seventh experiment, as shown in Figure 17. The values are shown in Table 10.

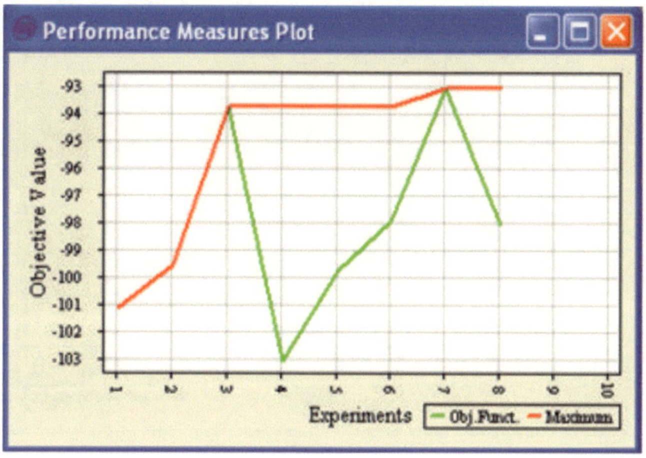

Figure 17. Performance measures plot for optimization using significant factors

Factor	Variable	Value
A	Type 1 operators	1*
B	Type 2 operators	1
C	Type 3 operators	1
D	Type 1 inspection posts	2
E	Type 2 inspection posts	1*
F	Type 3 inspection posts	1*
G	Type 4 inspection posts	1*
H	Type 5 inspection posts	1*
J	Type 6 inspection posts	1*
K	Type 7 inspection posts	1*

Note: The parameters identified with (*) were not used as input for optimization. They were kept at lower level (1).

Table 10. The best solution for optimization using significant factors

9.2. Optimization of the second study object

The optimization objective for the second simulation model was to find the best combination of model input variables in order to maximize the manufacturing cell's throughput. As presented in Table 3, the model possesses 12 input variables which are varied from the lower level (1) to the upper level (2).

In the first optimization phase, the 12 model input variables were selected and the optimization software was set up for experimentation. The results found can be seen in Figure 18.

The optimizer converged with 173 experiments. The best result found was 452,400, which was obtained in experiment 10 (Figure 18). The obtained values are shown in Table 11.

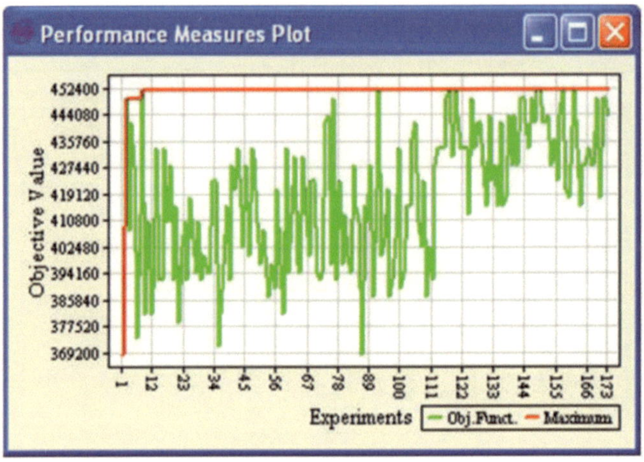

Figure 18. Performance measures plot for optimization using all factors

Factor	Variable	Value
A	Type 1 operators	2
B	Type 2 operators	2
C	Type 3 operators	1
D	Type 1 machines	2
E	Type 2 machines	2
F	Type 3 machines	2
G	Type 4 machines	2
H	Type 5 machines	1
J	Type 1 inspection posts	2
K	Type 2 inspection posts	2
L	Type 3 inspection posts	2
M	Type 4 inspection posts	2

Table 11. Best solution for optimization using all factors

The sensitivity analysis for the second study object identified five factors with significant effects which will be used for simulation optimization inputs (Table 12). The other model input variables were kept at their lower level (*).

Factor	Variables	Value range
A	Number of type 1 operators	1 - 2
B	Number of type 2 operators	1 - 2
E	Number of type 2 machines	1 - 2
G	Number of type 4 machines	1 - 2
H	Number of type 5 machines	1 - 2

Table 12. Significant factors for the second study object

The results are shown in Figure 19.

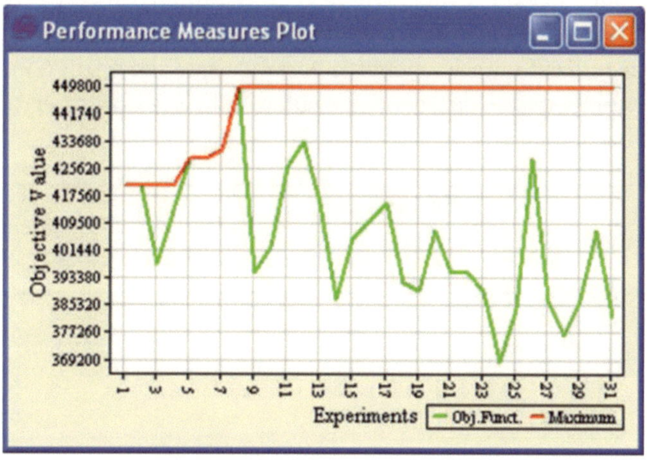

Figure 19. Performance measures plot for optimization using significant factors

Simrunner® converged after 31 experiments. The best value found was 449,800, which was attained in the eighth experiment carried out using the optimizer. The factors' values can be seen in Table 13.

Factor	Variable	Value
A	Type 1 operators	2
B	Type 2 operators	2
C	Type 3 operators	1*
D	Type 1 machines	1*
E	Type 2 machines	2
F	Type 3 machines	1*
G	Type 4 machines	2
H	Type 5 machines	2
J	Type 1 inspection posts	1*
K	Type 2 inspection posts	1*
L	Type 3 inspection posts	1*
M	Type 4 inspection posts	1*

Note: The parameters identified with (*) were not used as input for optimization. They were kept at lower level (1).

Table 13. Best solution for optimization using significant factors

10. Results analysis

10.1 First study object

Table 14 presents a comparison of the results attained utilizing the three methods for the first study object. As far as the number of experiments executed, the advantage of using sensitivity analysis to identify the significant factors becomes obvious. The commercial optimizer carried out 296 experiments when all of the input variables were chosen; when only the significant factors were utilized, merely 8 experiments were executed. Summing up the 64 experiments utilized with fractional factorial design, the result (72) is still four times smaller than the number of experiments executed with the optimizer when all 10 input variables were utilized.

Parameter	Optimization using all factors	Optimization using significant factors	Design of experiments
A	2	1*	1
B	2	1	1
C	1	1	1
D	2	2	2
E	1	2	2
F	1	1*	1
G	1	1*	1
H	2	1*	1
J	1	1*	2
K	1	1*	1
Result (WIP)	92	93	93
Confidence Interval (95%)	(83 – 100)	(86 – 99)	-
Number of runs	296	8	64

Note: The parameters identified with (*) were not used as input for optimization. They were kept at the lower level (1).

Table 14. Optimization results for the three procedures of the first study object

In respect to the responses found, it should be highlighted that, due to the simulation model's stochastic character, the response presented by the optimizer should be analyzed with care while considering both the average value and confidence interval of each result found.

Analyzing only the average optimization result found, it can be noted that the result found by the optimizer, when all 10 decision variables were manipulated was greater, reaching a WIP result of 92. However, when the response's confidence interval is analyzed, it can be said that the optimization's responses, when considering only the significant factors and their respective confidence intervals, are equal. The advantage of the response found using the sensitivity analysis is that only two factors (D and E) had to remain at the upper level, while the rest were kept at the lower level in order to minimize WIP.

The results in Table 5 were found with only the use of fractional factorial design and were selected using the best results during the experimentation process. This approach, however, does not take into consideration any simulation optimization approach and should be viewed with caution. The result using only DOE shows the possibility of using experimental design with optimization. This possibility was not explored in detail here, as it was not this chapter's objective; however, many authors [1, 4, 18, 19] present optimization techniques using only experimental design.

10.2. Second study object

Table 15 shows a comparison of the results obtained using the three methods for the second study object.

Parameter	Optimization using all factors	Optimization using significative factors	Design of experiments
A	2	2	2
B	2	2	2
C	1	1*	2
D	2	1*	2
E	2	2	2
F	2	1*	2
G	2	2	2
H	1	2	2
J	2	1*	2
K	2	1*	2
L	2	1*	2
M	2	1*	2
Result (WIP)	452400	449800	449800
Confidence Interval (95%)	(445182 – 459617)	(440960 – 458639)	-
Number of runs	173	31	64

Note: The parameters identified with (*) were not used as input for optimization. They were kept at lower level (1).

Table 15. Optimization results for the three procedures analyzing the second study object

In relation to the number of experiments executed, once again, the sensitivity analysis showed itself to be efficient. Along with the reduction in the number of factors, the number of experiments fell from 173 to 31. With the addition of 64 experiments using fractional factorial design, the method was efficient with 95 experiments, a little more than half of the experiments when all factors were considered.

In relation to the optimization result, once again, it was necessary to perform a more detailed analysis of the responses. In spite of the average difference between the solutions presented with the optimizer (using all 12 and then only 5 significant factors) being around 2,600 pieces, it was verified that the solutions were within the same confidence interval. Thus the post-sensitivity analysis optimization solution's quality again showed itself to be efficient when comparing the optimization of all of the input variables.

As was true with the last case, the results in Table 7 were found with only the use of fractional factorial design and were selected using the best results during the experimentation process.

11. Conclusion

The objective of this chapter was to present how experimental design and analysis techniques can be employed in order to identify significant variables in discrete-event simulation models, thus aiding simulation optimization searches for optimal solutions.

To develop this application, the main concepts of simulation optimization were presented during this chapter. In following, two applications were developed to verify how fractional factorial design can be used in sensitivity analysis for simulation models, identifying its advantages, disadvantages and effects on model optimization.

For optimization, the identification of the significant variables was extremely important, as it enabled the reduction of the search space and computational potential necessary to perform the search for an optimal solution. Optimization was performed for the two applications in two distinct forms, utilizing simulation optimization.

The first simulation optimization approach was to use all of the models' input variables. No previous studies were performed to determine if the models' variables exercised significant effects on overall system performance. The second approach relied on sensitivity analysis in order to identify the variables which influenced system performance. After identifying the significant variables, model optimization was utilized while using the reduced search space. The third approach involved using only the experimentation's results without using any simulation optimization procedure.

By analyzing the results, the advantages of using sensitivity analysis become evident, not only due to the reduction in necessary computational potential for the optimization process, but also for the greater level of detail and knowledge acquired about the process under study. By using this experimentation, it is possible to verify the process's variables which exercise the greatest effects on overall system performance, thus being able to determine the effect each variable has on the process as well as their interactions. These interactions would be very difficult to define and easy to disregard in simulation projects without the use of DOE.

It should not go without noting, however, that one must take extreme caution during execution of these experiments, as just one experiment realized under incorrect conditions or out of the correct matrix order can lead to erroneous results. In order to analyze the results obtained during experimentation, the user should have a solid understanding of DOE and statistics. Those erroneous conclusions in simulation could possibly lead to incorrect implementation, which could generate very tangible costs in the real world. Thus, it is recommended that one research further the concepts shown in this chapter.

One approach that is commonly used for simulation model optimization which was not explored in great detail in this chapter is the development of a mathematical metamodel, which represents a determined model output, according to optimization. This approach has a vast field of application and could have been applied in the problems presented. It is also recommended that the reader study this topic further as well [18, 43, 46]. In this sense, the use of Kriging metamodeling for simulation has established itself in the scientific simulation community, which can be seen in [46, 47, 48, 49], thus demonstrating its promising research field.

The use of discrete-event simulation along with optimization is still scarce; nonetheless, in the last decade, important studies about this area of operational research have started to be realized, supporting the wider acceptance of this approach while also investigating the barriers to its continuous improvement. The use of sensitivity analysis in DOE enables a reduction in search space while increasing the optimization process's efficiency and speed.

Simulation optimization helps take simulation from being merely a means of scenario evaluation to a much greater solution generator. In doing so, sensitivity analysis plays a crucial role in this process, as it helps overcome the time and computational potential barriers presented by simulation models with large numbers of variables, thus making optimization an even greater tool for aiding decision-making.

In respect to future research possibilities, a potentially rich area in terms of investigation would be the examination of experimental designs which would reduce the number of experiments needed in order to identify the significant factors in pre-optimization phases. Another point which could be investigated more profoundly is the inclusion of qualitative techniques, such as brainstorming, cause and effect diagrams and Soft Systems Methodology, in order to select the factors to be utilized in experimentation. A field which is little-explored is sensitivity analysis in the optimization of multiple-objective models.

Author details

José Arnaldo Barra Montevechi, Rafael de Carvalho Miranda and Jonathan Daniel Friend
Universidade Federal de Itajubá (UNIFEI), Instituto de Engenharia de Produção e Gestão (IEPG), Itajubá, MG, Brazil

Acknowledgement

The authors extend their sincere gratitude to the Brazilian educational funding agencies of FAPEMIG, CNPq, the engineering support program CAPES, and the company PADTEC for their continued support during the development of this project.

12. References

[1] Banks J, Carson II JS, Nelson BL, Nicol DM (2005) Discrete-event Simulation. New Jersey: Prentice-Hall.

[2] Bruzzone AG, Bocca E, Longo F, Massei M (2007) Training and recruitment in logistics node design by using web-based simulation. Int. J. Internet Manuf. Serv. 1(1): 32-50.

[3] Sargent RG (2009) Verification and validation of simulation models. In: Winter Simulation Conference, Proceedings... Austin, TX, USA.

[4] Law AM (2007) Simulation modeling and analysis. New York: McGraw-Hill.

[5] Jahangirian M, Eldabi T, Naseer A, Stergioulas LK, Young T (2010) Simulation in manufacturing and business: A review. Eur J Oper Res. 203(1):1-13.
[6] Ryan J, Heavey C (2006) Process modeling for simulation. Comput Ind. 57(5): 437-450.
[7] Law AM, Mccomas, MG (2002) Simulation-Based Optimization, In: Winter Simulation Conference, Proceedings... San Diego, CA, USA.
[8] Harrel CR, Mott JRA, Bateman RE, Bowden RG, Gogg TJ (1996) System improvement using simulation. Utha: Promodel Corporation.
[9] Fu MC (2002) Optimization for Simulation: Theory vs. Practice. J. Comput. 14(3): 192-215.
[10] Fu MC, Andradóttir S, Carson JS, Glover F, Harrell CR, Ho, YC, Kelly JP, Robinson SM (2000) Integrating optimization and simulation: research and practice. In: Winter Simulation Conference, Proceedings... Orlando, FL, USA.
[11] Harrel CR, Ghosh BK, Bowden R (2004) Simulation Using Promodel. New York: McGraw-Hill.
[12] Law AM, Kelton WD (2000) Simulation modeling and analysis. New York: McGraw-Hill.
[13] Banks J, Carson II JS, Nelson BL, Nicol DM (2000) Discrete event system simulation. New Jersey: Prentice-Hall.
[14] April J, Better M, Glover F, Kelly JP, Laguna M (2005) Enhancing business process management with simulation optimization. In: Winter Simulation Conference, Proceedings... Monterey, CA, USA.
[15] Andradóttir S (1998) Simulation optimization. In: Banks J, editor, Handbook of Simulation. New York: John Wiley & Sons. pp. 307-333.
[16] Biles WE (1979) Experimental design in computer simulation. In: Winter Simulation Conference, Proceedings... San Diego, CA, USA.
[17] Biles WE (1984). Experimental design in computer simulation. In: Winter Simulation Conference, Proceedings... Dallas, TX, USA.
[18] Montgomery DC (2005) Design and Analysis of Experiments. New York: New York: John Wiley & Sons, Inc.
[19] Kleijnen JPC (1998). Experimental design for sensitivity analysis, optimization, and validation of simulation models. In: Banks J, editor. Handbook of Simulation. New York: John Wiley & Sons. p. 173-223.
[20] Carson Y, Maria A (1997) Simulation optimization: methods and applications. In: Winter Simulation Conference, Proceedings... Atlanta, GA, USA.
[21] Azadeh A, Tabatabaee M, Maghsoudi A (2009) Design of Intelligent Simulation Software with Capability of Optimization. Aust. J. Basic Appl. Sci. 3(4): 4478-4483.
[22] Fu MC (1994) Optimization via simulation: A review. Ann Oper Res. 53:199-247.
[23] Rosen SL, Harmonosky CH, Traband MT (2007) Optimization of Systems with Multiple Performance Measures via Simulation: Survey and Recommendations. Comput. Ind. Eng. 54: 327-339.
[24] Bettonvil BWM, Castillo E, Kleijnen JPC (2009) Statistical testing of optimality conditions in multiresponse simulation-based optimization. Eur J Oper Res. 199(2): 448-458.

[25] Coello CAC, Lamont GB, Van Veldhuizen DA (2007) Evolutionary Algorithms for Solving Multi-Objective Problems (Genetic and Evolutionary Computation). New York: Springer.

[26] Holland JH (1992) Adaptation in Natural and Artificial Systems. Cambridge: MIT Press.

[27] Martí R, Laguna M, Glover F (2006) Principles of Scatter Search. Eur J Oper Res.169(2): 359-372.

[28] Glover F, Laguna M, Martí R (2005) Principles of Tabu Search, In: Gonzalez T, editor, Approximation Algorithms and Metaheuristics. London: Chapman & Hall/CRC.

[29] Ripley B (1996) Pattern Recognition and Neural Networks. Cambridge: University Press.

[30] Aarts EHL, Korst J, Michiels W (2005) Simulated Annealing. In: Burke EK, Kendall G, editors. Introductory tutorials in optimisation, decision support and search methodologies. New York: Springer. pp. 187-211.

[31] April J, Glover F, Kelly JP, Laguna M (2003) Practical introduction to simulation optimization. In: Winter Simulation Conference, Proceedings... New Orleans, LA, USA.

[32] Banks, J. Panel Session: The Future of Simulation. In: Winter Simulation Conference, Proceedings... Arlington, VA, USA, 2001.

[33] Tyni T, Ylinen J (2006) Evolutionary bi-objective optimization in the elevator car routing problem. Eur J Oper Res. 169(3):960-977.

[34] Montgomery DC (2009) Introduction to Statistical Quality Control. New York: John Wiley & Sons, Inc.

[35] Montgomery DC, Runger GC (2003) Applied Statistics and Probability for Engineers. New York: John Wiley & Sons, Inc.

[36] Kelton WD (2003) Designing simulation experiments. In: Winter Simulation Conference, Proceedings... New Orleans, LA, USA.

[37] Kleijnen JPC, Sanchez SM, Lucas TW, Cioppa TM (2005) State-of-the-Art Review: A User's Guide to the Brave New World of Designing Simulation Experiments. J. Comput. 17(3): 263–289.

[38] Montevechi JAB, Pinho AF, Leal F, Marins FAZ (2007) Application of design of experiments on the simulation of a process in an automotive industry. In: Winter Simulation Conference, Proceedings... Washington, DC, USA.

[39] Sanchez SM, Moeeni F, Sanchez PJ (2006) So many factors, so little time.... Simulation experiments in the frequency domain. Int J Prod Econ. 103: 149–165.

[40] Kleijnen JPC (2001) Experimental designs for sensitivity analysis of simulation models. In: Eurosim, Proceedings… Delft, Netherlands.

[41] Chung CA (2004) Simulation Modeling Handbook: a practical approach. Washington, DC: CRC Press.

[42] Landsheer JA, Wittenboer GVD, Maassen GH (2006) Additive and multiplicative effects in a fixed 2 x 2 design using ANOVA can be difficult to differentiate: demonstration and mathematical reason. Soc Sci Res. 35: 279–294.

[43] Montevechi JAB, Almeida Filho RG, Paiva AP, Costa RFS, Medeiros AL (2010) Sensitivity analysis in discrete-event simulation using fractional factorial designs. J. Simulat. 4: 128-142.

[44] Ye KQ, Hamada M (2001) A step-down Lenth method for analyzing unreplicated factorial designs. J Qual Technol. 33(2):140–153.

[45] Simrunner User Guide. ProModel Corporation: Orem, UT. USA. 2002.

[46] Kleijnen JPC, van Beers W, van Nieuwenhuyse I (2010) Constrained optimization in simulation: A novel approach. Eur J Oper Res. 202 (1): 164-174.

[47] Kleijnen JPC (2009) Kriging metamodeling in simulation: A review. Eur J Oper Res. 192(3): 707–716.

[48] Ankenman B, Nelson BL, Staum J (2010) Stochastic Kriging for Simulation Metamodeling. Oper. Res. 58(2):371–382.

[49] Biles WE, Kleijnen JPC, van Beers WCM, van Nieuwenhuyse I (2007) Kriging metamodeling in constrained simulation optimization: an explorative study. In: Winter Simulation Conference, Proceedings... Washington, DC, USA.

Section 2

Novel Integration of Discrete Event Simulation with Other Modeling Techniques

Chapter 4

Discrete Event Simulation Combined with Multiple Criteria Decision Analysis as a Decision Support Methodology in Complex Logistics Systems

Thiago Barros Brito, Rodolfo Celestino dos Santos Silva,
Edson Felipe Capovilla Trevisan and Rui Carlos Botter

Additional information is available at the end of the chapter

http://dx.doi.org/10.5772/50107

1. Introduction

Discrete Event Simulation (DES) is a decision support tool that is extensively used to solve logistics and industrial problems. Indeed, the scope of DES is now extremely broad in that it includes manufacturing environments, supply chains, transportations systems and computer information systems [1]. However, although its usage spreads dramatically, few authors, practitioners or users are able to fully understand and apply the methodology in order to derive its full potential.

While alone, the DES methodology is a tool that improves user comprehension of a system, it has sometimes been incorrectly stigmatized as a method, a "crystal ball." Indeed, a DES model should not be built to accurately predict the behavior of a system, but rather used to allow decision makers to fully understand and respond to the behavior of the variables (elements, resources, queues, etc.) of the system and the relations between those variables. However, depending on the complexity of the system, a deeper analysis and evaluation of the system behavior and variable tradeoff analyses may be a complicated task, since logistics problems, by nature, are composed of several elements interacting among themselves simultaneously, influencing each other in a complex relationship network, often under conditions that involve randomness. Further, the observation and evaluation of numerous decision criteria is required, led by multiple goals (often intangible and even antagonistic) and commonly running across long time horizons where the risks and uncertainties are salient elements.

In order to expand the capacity of DES to support decision making, other decision support methodologies may be incorporated, thereby adding greater value to the model and strengthening the overall capacity of the decision-making process. Consequently, the proposal of this chapter is to incorporate Multiple Criteria Decision Analysis (MCDA) into a DES model.

In this context, the DES model is built to analyze the operational performance of the system's variables, based on several alternative system configurations. From this point on, a multi-criteria decision model should be applied to the DES results, bringing to light and taking into account an evaluation of the decision-making priorities and judgments of decision makers over the decision criteria and thus formally studying the tradeoff between the performances of the decision criteria in the DES model. Therefore, the main objectives of this chapter are to:

- Understand the capabilities of DES as a decision support methodology in complex logistics systems;
- Show the most important aspects of a decision-making process;
- Build and implement a Decision Support System (DSS) that merges the DES and MCDA methodologies to serve as a catalyst to improve the decision-making process;
- Present a real case study to analyze the establishment and operational configuration of a new steel production plant, an example of a complex and multifaceted logistics system; and
- Draw conclusions on the application of this hybrid DSS methodology.

2. The application of DES in complex logistics systems as a DSS

A DES model is a mathematical/logical structure that represents the relationships among the components of a system. It has long been one of the mainstream computer-aided decision-making tools because of the availability of powerful computers. Traditionally, DES has been efficiently employed to simulate complex logistics systems owing to its capacity to replicate the behavior of the system, to represent all its relevant physical aspects and to provide decision-making insights into how to respond.

The DES methodology presented in this paper is based on the steps proposed by [2]. Those steps are summarized and graphically represented by [3], which divide the development of the model into three main stages (Figure 1):

a. Conception: definition of the system and its objectives, as well as data collection and conceptual modeling;
b. Implementation: preparation of the computer model itself, verification and validation; and
c. Analysis: simulation runs and sensitivity and results analysis.

In fact, a DES methodology represents a wider concept, with possible applications in numerous industries and expertise areas, from ordinary daily activities (e.g., the service process in a bank) to situations of elevated complexity (e.g., understanding the evolution of a country's economic indicators or its weather forecasting system).

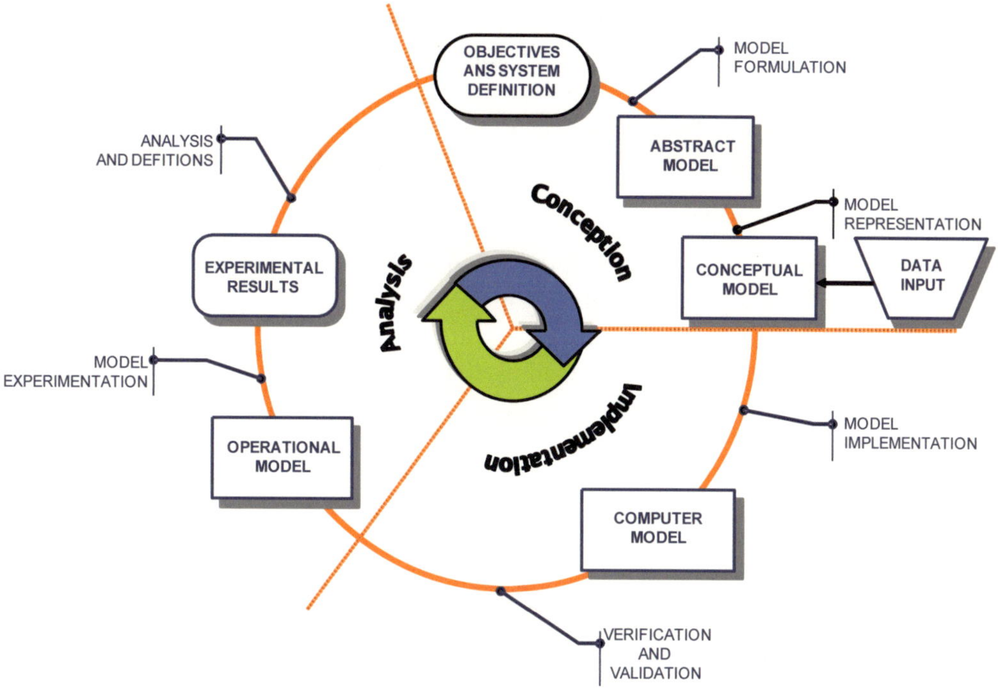

Figure 1. Development of a simulation model [3]

However, the work of [3] defines the DES methodology in the reverse way, namely by clarifying what a DES model is not:

- A crystal ball: the simulation is not able to predict the future, but it can predict, within a selected confidence interval, the behavior of the system;
- A mathematical model: the simulation does not correspond to a mathematical/analytical set of expressions, whose outputs represent the behavior of the system;
- An optimization tool: the simulation is a tool of analysis of scenarios that can be combined with other tools of optimization;
- A substitute for logical/intelligent thought: the simulation is not able to replace human reasoning in the decision-making process;
- A last resource tool: currently, the simulation is one of the most popular techniques applied in operational research (OR); or
- A panacea to resolve all considered problems: the simulation technique works efficiently in a specific class of problems.

However, the complete definition of the DES methodology must be based on the advantages of its use. The characterization of the simulation tool as the concatenation of the procedures of building of a model that represents a system and its subsequent experimentation that aims at observing and understanding the behavior of the system already suggests its main purpose, namely to allow the observer/modeler to carry out "what if" analysis using the system. Indeed, "what if" is the best statement to illustrate the purpose of the simulation methodology. [4] emphasizes the potential of "what if" analysis when affirming that the decision maker, in possession of a DES model, is capable of assuming any appropriate situation or scenario and analyzing the response of the system under such circumstances. Asking "what if" means nothing more than exploring the model, challenging its parameters and examining the impact of the proposed changes on the system.

Then, one can define the main functions of the DES simulation technique as:

- To analyze a new system before its implementation;
- To improve the operation of an already existent system;
- To better understand the functioning of an already existent system; and
- To compare the results from hypothetical situations ("what if" analysis).

Further, the main reasons for its usage include the following [4]:

- The real system still does not exist; the simulation is used as a tool to project the future;
- Experimenting with the real system is expensive; a simulation methodology is used in order to avoid unnecessary expenses with regard to system stoppages and/or modifications to the *modus operandi* of the system; and
- Experimenting with the real system is not appropriate; simulation should be used in order to avoid replicating extreme situations with the real system (e.g., a fire in a building).

A disadvantage of simulation is that even though one can explore wide-ranging problems, they cannot usually be "solved." The simulation methodology does not provide the user with information about the "correct" solution of the problem explored. Instead, it provides subvention for the pursuit of alternatives that best fit the needs of the user's understanding of the problem. Thus, each user, through his or her own vision of the problem, can find particular (and often different) answers for the same model. This characteristic is emphasized by [5] in the work presented in a compilation organized by [6], in which the ultimate goal of modeling and the simulation methodology is discussed.

This discussion begins with the seemingly endless appeal of computational models and the promise that one day, supported by the growing power of computational processing, users will be able to completely and accurately represent a given system using the "perfect" model. However, it is unlikely that a model representing 100% of a given system will ever be built. Even the simplest of models carries a huge list of internal and external relationships between its components in a process under constant renewal and adaptation.

This conclusion reflects the inevitable necessity of working with models that are "incomplete." This is equivalent to carrying out simulation studies within the boundaries that govern the interpretation and representation of real systems. Decision makers are rarely conceptually capable of recognizing the validity of an "incomplete" model, resulting in their inability to work under such boundary conditions. This means that, under the watchful eyes of an "unprepared" decision maker, working with an "incomplete" model may not seem to be an alternative that provides valid results or allows useful analysis.

DES helps frame the problem and establish a defensible course of action, making good decisions and setting priorities is a further and much harder task. A DES model uses analysis to break things down in order to provide information only, not necessarily the right answers or directions for the decision maker. Thus, DES modeling could offer great potential for modeling and analyzing logistics processes. For example, DES models can dynamically model different samples of parameter values such as arrival rates or service intervals, which can help discern process bottlenecks and investigate suitable alternatives. However, while the DES output is tangible, decision making must often rely on intangible information, which raises the question of how to help organizational decision makers harness the incredible complexity of the interaction between logistics problem's variables and the wealth of data available from the analysis of DES models.

3.1. DSSs

DSSs, a type of information system designed to support semi-structured or unstructured managerial activity [10], are ideally suited to bridge the gap between information (tangible and intangible) and decision makers. A properly designed DSS (such as that shown in Figure 2) is an interactive software-based system intended to help decision makers compile useful information from a combination of raw data, documents, personal knowledge and business models in order to identify problems and help make decisions.

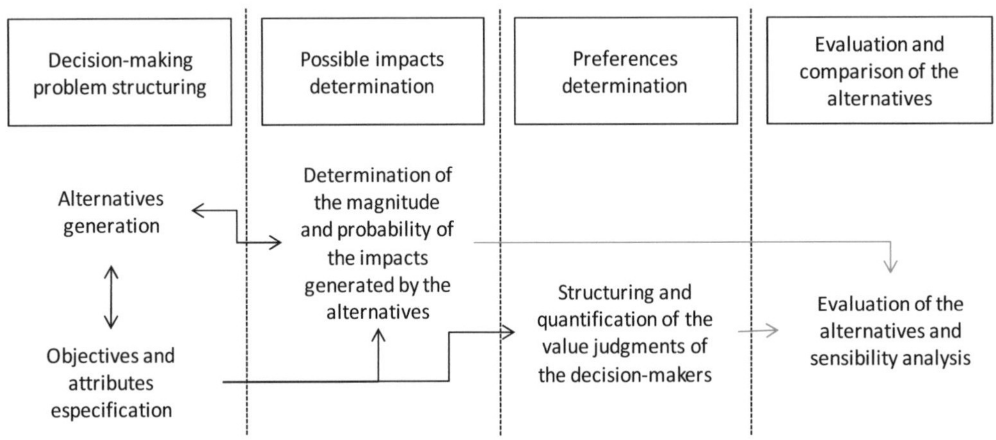

Figure 2. Structuring a DSS application [11].

DSSs, especially in the form of spreadsheets, have become mainstream tools that organizations routinely use to improve managerial decision making [12] often by importing data from enterprise-wide information systems into spreadsheets to address specific business problems. Moreover, DSSs also have the potential to serve as a catalyst to improve the decision-making process, as they provide the capability to organize and share as well as to create knowledge, providing structure and new insights to managers [13].

The most important capability of a DSS might be the possibility of carrying out tradeoff studies. A tradeoff study is the choice of one alternative solution when you have limited decision-making resources that may result in long- or short-term outcomes [14,15]. The main objective of a tradeoff study is thus to arrive at a single final score for each of a number of competing alternative scenarios, using normalizing criteria scoring functions and combining these scores through weighted combining functions.

However, the biggest contribution of a DSS application to evaluating a logistics problem is in pointing out solutions based on decision-making judgments, thus capturing companies' aspirations and worries. For this reason, when conducting anything other than a rough or obvious tradeoff study, careful and honed expert attention must be given to properly choose the criteria scoring functions, weights and inputs – especially if they are in any way subjective. This approach requires, during the process of capturing decision-making judgments, the adoption of an OR intervention tool that should pursue the so-called *facilitated modeling process*. This process requires the operational researcher to carry out the whole intervention jointly with the client, from helping structure and define the nature of the problem of interest to supporting the evaluation of priorities and development of plans for subsequent implementation [16].

Facilitated modeling process

…ional way of conducting OR intervention in logistics problems is so-called *expert* … namely when the decision maker hires OR consultants to objectively analyze a problem situation. The result of this kind of intervention is often the recommendation of an optimal (or semi-optimal) solution. Nevertheless, when dealing with problems at a strategic level, complexity rises and the expert mode of intervention may not be appropriate. [16] present two of the main reasons for its inadequacy:

- The lack of agreement on the scope and depth of the problem situation to be addressed; and
- The existence of several stakeholders and decision makers with distinct and often conflicting perspectives, objectives, values and interests.

Facilitated modeling intervention aims to overcome these issues by structuring decisions in complex and strategic logistics problems. It mainly helps in the negotiation of conflicts of interest during all phases of a decision-making process, taking into consideration different opinions and ideas related to the scope and definition of the problem as well as divergences in the output analysis, values and interest in the results.

In a facilitated modeling approach, the OR consultant must work not only as an analyst, but also as a facilitator and negotiator of conflicts in order to reach a common, satisfactory and useful decision about the problem definition, investigation and resolution. Almost every step taken in the intervention – from defining the problem to creating and analyzing models and providing recommendations – is conducted interactively with the team, in a so-called "helping relationship" [17] between OR consultants and their clients. In Figure 3, [16] define the activities of an OR consultant working as a facilitator in all steps of a facilitated modeling process.

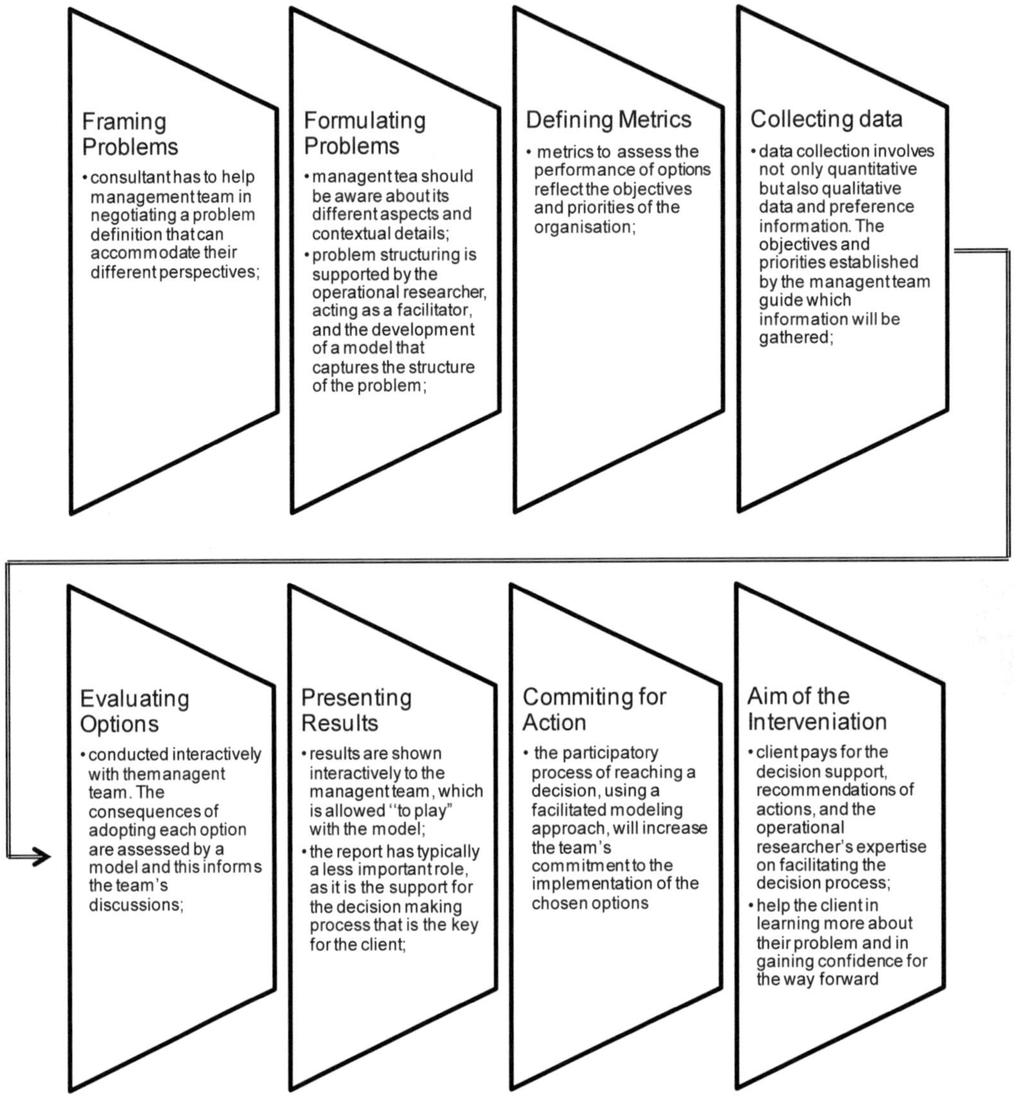

Figure 3. Activities of an OR consultant in a facilitated modeling process [16]

Further literature review based on [16] describes the four main assumptions taken under the facilitated intervention modes:

- Even the tangible aspects of problem framing and formulating, defining metrics and evaluating results have their salience and importance depending on how decision makers subjectively interpret them [18,19]. Different decision makers will perceive a given tangible variable in diverse ways because of their distinct interests and goals. This complicates problem modeling for decision makers [16];
- Following from the above consideration, subjectivity is unavoidable and thus it should be considered when solving a problem. The different perceptions of a problem as well

as distinct points of view and backgrounds may lead to a much better interpretation of a given problem and bring new ideas and concepts, leading to a better result [20,21];

- Despite the fact that experts recommend optimal (or semi-optimal) solutions, decision makers are rarely interested in the best alternative, but rather in a satisfactory one. Satisfactory alternatives also represent a feasible solution in the political, financial and environmental fields. Further, all logistics systems are inevitably too complex to be integrally modeled and they are thus subject to necessary simplifications and assumptions. Any model should thus be seen as a guide, a general indicator of the system behavior, rather than a precise indicator of the performances of the system's variables [22,23]; and
- The decision maker's involvement in the whole process increases the commitment to implement the proposed solution. This involvement increases confidence in the decision-making process. It is a physiological factor of having our voice heard and ideas, preferences and beliefs taken into consideration during all steps of the process [24–26].

It is important to note that neither of the two modes of intervention (i.e., expert or facilitated) is necessarily the best. [22] and [26] argue that for operational and well-defined problems, when there is a clear objective to be optimized or an unquestionable structure of the problem, the expert mode is usually appropriate. However, complex problems may require a facilitated intervention. In this case, the facilitator encourages divergent thinking while helping participants explicitly explore their particular perspectives of the problem. The next step is to stimulate and drive convergent thinking, consolidating a single and fully representative interpretation and perspective of the problem.

Consequently, facilitated modeling is the doorway to building an efficient DSS application. In this paper, we propose the employment of facilitated modeling via the implementation of an MCDA model. Section 4 describes the development and employment of a DSS tool to support strategic decisions about the planning and sizing of a complex logistics system – in this case, a steel production plant and its logistical elements (stockyards, transportation fleet, etc.). Such a tool is able to analyze and evaluate its performance and execute a tradeoff study of possible configurations and operational results.

4. Hybrid DSS: A combination of DES and MCDA

The developed DSS tool represents a hybrid software application combining the techniques of DES modeling with MCDA. The DES methodology will be supported by the Scenario Planning (SP) methodology, which uses hypothetical future scenarios to help decision makers think about the main uncertainties they face and devise strategies to cope with these uncertainties [27]. The SP methodology can be described as the following set of steps:

- Define a set of n strategic options (ai).
- Define a set of m future scenarios (sj).
- Each decision alternative is a combination of a strategic option in a given scenario (ai–sj).
- Define a value tree, which represents the fundamental objectives of the organization.

- Measure the achievement of each decision alternative (ai–sj) on each objective of the value tree using a 100–0 value scoring system.
- Elicit the weights of each objective in the value tree using swing weighting (anchoring on the worst and best decision alternatives in each criterion).
- Aggregate the performances of each decision alternative (ai–sj) using the weights attached to the objectives in the value tree, finding an overall score for the decision alternative.

The SP approach is an extension of MCDA. The SP/MCDA methodology was thus applied in this work using the propositions of [27], which confirm the use of the MCDA methodology as a supporting tool to decision makers in situations of high complexity with potentially significant and long-term impacts. MCDA is a structured DSS technique for dealing with problems in which multiple and complex criteria influence decision making [28], as it allows for the visualization of the rational/logical structure of the problem by representing and quantifying the importance of its elements, relating them to the overall goal and allowing the execution of further tradeoff studies as well as benchmark and sensitivity analyses. The methodology organizes and synthesizes information, includes measures objectively and considers the value judgments of decision makers [29] in an interactive and iterative process. The value judgments of decision makers are captured as preference compensation, thus creating a robust tradeoff instrument.

Several authors have reviewed the utilization of the MCDA methodology as a decision support tool. The 10 major advantages of MCDA, summarized by [28], are the maintenance of the unity of the problem, complexity understanding, criteria interdependence relationship representation, capability of measuring criteria preference, maintenance of consistency, synthesis, tradeoff evaluation, consideration of decision makers' value judgments and consensus reaching. Thus, the goal sought by the MCDA methodology is to identify good and robust alternatives, granting coherence and offering a good tradeoff between different objectives that guide problem resolution. In that way, the multi-criteria analysis in this work will be performed after the results of the DES model have been obtained.

5. Case study

5.1. Problem and objectives

A Brazilian steel company is establishing a new plant in the country's northeast region. The inputs to the plant production as well as the finished goods will all be handled through a private port located very close to the plant. Iron ore and coal are among the main steelmaking process inputs. Coal is imported from various locations around the world and is delivered to the terminal by a chartered vessel fleet, according to a procurement schedule. Iron ore is owned by the company and thus it comes from two distinct Brazilian regions, northeast (NE) and southeast (SE), with remarkable differences in physical properties. The transportation of iron ore from its original locations to the company's private port will be performed by the company's private dedicated fleet, which will operate in a closed-loop circuit. The company's private port operates two berths for unloading, which are able to accommodate small capesize vessels (DWT 120,000 tons). One berth is dedicated exclusively to iron ore unloading and the other to coal unloading.

Thus, the main objectives of this study are (i) to size the company's own vessel fleet (dedicated to supplying iron ore to the plant) and (ii) to determine the storage area assigned to the two types of iron ore (SE and NE). This is because they must be stored separately owing to their physical characteristics and properties in order to avoid any restriction or interruption in the plant steelmaking process based on the poor supply of inputs. This work does not cover the transportation, storage or processing of coal.

5.2. Problem definition

The first step of the problem is the intervention of the OR consultant as a facilitator that focuses on identifying the decision-making group and assessing how it comprehends and evaluates the problem, scopes the decision situation and structures the problem efficiently. These steps correspond to Steps 1 to 4 in Figure 4. The aim here is to put together the full problem representation by considering all the aspects of the facilitated modeling process presented in Section 3.2.

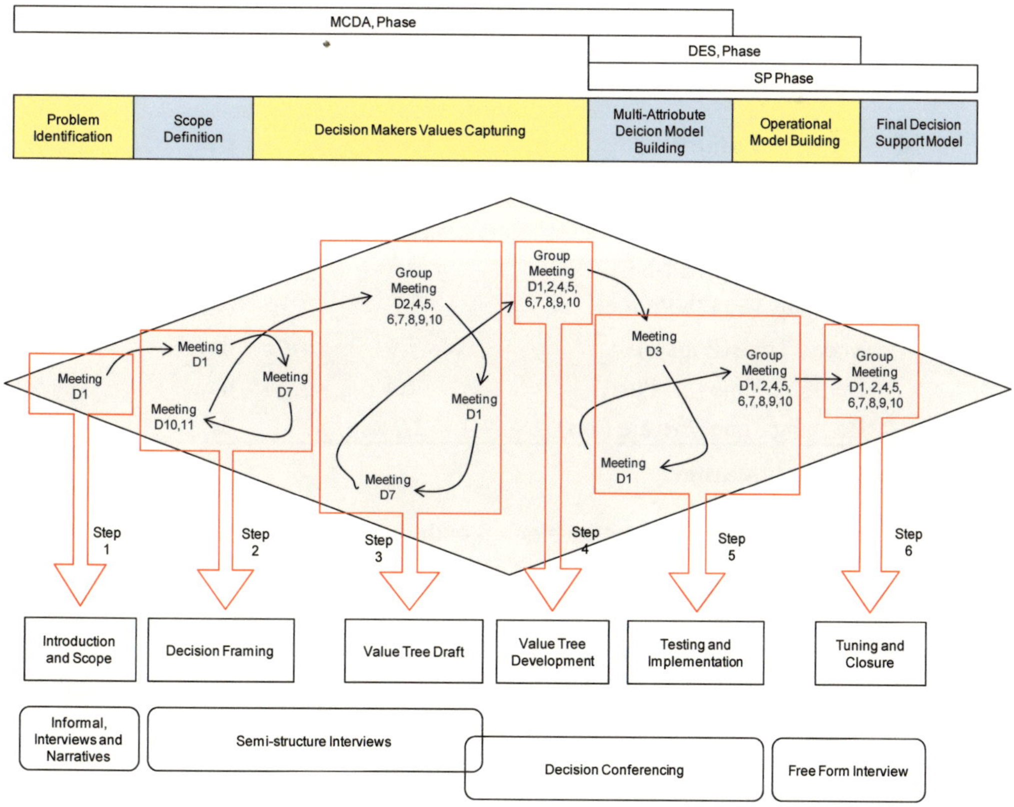

Figure 4. Complete modeling process of a hybrid DSS application (based on [30]).

The next step corresponds to the DES+SP phase of the problem resolution. Based on all the information derived from Steps 1 to 4 in Figure 4 by the OR consultant, the DES model representing the real system should be able to evaluate all the results and variables necessary to help measure system performance, according to the decision maker's criteria. Further, the DES model is built to analyze the proposed logistics system based on several possible system configurations. From this point on, a DSS application, based on a multi-criteria analysis of the results obtained from the DES model of each proposed alternative, was carried out. Through this analysis, it was possible to:

- Determine the "best" size of the iron ore supply vessel fleet required to meet demand for the planned cargo; and
- Assess the capacity of the stockyards for the two types of iron ore (SE and NE).

5.3. Input parameters

All input parameters were provided by the company or derived from the in-depth statistic analysis of the available data. In all considered scenarios, an annual iron ore demand of 5 MTPY (million tons per year) was considered. As mentioned before, iron ore is supposed to be supplied by a dedicated vessel fleet operating in closed-loop system. Moreover, the project fleet is composed of small capesize vessels, while the largest ship able to dock at the port has a 120,000-ton capacity. Table 1 lists the input data for all scenarios.

Parameter	Value	Unit
Planned Demand	5	mtpy
Vessels Capacity	120.000	tonnes
Travel Time (Plant-NE)	2.7	days
Berthing Time (NE Port)	1.5	days
Travel Time (Plant-NE)	7.9	days
Berthing Time (SE Port)	1.4	days
Berthing Time (Private Port)	3.25	days

Table 1. Input data for all scenarios.

However, a number of variables were considered in the simulation run process:

- Company fleet: number of vessels in the company's private fleet;
- SE/NE iron ore percentage: the iron ore employed in the steelmaking process is originally from either the SE or the NE regions of Brazil (see Figure 5). Owing to the specific physical and technical characteristics of each iron ore type, the percentage of SE iron ore may vary from 30% to 40% of the final composition of the steel process output. Although the production department prefers working with the maximum percentage of SE iron ore because of its enhanced physical properties, the procurement and transportation departments prefer working with the minimum percentage of SE iron

ore given the larger distance from the company's private port to the SE port compared with to the NE port;

- Stocks capacities: storage capacities (in tons) for each type of iron ore (SE and NE); and
- Chartering: this variable determines whether vessels are chartered during the periods when the vessels of the company fleet are docked for maintenance. Dockage is carried out every 2 and ½ years, and ships may be unavailable from 7 to 40 days. Chartering vessels with the same operational characteristics is particularly difficult, especially for short time periods.

Thus, with the variation of the proposed variables, it was possible to create a hall of simulation scenarios, which will be evaluated later.

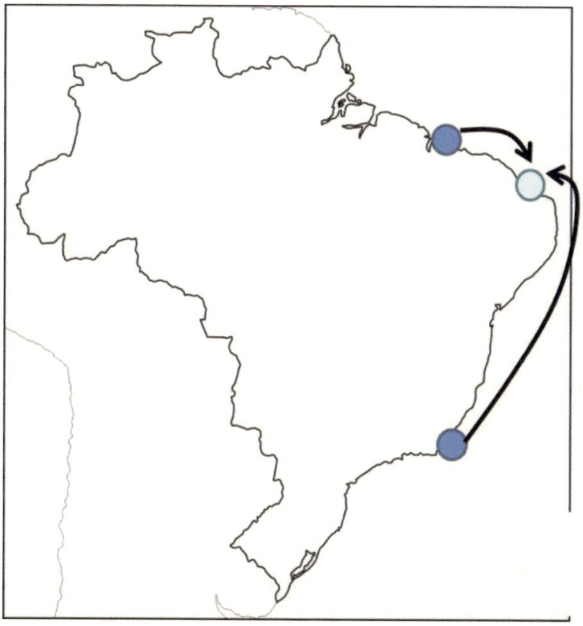

Figure 5. Representation of the iron ore transportation process from the SE and NE ports to the company's private port.

5.4. Scenario creation

Ten viable scenarios were created for further evaluation using MCDA. These scenarios cover a range of input parameters and variables of the DES model, as listed in Table 2.

In Table 2, the first seven scenarios simulate a two-vessel operation, while the last three scenarios encompass a three-vessel fleet. Next, the first alternated variable is the necessity of vessels chartering during the fleet docking period. Thereafter, until scenario 6, the proportion of iron ore from each source (NE and SE) changes. Scenario 7 is a sensitivity analysis of Scenario 4, with a reduced storage capacity. From Scenarios 8–10, the proportion of iron ore from SE and NE is altered, but under the assumption of a three-vessel operation.

Scenarios	Vessels Fleet	% Min. SE Iron Ore	Stock Capacity (tonnes)		Rely on chartering ?
			NE	SE	
Scenario 1	2	30	550,000	225,000	No
Scenario 2	2	30	550,000	225,000	Yes
Scenario 3	2	35	500,000	275,000	No
Scenario 4	2	35	500,000	275,000	Yes
Scenario 5	2	40	475,000	300,000	No
Scenario 6	2	40	475,000	300,000	Yes
Scenario 7	2	35	375,000	275,000	Yes
Scenario 8	3	30	185,000	235,000	No
Scenario 9	3	35	170,000	275,000	No
Scenario 10	3	40	155,000	315,000	No

Table 2. Description of the analyzed scenarios.

This table identifies a clear tradeoff between the number of vessels in the company fleet and the storage capacity required for each iron ore type, for example, by comparing Scenario 1 with Scenario 8. The simulation results are presented in Section 5.7.

5.5. Decision criteria: Value functions and multi-criteria analysis

The decision-making process implies capturing the value judgments of decision makers through the assignment of value functions to the relevant criteria and sub-criteria and the further positioning of the results of the scenarios on a value function scale. All evaluations and considerations were performed with the participation of representatives of the following areas of the company: Operations, Procurement, Transportation (Railroad and Navigation), Inventory Management and Finance.

The relevant criteria and sub-criteria considered in the system characterization, their descriptions and value functions are described below. The assignment of the scores associated with all decision criteria to each of the 10 previously considered scenarios is presented, as derived from the DES results.

- Power plant stoppages: Number of days per year that the plant stops production because of the lack of iron ore supply. The value function of this criterion is given as follows: when no interruption occurs in the operation of the steel production plant (0 days of interruption), the scenario gets a maximum score (1). If there is only 1 day of interruption, the scenario gets a score of 0.5. Two days of interruption corresponds to a score of 0.25 and 3 days to a score of 0.125. Thereafter, the score varies linearly until the scenario with 18 days of interruption, which scores 0. Between intervals, the value function varies linearly and thus aims at representing the extremely high costs of production resuming after any stoppage (Figure 6).

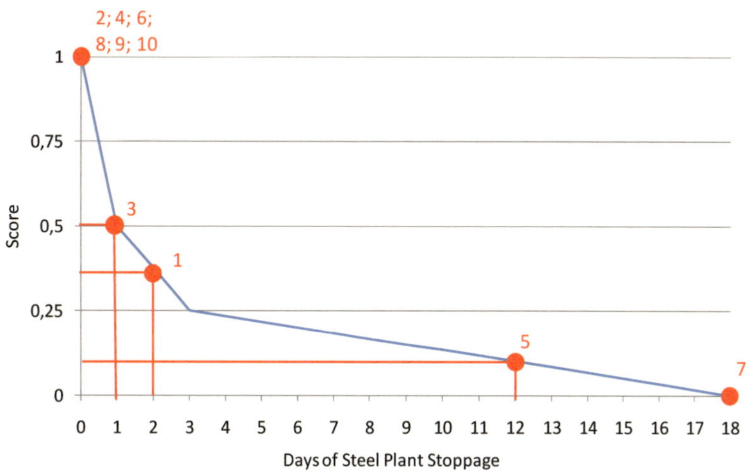

Figure 6. Determination of value function – days of production plant stoppage.

- Investment net present value (NPV): As the system modeled represents the internal logistics operation of the company, there is no revenue generation. Investment NPV is therefore directly related to the need for financial investment into the project (size of the company's fleet, need for vessel chartering, etc.). The results for Investment NPV are obtained based on the parameters provided by the company (Table 3).

Parameter	Unit
Vessel Acquisition Value	Mi US$
Financed Percentage	%
Interests	%
Amortization Period	years
Grace Period	years
Vessel's Service Life	years
Return Rate	%/year
NPV Financed (per vessel)	Mi US$
NPV Own Capital (per vessel)	Mi US$
Chartering Costs (per vessel)	US$/day

Table 3. Economic parameters of the investment.

The Investment NPV value function displays linear behavior, with a maximum score (1) assigned to the lowest total Investment NPV scenario and a minimum score (0) to the highest Investment NPV scenario (Figure 7).

- Annual fleet operational costs: This takes into account all the operational costs of the company fleet, such as fuel, port costs and running costs (crew, insurance, administrative costs, taxes, etc.). The components of the fleet operational costs are presented in Table 4.

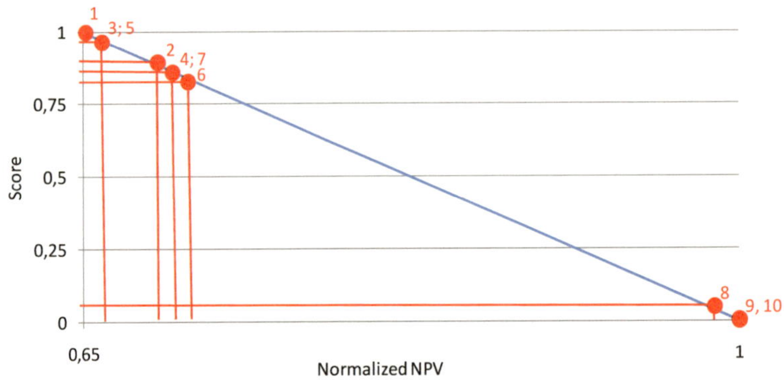

Figure 7. Determination of value function – NPV.

Parameter	Unit
Fuel Cost (at route)	(US$/day)/vessel
Fuel Cost (at port)	(US$/day)/vessel
Running Costs	(US$/day)/vessel
Mooring Cost at Plant Port	(US$/mooring)/vessel
Mooring Cost at NE Port	(US$/mooring)/vessel
Mooring Cost at SE Port	(US$/mooring)/vessel

Table 4. Components of the fleet operational costs.

Similar to NPV, the value function of this criterion is linear, with a maximum score (1) assigned to the scenario with the lowest total operational costs and a minimum score (0) assigned to the highest operational costs (Figure 8).

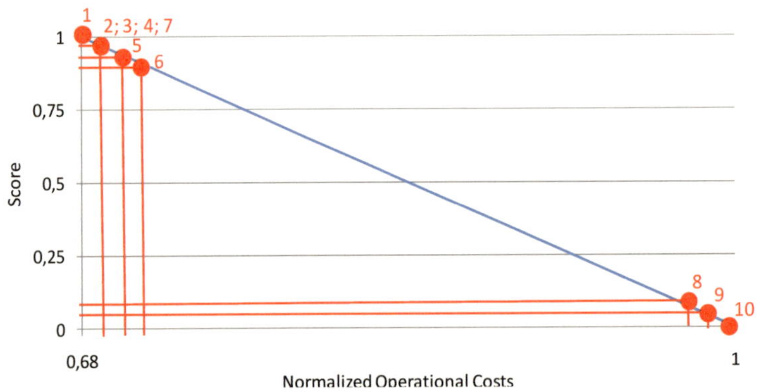

Figure 8. Determination of value function – operational costs.

- Stock below the safety level: This represents the time percentage that the plant's stock remains below the minimum inventory safety level, but it results in no interruption to the steelmaking process. The safety stock level is defined as 15 days of the plant's input consumption. This parameter aims at representing the risk of interruption to plant production. A value function of this criterion assigns a maximum score (1) to a zero percentage (0%) of observation days of stock below the safety level and a minimum score (0) to the highest percentage. The variation between these extremes is linear (Figure 9).

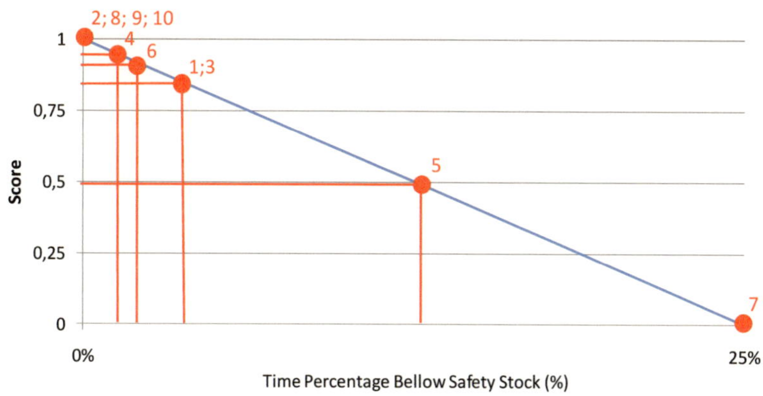

Figure 9. Determination of value function – time below the safety stock level.

- SE/NE iron ore percentages: Operationally, the plant, owing to its physical characteristics, would rather work with SE than it would with NE iron ore. The scenarios are simulated within a discrete distribution of the percentage of SE iron ore (40%, 35% and 30%) and the value function is given as follows: 40% - valued as maximum (1), 35% - assigned with an intermediate score (0.5) and 30% - valued as minimum (0) (Figure 10).

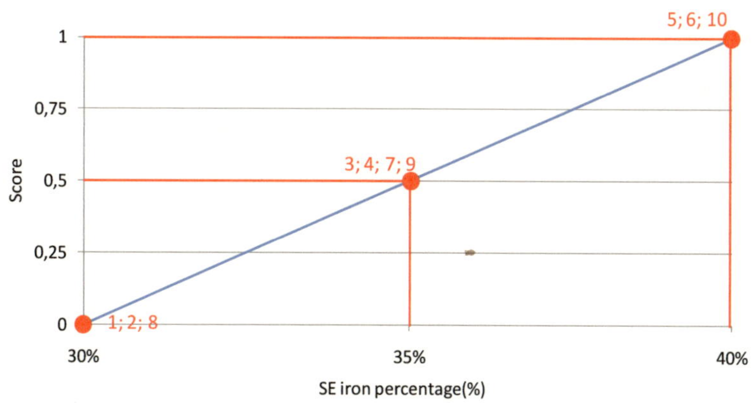

Figure 10. Determination of value function – SE/NE iron ore origin percentage.

- Stock capacity: The company project includes a stockyard that is able to store 775,000 tons of iron ore. For obvious reasons, configurations with lower storage areas are preferred, representing less area commitment. Thus, in accordance with the established value function, the scenario with lower storage capacity gets a maximum score (1) and that with a higher capacity gets a minimum score (0), with linear variation between these extremes (Figure 11).

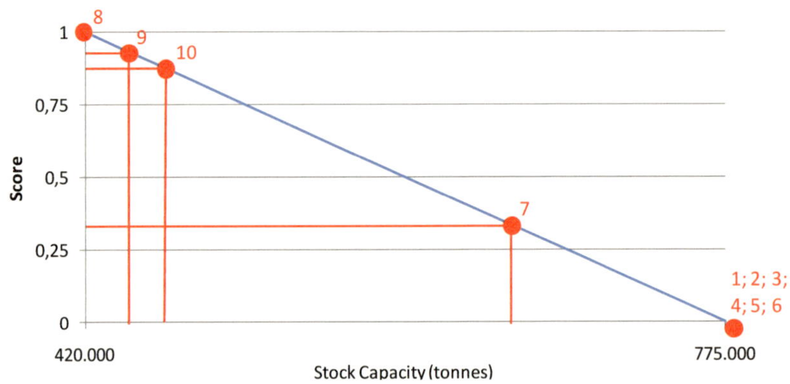

Figure 11. Determination of value function – stock capacity.

- Average supported queuing time: This refers to the average time that vessels can queue at the iron ore terminals without affecting the delivery of inputs. Vessels have to obey the queuing disciplines in both iron ore terminals. This is an uncertain parameter, since a scenario that supports lower queues is riskier than one that supports high levels of the queuing in terms of the fulfillment of planned demand. Moreover, the behavior of queue patterns at Brazilian iron ore terminals is regulated by fluctuations in global demand. The scenario with the largest average supported queuing time scores 1 (maximum), while the shortest time scores 0 (minimum) (Figure 12).

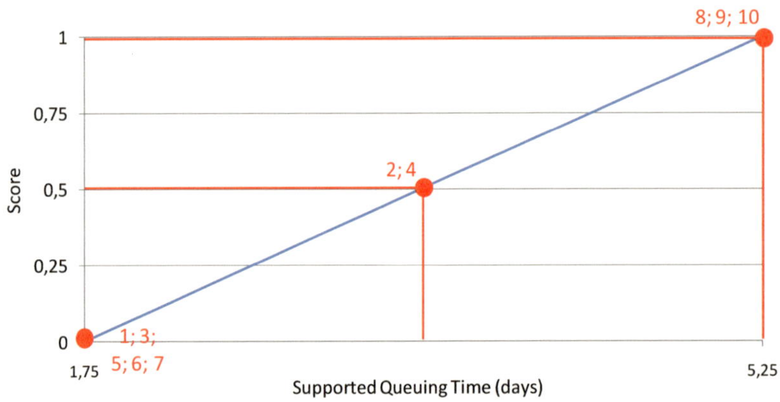

Figure 12. Determination of value function – supported queuing time.

- Chartering: This criterion assumes only binary values, namely relying or not on chartering spare vessels. Thus, scenarios with no chartering reliance receive a maximum score (1) and scenarios where chartering spare vessels is considered to be an option receive a minimum score (0). As previously mentioned, such behavior occurs because of the difficulty in chartering vessels that meet the specific operational characteristics demanded, especially for short time periods (Figure 13).

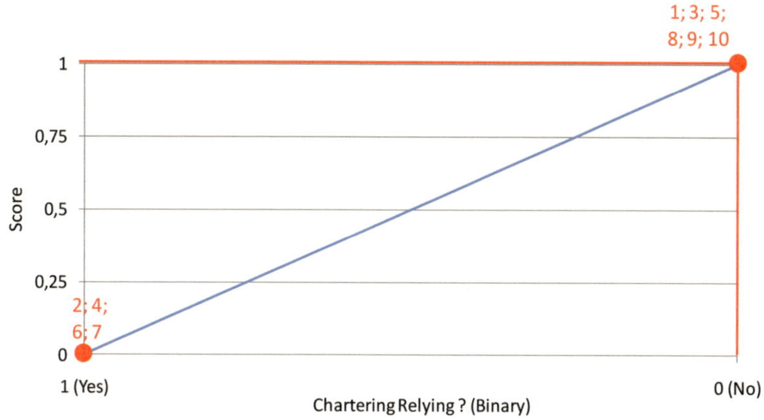

Figure 13. Determination of value function – chartering.

- New mission allocation waiting time: This represents the average number of hours that each vessel of the company fleet waits to be allocated to a new mission (new route to any of the iron ore suppliers). Thus, a higher new mission waiting time, on one hand means fleet idleness, whereas, on the other hand, represents less risk to input supply to the plant. The value function assigns, for the lowest waiting time value observed, the maximum score (1) and to waiting times greater than 24 hours, the minimum score (0). Between 0 and 24 hours, the variation of the value function is linear (Figure 14).

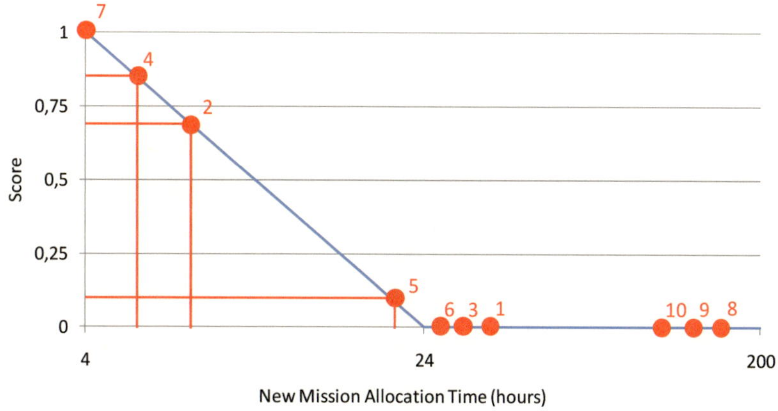

Figure 14. Determination of value function – new mission allocation time.

5.6. Model validation

Because the real system is still a future project, there is no historic operation database for validating the model's results. Thus, in order to validate the model, the analytical calculations of the fleet's operational parameters were compared.

Suppose the following initial scenario (fully deterministic):

- 30% of the cargo comes from SE;
- Vessel fleet composed of three Panamax class ships (70,000 tons);
- No restriction on storage;
- Queues at loading terminals of 5 days in the NE terminal and 7 days in the SE terminal;
- Travel times of 1.5 days (one way) from the plant port to the NE terminal and 4 days (one way) from the plant port to the SE terminal;
- 1 day mooring time at the loading terminals and 2.5 days at the unloading terminals;
- One unloading berth at the plant terminal;
- No downtime (offhire) nor docking; and
- No unloading queues at either terminal;

Vessels cycle times can be calculated as shown in Table 5.

	Empty Trip	Loading Queue	Loading	Loaded Return Travel	Unloading Queue	Unloadin	Total
NE	1,50	5,00	1,00	1,50	0,00	2,50	**11,50**
SE	4,00	7,00	1,00	4,00	0,00	2,50	**18,50**

Table 5. Cycle time composition (in days).

As the availability of vessels in these analytical calculations is 100%, in 25 years we have 9,125 days of operation. Using the cycle times data shown in Table 5, and keeping the proportions of SE iron ore at 30%, we make the following calculations:

- 11.5 days / cycle × 70% × # of cycles + 18.5 days / cycle × 30% × # of cycles = 9,125 days.

Thus, the amount of full cycles (round trips) per vessel is 670, i.e., 469 cycles between the plant and the NE terminal and 201 cycles between the plant and the SE terminal. Through these calculations, under these conditions (with no queuing when unloading) and with a three-vessel fleet, it would be possible to operationalize 2,010 cycles in 25 years, adding up 140.7 million tons, or 5,628 MTPY. Further, considering 2.5 days of berth occupancy for each unloading process, we reach a berth occupation rate of 55% (5,025 days in 9,125 available days).

A DES model run was then carried out under the same criteria. The results obtained from the DES simulation model are shown in Table 6, compared with the analytical results.

The 98% average adherence of the DES simulation model was considered to be satisfactory and thus the model was validated.

5.7. DES simulation result

Twenty replications (of 25 years each) of the DES model were run for each scenario described in Section 5.4. The results are shown in Table 7.

Description	# cycles in 25 years	Demanda (million tonnes)	Berth Occupancy Rate
Analytic Calculation	2.010	140,70	55%
DES Simulation Model	1.961	137,25	54%
Accurancy	98%	98%	98%

Table 6. Cycle time composition (in days).

Scenarios	% Demand Met	Lack of Inputs (days/year)	NPV Total (norm.)	Total Annual Operational Costs (norm.)	% Time Below Safety Stock	Average Suppported Queuing Time (days/cycle)		New Mission Allocation Time (h/cycle)
						NE	SE	
Scenario 1	99	2	0.65	0.68	5	1.75	1.25	44
Scenario 2	100	0	0.70	0.69	0	3.50	2.50	11
Scenario 3	99	1	0.66	0.69	5	1.75	1.25	35
Scenario 4	99	0	0.71	0.69	2	3.50	2.50	7
Scenario 5	99	12	0.66	0.70	13	1.75	1.25	22
Scenario 6	100	0	0.72	0.71	3	1.75	1.25	29
Scenario 7	99	18	0.71	0.69	25	1.75	1.25	4
Scenario 8	100	0	0.99	0.95	0	5.25	3.75	161
Scenario 9	100	0	1.00	0.97	0	5.25	3.75	146
Scenario 10	100	0	1.00	1.00	0	5.25	3.75	118

Table 7. Results obtained by the DES model.

The analysis in Table 5 demonstrates that those scenarios operating with fleets of three vessels (Scenarios 8–10) reached a higher performance level regarding the operational criteria and service levels (average supported queuing time, time below safety stock level, days of input lacking). Furthermore, these scenarios are less risky to the system, less susceptible to uncertainties, less demanding on storage areas and more tolerant of queues at the iron ore supplier's terminals. However, the costs of these configurations are higher compared with the other scenarios in terms of the initial investment needed or the operational costs.

Among the first seven scenarios, which assume a two-vessel fleet, the comparison of similar scenarios in which variations only concern the reliability or not of chartering spare vessels (e.g., Scenarios 1 and 2, 3 and 4, 5 and 6) allows us to conclude that the chartering process is responsible for improving the operational results despite leading to increased costs. Moreover, it is noticeable that a higher percentage of SE iron ore incurs higher costs because of the greater distance between the input supplier and the steel production plant. Section 5.7 contemplates the MCDA.

5.8. MCDA

The decision-making process was based on the assignment of weights to the decision criteria listed in Section 5.5. The process is now presented. The following methodological step is the assignment of scores associated with all the decision criteria in each of the 10 previously considered scenarios. Table 8 shows the importance of classifying the decision criteria and calculating the normalized weights associated with each of them. The criteria order of importance was defined unanimously by the group of decision makers.

Criterion #	Criterion	Priority	Weight (100/Priority)	Normalized Weight
1	Power Plant Stoppages	1	100.0	30
2	Net Investment Present Value (NPV)	2	50.0	15
3	Total Annual Operational Costs	2	50.0	15
4	% Time Below Safety Stock	3	33.3	10
5	Average Queuing Supported Time	4	25.0	8
6	Stocks Capacities	5	20.0	6
7	NE/SE Iron Ore Input Proportion	5	20.0	6
8	Vessels Chartering	6	16.7	5
9	New Mission Allocation Time	6	16.7	5
	Sum		**332**	**100**

Table 8. Importance of the decision criteria and normalized weights.

The criterion considered to be most important for the company was the number of days per year when the plant stops production owing to poor supply. This is an extremely critical criterion. Subsequently, the criteria related to costs are the most important (i.e., NPV and operational costs), followed by those related to operational risks (i.e., the safety stock level and uncertainty related to the average supported queuing time at iron ore terminals). After those criteria, the subsequent priorities are storage capacity, proportion of NE/SE iron ore input, stipulation of chartering vessels and new mission waiting time. From the simulation results shown in Table 7, the scores associated with all considered scenarios are presented in Table 9.

Scenario	Criterion 1	Criterion 2	Criterion 3	Criterion 4	Criterion 5	Criterion 6	Criterion 7	Criterion 8	Criterion 9
Scenario 1	0.38	1.00	1.00	0.80	0.00	0.00	0.00	1.00	0.00
Scenario 2	1.00	0.86	0.97	1.00	0.00	0.00	0.50	0.00	0.65
Scenario 3	0.50	0.97	0.97	0.80	0.50	0.00	0.00	1.00	0.00
Scenario 4	1.00	0.83	0.97	0.92	0.50	0.00	0.50	0.00	0.85
Scenario 5	0.10	0.97	0.94	0.48	1.00	0.00	0.00	1.00	0.10
Scenario 6	1.00	0.80	0.91	0.88	1.00	0.00	0.00	0.00	0.00
Scenario 7	0.00	0.83	0.97	0.00	0.50	0.35	0.00	0.00	1.00
Scenario 8	1.00	0.03	0.16	1.00	0.00	1.00	1.00	1.00	0.00
Scenario 9	1.00	0.00	0.09	1.00	0.50	0.93	1.00	1.00	0.00
Scenario 10	1.00	0.00	0.00	1.00	1.00	0.86	1.00	1.00	0.00

Table 9. Score by scenario and by criterion.

Thus, the application of the normalized weights considered for each criterion (Table 8) results in a final score for each scenario. The scenarios are ranked in Table 10.

Rank #	Scenario	Final Score
1	Scenario 4	0.78
2	Scenario 2	0.74
3	Scenario 6	0.72
4	Scenario 10	0.64
5	Scenario 9	0.62
6	Scenario 3	0.61
7	Scenario 8	0.60
8	Scenario 1	0.55
9	Scenario 5	0.50
10	Scenario 7	0.38

Table 10. Ranking of final scores for the 10 scenarios.

Table 10 shows that the scenario that has the highest final score is Scenario 4. The final scores of Scenarios 2 and 6 are, however, close to that of Scenario 4. Scenario 2 differs from Scenario 4 only by showing a smaller proportion of SE iron ore, while Scenario 6 employs a higher proportion of SE iron ore than does Scenario 4. However, Scenario 6 supports less queuing time compared with Scenarios 4 and 2.

Scenario 10 is ranked fourth, virtually tied with Scenarios 9, 8 and 3. Scenario 3 is similar to Scenario 4, but with no vessels chartering and a lower average supported queuing time. The difference between Scenarios 10, 9 and 8, which are those with a dedicated three-vessel fleet operation, is in the proportion of SE iron ore employed in the steelmaking process: 40%, 35% and 30%, respectively.

Given the proximity of the final scores of the three best-ranked scenarios (Scenarios 4, 2 and 6), a reasonable configuration is thus chosen between them. These three scenarios are composed by fleets of two vessels, which leads to close NPV values and total operational costs, similar total storage capacities (775,000 tons), a reliance on chartering vessels during fleet docking periods and no interruptions in the steelmaking process. Therefore, the final selection between these three scenarios is based on the average supported queuing time in the supplier's terminal and the SE iron ore percentage.

Scenario 2, second in the overall ranking, has the lowest SE iron ore percentage (30%), while Scenario 6, third in the overall ranking, has the highest SE proportion (40%). However, Scenario 6 supports only 50% of the average queuing time of Scenarios 2 and 4 (1.75 days versus 3.5 days). The final recommendation is thus Scenario 4 because its high average queuing time compared with Scenarios 2 and 6 and its intermediate percentage of SE iron ore.

5.9. Sensitivity analysis

After obtaining the first recommended alternatives, further analyses may be performed through a sensitivity analysis by changing the weights of the criteria and priorities as well as through the generation of new alternative solutions. Another alternative is the reapplication of the MCDA model, after the elimination of the less promising alternatives (in this case, Scenarios 1, 5 and 7, which obtained final scores lower than 0.60). Following the removal of these scenarios, there will be a redistribution of the normalized scores and thus the evaluation of the remaining alternatives will become a more robust process. Although the range of evaluation scenarios and possible solutions may be lost, the decision-making process certainly becomes more meticulous and accurate.

In addition, sensitivity analysis regarding other aspects such as value functions may be performed in order to observe the behavior and responses of the system as a whole to variations in data inputs. Another point to consider is the participation of several specialists to establish the criteria and their importance weights, as this commitment increases credibility to the study.

6. Conclusion

Firstly, it is important to keep in mind that the DSS methodology proposed in this chapter is not a solution optimizer methodology that necessarily indicates the best decisions to make. This chapter contributes to the decision-making literature by showing how DSSs can bridge the gap between enterprise systems and decision makers. Implementing the proposed DSS would provide companies with a distinct competitive advantage: when following the hybrid methodology steps exemplified, the proposed DSS tool could certainly guide and orientate decision making based on technical and practical fundamentals. Moreover, such a methodology may involve a team of several experts in the definition of criteria and weights, corroborating decision-making credibility. In that way, human evaluation capability and judgments should never to be left alone in any decision-making process.

However, the main conclusion of this study confirms the efficacy of using DES in a broader and more complex environment compared with the development and application of a simplistic model. The proposed DSS tool works as a catalyst to improve the decision-making process, deriving the capabilities of a DES model and surpassing its shortcomings through the employment of MCDA to allow for further tradeoff studies. The DES and MCDA combined methodology has been shown to be effective as a complex logistics problem decision-making support tool. Further, the developed DSS tool, with some minor modifications, would be applicable for the evaluation of similar logistics systems.

Merging MCDA and DES can enhance the interaction between model development and users/customers, thereby improving model development and the analysis of the results. This interaction is an important quality issue in DES models, especially those that promote social change, namely those that help users make better decisions [31]. Therefore, quality improvement for DES can be investigated when using MCDA in combination.

Another important contribution of this chapter is the possibility of choosing alternatives based on various relevant and often antagonistic criteria, usually ignored by skewed decision-making processes, which are primarily guided by the financial aspects (costs/income) of each proposed solution. Moreover, in a conventional simulation study, scenario evaluations are usually based on a single criterion (related mostly to operational aspects) and the classification of two scenarios: viable or not viable. By observing, developing and working from a more extensive and complete evaluation perspective, including the participation of several experts in setting criteria and priorities, decision making becomes a more inclusive and trustful process.

6.1. Future research and recommendations

We believe that there is a great field to be explored in science management and DSSs by applying the presented hybrid methodology, especially in strategic environments such as Supply Chain Management and Supply Chain Strategy. For example, a manufacturing plant could be redesigned based on the company's objectives and marketing department's intentions using a specific set of products (for further discussion, see [32,33]).

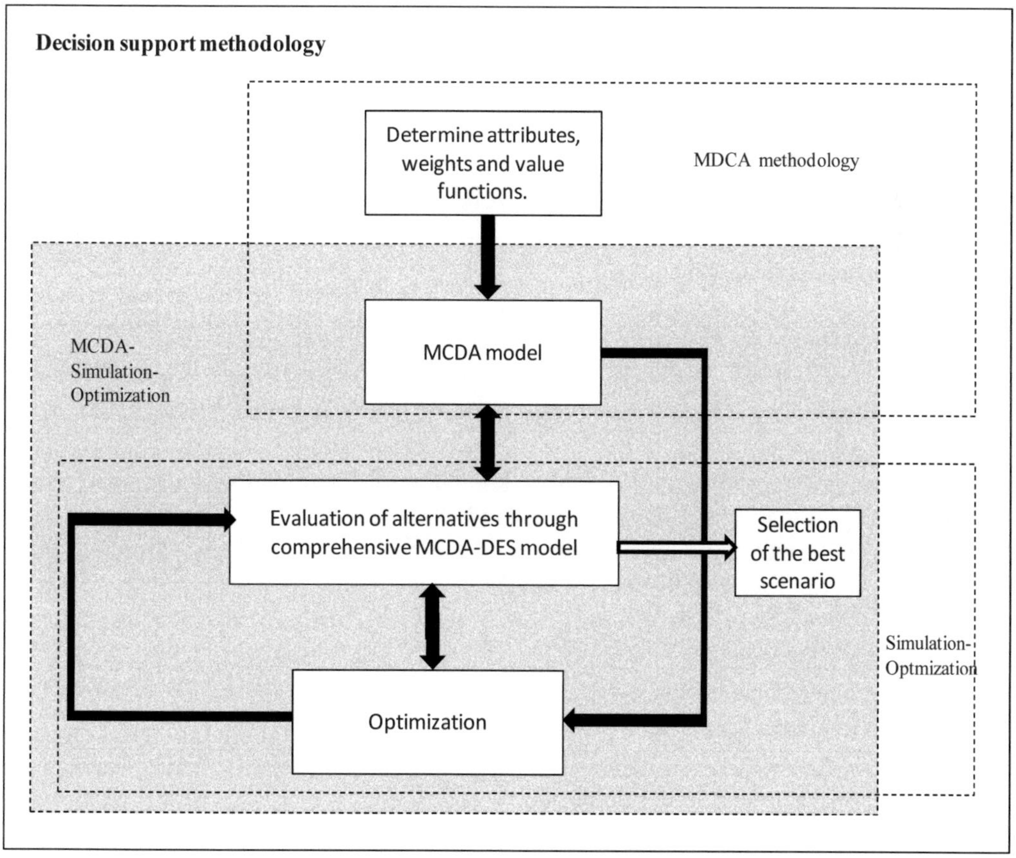

Figure 15. Framework of the simulation/optimization/MCDA methodology.

In addition, MCDA has a potential interface in simulation/optimization problems during the definition of the objective function. Converting objectives and values into an input/output assessment framework improves the scope of the study. In logistics systems, for example, DES has a greater capability to deal with randomness, increase the comprehension of the system and thus generate new ideas and solutions. Further, MCDA increases the visualization, measurement and weight of values and objectives through a set of attributes, while the methodologies of optimization for simulation (see [34]) enhance the elaboration, comparison and determination of the optimal or most efficient scenario. A framework for a more complex methodology for a DSS is presented in Figure 15, illustrating how these three methodologies may be implemented.

Author details

Thiago Barros Brito*, Rodolfo Celestino dos Santos Silva, Edson Felipe Capovilla Trevisan and Rui Carlos Botter
University of Sao Paulo, Department of Naval Engineering,
CILIP (Innovation Center for Logistics and Ports Infrastructure), Sao Paulo, Brazil

7. References

[1] Altiok, T., Melamed, B. (2007). Simulation modeling and analysis with Arena. Academic Press.
[2] Pedgen, C.D., Shannon, R.E., Sadowski, R.P. (1995). Introduction to simulation using SIMAN, McGraw-Hill. 2nd Edition. New York.
[3] Chwif, L., Medina, A.C. (2006). Modeling and Simulation of Discrete Events: Theory & Practice, 2nd Edition. São Paulo.
[4] Freitas,, P.J.F. (2001). Introduction to Systems Modeling and Simulation. Visual Books Ltd, 2nd Edition, São Paulo.
[5] De Geu, A.P. (1994). Foreword: Modeling to predict or to learn? System Dynamics Series, p. xiii – xv, Productivity Press, Portland, OR. Dynamics Society, July 23-27, Nijmegen, the Netherlands.
[6] Morecroft, J.D.W., Stermann, J.D. (1994). Modeling for Learning Organizations. System Dynamics Series, Productivity Press, Portland, OR.
[7] Chwif, L. (1999). Discrete Event Simulation Model Reduction in Design Step: A Causal Approach. PhD Thesis, University of Sao Paulo.
[8] Wack, P. (1985). Scenarios: the gentle art of re-perceiving. Harvard Business Review, September – October.
[9] Zeleny, M. (1982). Multiple Criteria Decision Making. McGraw-Hill Book Company, 1st Edition, New York.
[10] Turban, E., Aronson, J.E., Liang, T.P., Sharda, R. (2007) Decision Support and Business Intelligence Systems, Prentice Hall.

* Corresponding Author

[11] Belton, V., Stewart, J.T. (2001). Multiple Criteria Decision Analysis – An Integrated Approach. Kluwer Academic Publishers, London.
[12] Arnott, D., Pervan, G. (2005). A critical analysis of decision support systems research, Journal of Information Technology, 20 (2).
[13] Holsapple, C.W., Whinston, A.B. (2000) Decision Support Systems: A Knowledge-based Approach, West Publishing, St. Paul, MN.
[14] Smith, E.D. (2006). Tradeoff Studies and Cognitive Biases. PhD Thesis, Arizona University.
[15] Landman, J.R. (1993). The Persistence of The Possible. Oxford University Press, New York, NY.
[16] Franco, L.A., Montibeller, G. (2010). Facilitated Modeling In Operational Research. European Journal of Operational Research 205, pp. 489–500.
[17] Schein, E.H. (1998). Process Consultation Revisited: Building the Helping Relationship. Addison Wesley.
[18] Eden, C. (1982). Problem Construction and the Influence of OR. Interfaces 12 (2), pp. 50–60.
[19] Eden, C., Jones, S., Sims, D., Smithin, T. (1981). The Intersubjectivity of Issues and Issues of Intersubjectivity. The Journal of Management Studies 18 (1), pp. 37– 47.
[20] Rosenhead, J., Mingers, J., (2001). A New Paradigm of Analysis. In: Rosenhead, J., Mingers, J. (Eds.), Rational Analysis for a Problematic World Revisited: Problem Structuring Methods for Complexity, Uncertainty, and Conflict. Wiley, Chichester, pp. 1–19.
[21] Eden, C., Sims, D., 1979. On the Nature of Problems in Consulting Practice. OMEGA: The International Journal of Management Science 7 (2), pp. 119–127.
[22] Eden, C., Ackermann, F. (2004). Use of 'Soft OR' Models by Clients: What do they want from them? In: Pidd, M. (Ed.), Systems Modelling: Theory and Practice. Wiley, Chichester, pp. 146–163.
[23] Phillips, L. (1984). A Theory of Requisite Decision Models. Acta Psychologica 56 (1–3), pp. 29–48.
[24] Friend, J., Hickling, A., 2005. Planning Under Pressure: The Strategic Choice Approach, 3rd Edition, Elsevier.
[25] Phillips, L., 2007. Decision Conferencing. In: Edwards, W., Miles, R., Jr., von Winterfeldt, D. (Eds.), Advances in Decision Analysis: From Foundations to Applications. Cambridge University Press, New York, pp. 375–399.
[26] Rosenhead, J., Mingers, J. (2001). A New Paradigm of Analysis. In: Rosenhead, J., Mingers, J. (Eds.), Rational Analysis for a Problematic World Revisited: Problem Structuring Methods for Complexity, Uncertainty, and Conflict. Wiley, Chichester, pp. 1–19.
[27] Montibeller, G., Franco L.A. (2007). Decision And Risk Analysis for the Evaluation Of Strategic Options. In: Supporting Strategy: Frameworks, Methods and Models. ed. F.A. O'Brien, and R.G. Dyson. pp. 251–284. Wiley, Chichester.
[28] Saaty, T.L. (2001). Decision making for leaders. RWS Publications. Pittsburgh.

[29] Montibeller, G., Franco L.A. (2008). Multi-criteria Decision Analysis for Strategic Decision Making. In: Handbook of Multicriteria Analysis, Volume 103, Part 1, pp. 25–48, Springer, 1st Edition, Gainesville.

[30] Barcus, A., Montibeller, G. (2008). Supporting the Allocation of Software Development Work in Distributed Teams With Multi-Criteria Decision Analysis. Omega 36 (2008), pp. 464–475.

[31] Robinson, S. (2002). General concepts of quality for discrete-event simulation. European Journal of Operations Research 138, pp. 103–117.

[32] Fisher, M.L. (1997). What is the right supply chain for your product? Harvard Business Review. March-April 1997, Harvard Business Review Publishing, Boston, MA.

[33] Mentzer, J.T., DeWitt, W., Keebler, J.S., Nix, N.W., Smith, C.D., Zacharia, Z.G. (2001). Defining Supply Chain Management. Journal of Business Logistics, 22 (2).

[34] Optimization for Simulation: Theory vs. Practice. INFORMS Journal on Computing, 14 (3), Summer 2002 pp. 192–215.

Section 3

Applications of Discrete Event Simulation Towards Various Systems

Chapter 5

Human Evacuation Modeling

Stephen Wee Hun Lim and Eldin Wee Chuan Lim

Additional information is available at the end of the chapter

http://dx.doi.org/10.5772/49938

1. Introduction

The modeling of movement patterns of human crowds at the exit point of an enclosed space is a complex and challenging problem. In a densely populated space, if all the occupants are simultaneously rushing for the exits, shuffling, pushing, crushing and trampling of people in the crowd may cause serious injuries and even loss of lives. An analytical study of crowd dynamics through exits may provide useful information for crowd control purposes. Proper understanding of the evacuation dynamics will allow, for example, improvements of designs of pedestrian facilities. In particular, the dynamics of evacuation through a narrow door during an emergency is a complex problem that is not yet well understood. The possible causes for evacuation may include building fires, military or terrorist attacks, natural disasters such as earthquakes, etc. In the light of tightened homeland security, research on evacuation modeling has been gaining impetus and attracting the attention of researchers from various fields.

In the published literature, one of the first computational studies of human evacuation was reported by Helbing *et al.* [1]. They applied a model of pedestrian behavior to investigate the mechanisms of panic and jamming by uncoordinated motion in crowds and suggested an optimal strategy for escape from a smoke-filled room involving a mixture of individualistic behavior and collective herding instinct. Subsequently, two main approaches, referred to as cellular automata or the lattice gas model and the continuum modeling framework, have been pursued by researchers in this field for modeling studies of human evacuation over the last decade. In the cellular automata approach, the computational domain is discretised into cells which can either be empty or occupied by one human subject exactly. Each human subject is then simulated to either remain stationary or move into an empty neighboring cell according to certain transition probability rules. Kirchner and Schadschneider [2] applied such an approach to model evacuation from a large room with one or two doors and observed that a proper combination of herding behavior and use of knowledge about the surrounding was necessary for achieving optimal evacuation times. Perez *et al.* [3] used the same modeling approach and found that in situations where exit door widths could accommodate the simultaneous exit of more than one human subject at any given time, subjects left the room in bursts of different sizes. Takimoto and Nagatani [4] applied the lattice gas model to simulate the evacuation process from a hall and observed that the average escape time was dependent on the average initial distance from the exit. The same conclusion was reached by Helbing *et al.* [5] who applied the same modeling approach and compared escape times with experimental results. Subsequently, the authors extended their lattice gas model to simulate evacuation of subjects in the absence of visibility and found that addition of more exits did not improve escape time due to a kind of herding effect based on acoustic interactions in such situations [6]. Nagatani and Nagai [7] then derived the probability density distributions of the number of steps of a biased random walk to a wall during an evacuation process from a dark room, first contact point on the wall and the number of steps of a second walk along the wall. In a following study, the probability density distributions of escape times were also derived and shown to be dependent on exit configurations [8]. Qiu *et al.* [9] simulated escaping pedestrian flow along a corridor under open boundary condition using the cellular automata approach. It was found that transition times were closely dependent on the width of the corridor and maximum speed of people but only weakly dependent on the width of doors. More recently, a contrasting mathematical approach for modeling crowd dynamics that is based on the framework of continuum mechanics has also been introduced by some research workers [10]. Such an approach uses the mass conservation equations closed by phenomenological models linking mass velocity to density and density gradients. These closures can take into account movement in more than one space dimension, presence of obstacles, pedestrian strategies and panic conditions. However, it is also recognized that human evacuation systems do not strictly satisfy the classical continuum assumption [11] and so macroscopic models have to be considered as approximations of physical reality which in some cases, such as low density regimes, may not be satisfactory. Furthermore, such macroscopic models are derived based on the assumption that all individuals behave in the same way, or namely, that the system is homogeneous.

In the present study, a particle-based simulation approach known as the Discrete Element Method (DEM) was applied for modeling of human evacuation from a room with a single exit. The governing equations used in this method will be presented in the following section.

2. Mathematical model

2.1. Discrete Element Method

The molecular dynamics approach to modeling of granular systems, otherwise known as the Discrete Element Method (DEM), has been applied extensively for studies of various aspects of granular behavior. The method of implementation in this proposed study followed that used by the author in previous studies of various types of granular systems [12–20]. The translational and rotational motions of individual solid particles are governed by Newton's laws of motion:

$$m_i \frac{dv_i}{dt} = \sum_{j=1}^{N} \left(f_{c,ij} + f_{d,ij} \right) \tag{1}$$

$$I_i \frac{d\omega_i}{dt} = \sum_{j=1}^{N} T_{ij} \tag{2}$$

where m_i and v_i are the mass and velocity of ith particle respectively, N is the number of particles in contact with i^{th} particle, $f_{c,ij}$ and $f_{d,ij}$ are the contact and viscous contact damping forces respectively, I_i is the moment of inertia of ith particle, ω_i is its angular velocity and T_{ij} is the torque arising from contact forces which causes the particle to rotate.

Contact and damping forces have to be calculated using force-displacement models that relate such forces to the relative positions, velocities and angular velocities of the colliding particles. Following previous studies, a linear spring-and-dashpot model was implemented for the calculation of these collision forces. With such a closure, interparticle collisions are modeled as compressions of a perfectly elastic spring while the inelasticities associated with such collisions are modeled by the damping of energy in the dashpot component of the model. Collisions between particles and a wall may be handled in a similar manner but with the latter not incurring any change in its momentum. In other words, a wall at the point of contact with a particle may be treated as another particle but with an infinite amount of inertia. The normal ($f_{cn,ij}$, $f_{dn,ij}$) and tangential ($f_{ct,ij}$, $f_{dt,ij}$) components of the contact and damping forces are calculated according to the following equations:

$$f_{cn,ij} = -\left(\kappa_{n,i} \delta_{n,ij} \right) n_i \tag{3}$$

$$f_{ct,ij} = -\left(\kappa_{t,i} \delta_{t,ij} \right) t_i \tag{4}$$

$$f_{dn,ij} = -\eta_{n,i} \left(v_r \cdot n_i \right) n_i \tag{5}$$

$$f_{dt,ij} = -\eta_{t,i} \left\{ \left(v_r \cdot t_i \right) t_i + \left(\omega_i \times R_i - \omega_j \times R_j \right) \right\} \tag{6}$$

where $\kappa_{n,i}$, $\delta_{n,ij}$, n_i, $\eta_{n,i}$ and $\kappa_{t,i}$, $\delta_{t,ij}$, t_i, $\eta_{t,i}$ are the spring constants, displacements between particles, unit vectors and viscous contact damping coefficients in the normal and tangential directions respectively, v_r is the relative velocity between particles and R_i and R_j are the radii of particles i and j respectively. If $\left| f_{ct,ij} \right| > \left| f_{cn,ij} \right| \tan\phi$, then 'slippage' between two contacting surfaces is simulated based on Coulomb-type friction law, i.e. $\left| f_{ct,ij} \right| = \left| f_{cn,ij} \right| \tan\phi$, where tan ϕ is analogous to the coefficient of friction.

2.2. Simulation conditions

The geometry of the computational domain considered in this study was in the form of a room measuring 10 m × 10 m. A single exit located at the center of one of the walls of the room was simulated. The width of the exit was specified as 1 m. A total of 100 human subjects initially randomly distributed within the room were considered. During the evacuation process, each subject was simulated to move generally in the direction of the exit while interacting with other subjects through human-human collisions according to the governing equations of the model.

3. Results and discussions

Fig. 1 shows the top view of the evacuation process simulated. The exit of the room was simulated to be located at the centre of the bottom wall. The arrow symbols associated with each subject indicate the instantaneous direction of movement. The subjects were originally distributed randomly throughout the room and it was assumed that each subject sought to reach the exit in the most direct manner while obeying only basic laws of physics as defined by the governing equations of the DEM model. The typical phenomenon of jamming that is ubiquitous in various physical systems, such as the flows of granular materials for example, could be reproduced computationally with such an approach. It can be seen that there was a tendency for the subjects to first cluster round the exit of the room and then spread along the wall where the exit was situated. The limiting factor of the evacuation process in this case was the necessity for subjects to leave the room through the exit one at a time. The speed of movement during the initial stage of the evacuation process to form the human cluster around the exit did not play a significant role in determining the total amount of time required for the entire evacuation process to be completed. In other words, the limiting factor or bottleneck of the overall evacuation process in this case was movement of individual subjects through the exit. This is consistent with observations of other researchers utilizing other modeling approaches, such as cellular automata or the lattice gas model, for simulating such evacuation processes. This points towards the possibility of improving the evacuation time simply by increasing the width of the exit such that more than one subject can exit at any one time or by increasing the total number of exits of the room.

Fig. 2 shows the spatial distribution of collision forces that developed due to human-human collisions during the evacuation process. Here, the color contours indicate high (red) and low (blue) magnitudes of such collision forces. This ability to predict collision forces is a novel feature of the current approach for crowd dynamics modeling that is unavailable in all other approaches reported by other researchers in the literature to date. This will be important for subsequent estimations of the likelihood of the human subjects to sustain injuries as a result of the evacuation process and so will be crucial for casualty predictions. In terms of engineering designs of the interiors of buildings or any enclosed spaces, such predictions can also be applied in a reverse engineering sense with a view towards minimizing human casualties in such events of emergencies.

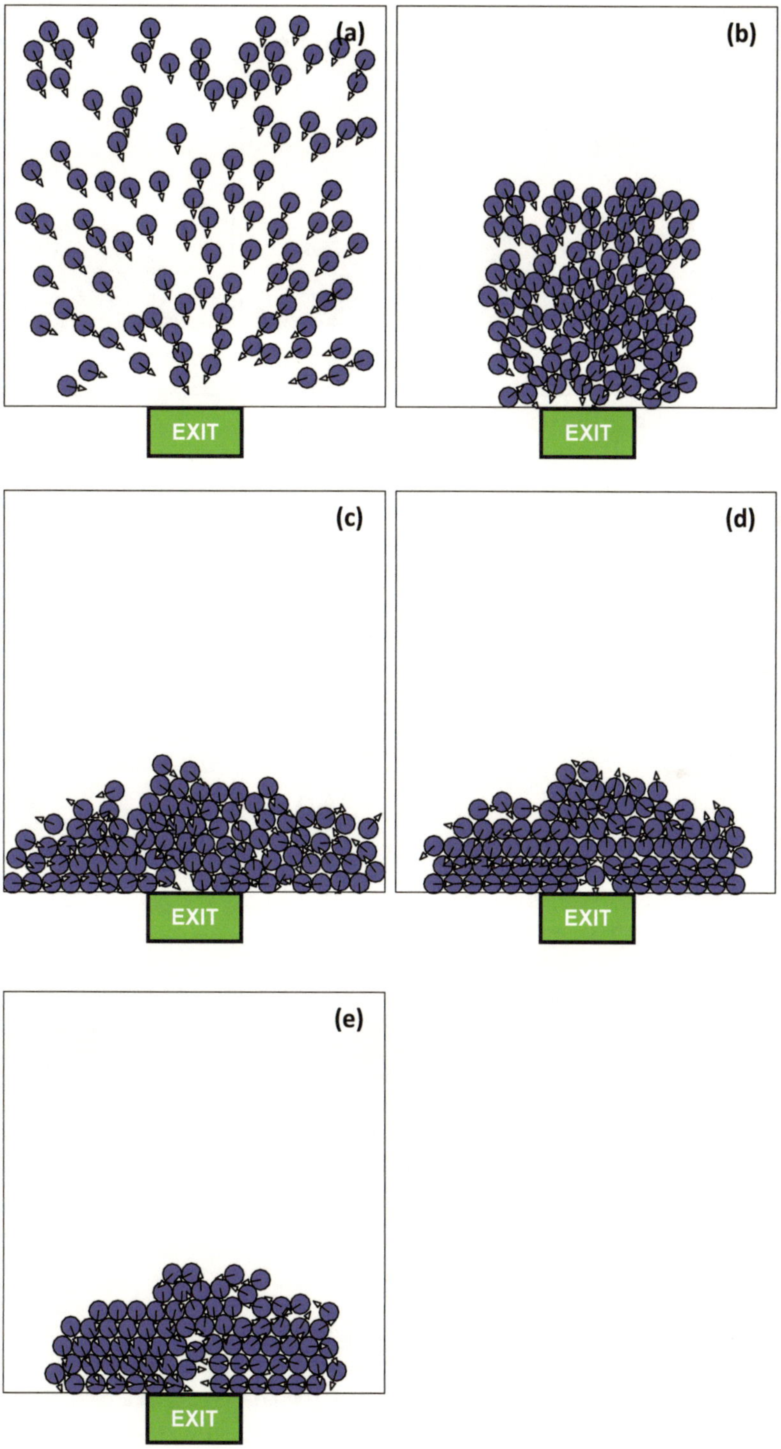

Figure 1. Top view of an evacuation process involving 100 human subjects from a room measuring 10 m × 10 m.

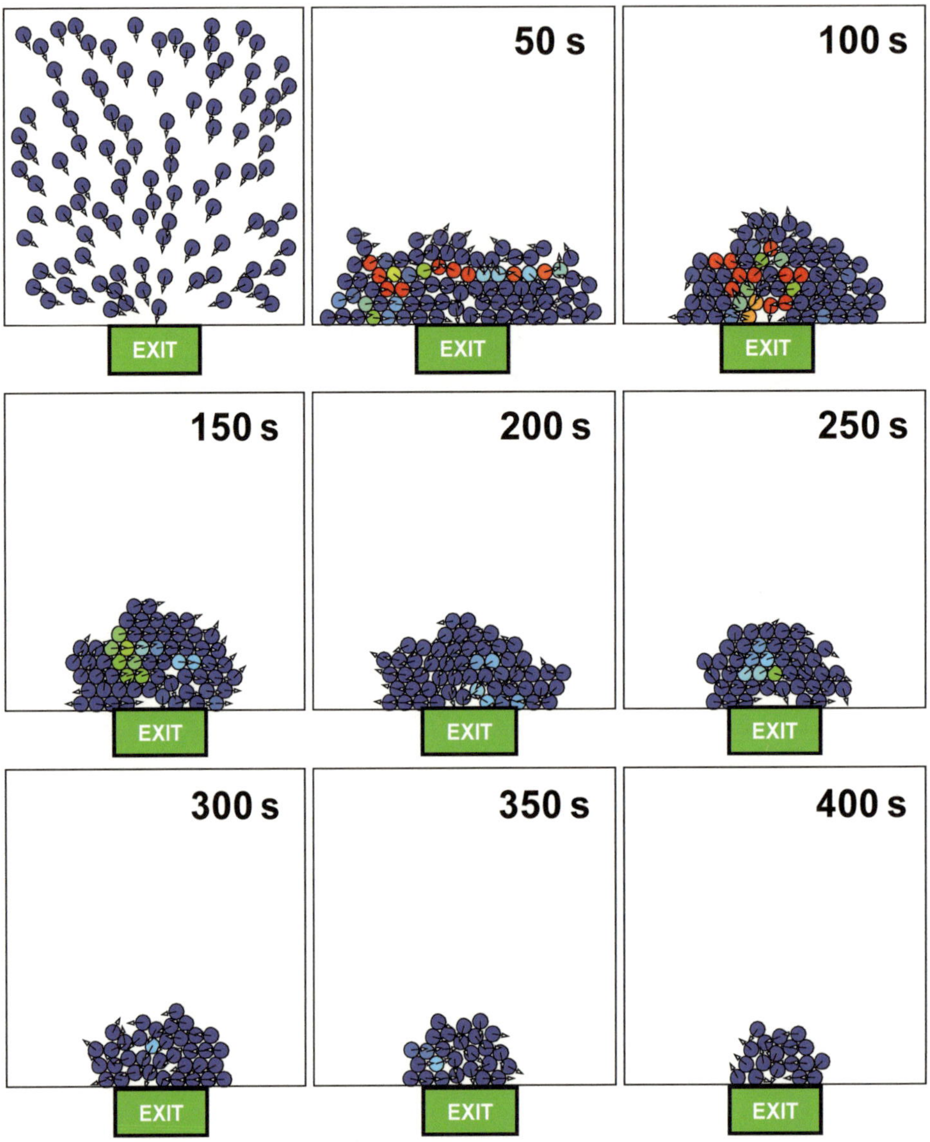

Figure 2. A novel feature of the current approach where collision forces developed due to human-human collisions during the evacuation process can be predicted by the algorithm.

4. Conclusions

An agent based model has been applied for modeling of the human evacuation process in this study. A relatively simple configuration consisting of a room without any obstacles and a single exit was considered and the evacuation of 100 subjects was simulated. The typical phenomenon of jamming that is ubiquitous in various physical systems, such as the flows of granular materials for example, could be reproduced computationally with such an approach. The evacuation process was observed to consist of the formation of a human cluster around the exit of the room followed by departure of subjects one at a time that created a significant bottleneck for the entire process.

The application of the agent based approach for extensive parametric studies of effects of various engineering factors on the evacuation process such as number of human subjects present, initial configuration of the subjects, placement and number of exits, presence of unmovable obstacles, size and shape of the enclosed space will be the subject of a future study.

In particular, in order to study human decisions underlying an evacuation process more closely, a multi-objective evolutionary algorithm for emergency response optimization can be applied. These algorithms are stochastic optimization methods that simulate the process of natural evolution [21]. Such an evolutionary approach is expected to discover and develop human factors and useful psychological models that determine decision-making processes in an emergency context.

5. Summary

An agent based model was applied for crowd dynamics simulation in this study. The computational domain consisted of a room without any obstacles and a single exit and the evacuation of 100 subjects from the room was simulated. The typical phenomenon of jamming that is typical of such systems was reproduced computationally with such an approach. The evacuation process was observed to consist of the formation of a human cluster around the exit of the room followed by departure of subjects one at a time that created a significant bottleneck for the entire process. Future work can adopt an evolutionary algorithm to closely predict human decision processes in an emergency context.

Author details

Stephen Wee Hun Lim and Eldin Wee Chuan Lim
National University of Singapore, Singapore

Acknowledgement

This study has been supported by the National University of Singapore.

6. References

[1] D. Helbing, I. Farkas, and T. Vicsek, "Simulating Dynamical Features of Escape Panic", Nature, vol. 407, pp. 487–490, 2000.

[2] A. Kirchner, and A. Schadschneider, "Simulation of Evacuation Processes using a Bionics-inspired Cellular Automaton Model for Pedestrian Dynamics", Physica A, vol. 312, pp. 260–276, 2002.

[3] G. J. Perez, G. Tapang, M. Lim, and C. Saloma, "Streaming, Disruptive Interference and Power-law Behavior in the Exit Dynamics of Confined Pedestrians", Physica A, vol. 312, pp. 609–618, 2002.

[4] K. Takimoto, and T. Nagatani, "Spatio-temporal Distribution of Escape Time in Evacuation Process", Physica A, vol. 320, pp. 611–621, 2003.
[5] D. Helbing, M. Isobe, T. Nagatani, and K. Takimoto, "Lattice Gas Simulation of Experimentally Studied Evacuation Dynamics", Physical Review E, vol. 67, pp. 067101, 2003.
[6] M. Isobe, D. Helbing, and T. Nagatani, "Experiment, Theory, and Simulation of the Evacuation of a room without Visibility", Physical Review E, vol. 69, pp. 066132, 2004.
[7] T. Nagatani, and R. Nagai, "Statistical Characteristics of Evacuation without Visibility in Random Walk Model", Physica A, vol. 341, pp. 638–648, 2004.
[8] R. Nagai, T. Nagatani, M. Isobe, and T. Adachi, "Effect of Exit Configuration on Evacuation of a room without Visibility", Physica A, vol. 343, pp. 712–724, 2004.
[9] B. Qiu, H. Tan, C. Zhang, L. Kong, and M. Liu, "Cellular Automaton Simulation of the Escaping Pedestrian Flow in Corridor", International Journal of Modern Physics C, vol. 16, pp. 225–235, 2005.
[10] V. Coscia, and C. Canavesio, "First-order Macroscopic Modelling of Human Crowd Dynamics", Mathematical Models and Methods in Applied Sciences, vol. 18, pp. 1217–1247, 2008.
[11] N. Bellomo, and C. Dogbe, "On the Modelling Crowd Dynamics from Scaling to Hyperbolic Macroscopic Models", Mathematical Models and Methods in Applied Sciences, vol. 18, pp. 1317–1345, 2008.
[12] E. W. C. Lim, C. H. Wang, and A. B. Yu, "Discrete Element Simulation for Pneumatic Conveying of Granular Material", AIChE Journal, vol. 52(2), pp. 496–509, 2006.
[13] E. W. C. Lim., Y. Zhang, and C. H. Wang, "Effects of an Electrostatic Field in Pneumatic Conveying of Granular Materials through Inclined and Vertical Pipes", Chemical Engineering Science, vol. 61(24), pp. 7889–7908, 2006b.
[14] E. W. C. Lim, and C. H. Wang, "Diffusion Modeling of Bulk Granular Attrition", Industrial and Engineering Chemistry Research, vol. 45(6), pp. 2077–2083, 2006.
[15] E. W. C. Lim, Y. S. Wong, and C. H. Wang, "Particle Image Velocimetry Experiment and Discrete-Element Simulation of Voidage Wave Instability in a Vibrated Liquid-Fluidized Bed", Industrial and Engineering Chemistry Research, vol. 46(4), pp. 1375–1389, 2007.
[16] E. W. C. Lim, "Voidage Waves in Hydraulic Conveying through Narrow Pipes", Chemical Engineering Science, vol. 62(17), pp. 4529–4543, 2007.
[17] E. W. C. Lim, "Master Curve for the Discrete-Element Method", Industrial and Engineering Chemistry Research, vol. 47(2), pp. 481–485, 2008.
[18] E. W. C. Lim, "Vibrated Granular Bed on a Bumpy Surface", Physical Review E, vol. 79, pp. 041302, 2009.
[19] E. W. C. Lim, "Density Segregation in Vibrated Granular Beds with Bumpy Surfaces", AIChE Journal, vol. 56(10), pp. 2588–2597, 2010.
[20] E. W. C. Lim, "Granular Leidenfrost Effect in Vibrated Beds with Bumpy Surfaces", European Physical Journal E, vol. 32(4), pp. 365–375, 2010.
[21] Georgiadou, P. S., Papazoglou, I. A., Kiranoudis, C. T., and N. C. Markatos, "Multi-objective evolutionary emergency response optimization for major accidents", Journal of Hazardous Materials, vol. 178, pp. 792–803, 2010.

Chapter 6

Discrete-Event Simulation of Botnet Protection Mechanisms

Igor Kotenko, Alexey Konovalov and Andrey Shorov

Additional information is available at the end of the chapter

http://dx.doi.org/10.5772/50101

1. Introduction

The common use of computers, connected to the Internet, as well as insufficient level of security, allow malefactors to execute large-scale infrastructure attacks, engaging in criminal activity a huge number of computing nodes. Attacks of such type have been traditionally performing by botnets. There are examples of successful large-scale attacks fulfilled by armies of bots. For example, attacks such as distributed denial of service (DDoS), aimed at government websites of Estonia in 2007 and Georgia in 2008 had led to the practical inaccessibility of these sites for several days. In 2009 and 2010 spying botnets "GhostNet" and "Shadow Network" have been occurred in many countries around the world.

Further research of these botnets has shown their presence on governmental servers, which contain important sensitive information. In 2009 a malware "Stuxnet" was discovered, which was capable to affect SCADA-systems and steal intellectual property of corporations. Report "Worldwide Infrastructure Security Report", published by Arbor Networks in 2010, shows that the total capacity of DDoS attacks in 2010 has grown considerably and has overcome the barrier of 100 GB/sec. It is noted that the power of DDoS-attacks has grown more than twice in comparison with 2009 and more than 10 times in comparison with 2005.

On this basis, it becomes obvious that existing modern botnets are a very important phenomenon in the network security. Thus, the task of researching botnets and methods of protection against them is important. One of the promising approaches to research botnets and protection mechanisms is simulation.

This paper is devoted to investigating botnets, which realize their expansion by network worm propagation mechanisms and perform attacks like "distributed denial of service" (DDoS). The protection mechanisms against botnets are of top-priority here. The main results of this work are the development of integrated simulation environment, including the libraries for implementing models of botnets and models of protection mechanisms. As distinct from other authors' papers (for example, [12, 13]), this paper specifies the architecture of the integrated simulation environment and describes the set of conducted experiments on simulation of botnets and protection mechanisms against them.

Comparing with previous research, the architecture of the integrated simulation environment has been substantially revised - more emphasis has been placed to extend the libraries of attacks and protection mechanisms. Also in this version of the simulation environment, we have applied a hierarchical component-based way of representation of architecture. The main attention in the paper is paid to the set of experiments, which provided the opportunity to compare protection methods against botnets on different stages of their life cycle.

The rest of the paper is organized as follows. Section 2 discusses the related work. Section 3 presents the architecture of the integrated simulation environment developed. Section 4 considers the attack and defense models. Section 5 contains the description of implementation and main parameters and the plan of the experiments. Section 6 describes the results of experiments. Concluding remarks and directions for further research are given in Section 7.

2. Related work

The current work is based on results of three directions of research: analysis of botnets as a phenomenon occurred in the Internet [2, 6, 8, 19, 21], including the studies of botnet taxonometry, approaches of creation and improving the techniques for counteraction against modern botnets, and enhancement of concepts and methods for efficient modeling and simulation of botnet infrastructure and counteraction.

At present moment using public proceedings we can find many interpretations of different aspects of botnet functionality. A group of researches, related to analysis of botnet as a network phenomenon, defines botnet lifecycle [6, 21], which is consisting of several stages: initial infection and spreading stage, stage of 'stealth' operation and attack stage. Centralized [21] and decentralized [6, 8, 34] kinds of architectures are considered as results of investigation of feasible node roles, and different types of botnet arracks are described.

The investigations, devoted to botnet counteraction methods, may be conditionally divided into two logical groups: methods, which are based on identification of predefined signatures [28], and methods which rely on detection of local and network anomalies [3, 10, 18, 32]. The second group of methods has a significant advantage against first group in ability to detect unknown threats not having specific knowledge of their implementation [15]. On the other hand, the second group is much more resource consuming and more subjected to false positive and false negative errors.

Due to significant differences of botnet lifecycle stages, the combined protection methods are used extensively which take into account specificities of each stage.

Defense techniques "Virus Throttling" [37] and "Failed Connection" [4] are used to oppose botnet propagation on spreading stage. Such techniques as Threshold Random Walk [20] and Credit-based Rate Limiting also require consideration.

Beyond many types of botnets attacks, we studied botnets which implement DDoS as an actual attack stage. We considered protection methods for different phases of DDoS attacks. Approaches Ingress/Egress Filtering and SAVE (Source Address Validity Enforcement Protocol) [17] are used as attack prevention mechanisms. They realize filtering of traffic streams for which IP spoofing was detected. Moreover, such techniques as SIM (Source IP Address Monitoring) [23] and Detecting SYN flooding [35] were taken into consideration as methods for discovering DDoS attacks.

We also investigated protection methods destined to detect botnets of different architectures. Botnet architecture is defined by the applied communication protocol. At present moment IRC-, HTTP- and P2P-related botnet architectures [21] are important for consideration.

Research on botnet modeling and simulation is based on a variety of methods and approaches. A large set of publications is devoted to botnet analytical modeling. For instance, a stochastic model of decentralized botnet propagation is presented in [26]. This model represents a botnet as a graph. Nodes of this graph represent the botnet states, and edges depict possible transitions between states. D.Dagon et al. [5] proposes an analytical model of global botnet, which describes dependencies between the activities of botnet nodes and the time zone for location of these nodes.

Another group of studies uses simulation as a main tool to investigate botnets and computer networks in general. Studies in this group mainly rely on methods of discrete-event simulation of processes being executed in network structures [29, 36], as well as on trace-driven models initiated by trace data taken from actual networks [22]. G.Riley et al. [25] use the GTNetS simulation environment to build network worm propagation model. A.Suvatne [30] suggests a model of "Slammer" worm propagation by using "Wormulator" [14] simulation environment. M.Schuchard [27] presents simulation environment which allows to simulate a large-scale botnet containing 250 thousands of nodes. Gamer at al. [7] consider a DDoS simulation tool, called Distack. It is based on OMNeT++ discrete simulation system. Li at al. [17] use own simulation environment and testbeds to estimate efficiency, scalability and cost of implementation of protection mechanism SAVE.

Other techniques, which are very important for investigation of botnets, are emulation, combining analytical, packet-based and emulation-based models of botnets and botnet defense (on macro level), as well as exploring real small-sized networks (to investigate botnets on micro level).

This paper describes the approach, which combines discrete-event simulation, component-based design and packet-level simulation of network protocols. Initially this approach was suggested for network attack and defense simulation. In the present paper, as compared with other works of authors, the various methods of botnet attacks and counteraction against botnets are explored by implementing comprehensive libraries of attack and defense components.

3. Simulation environment architecture

The proposed simulation environment realizes a set of simulation models, called BOTNET, which implement processes of botnet operation and protection mechanisms.

With narrowing the context of consideration, these models could be represented as a sequence of internal abstraction layers: (1) discrete event simulation on network structures, (2) computational network with packet switching, (3) meshes of network services, (4) attack and defense networks.

Specification of every subsequent layer is an extended specification of the previous one. Enhancement of specification is achieved by defining new entities to the preceding layer of abstraction. Proposed view on semantic decomposition of BOTNET models is shown in Fig.1. Hierarchy of abstraction layers reproduces the structure of simulation components and modules.

Simulation environment relies on several libraries - implemented by authors of the paper and third party libraries. Functionality of each library matches to the appropriate layer of abstraction. The library, which is related to attack and defense networks layer, is implemented by the authors. All components of simulation environment are implemented in C++ programming language with standard runtime libraries.

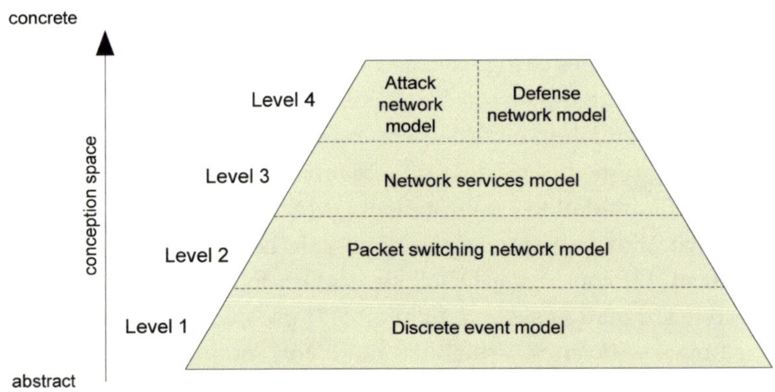

Figure 1. Hierarchy of Abstraction Layers

The diagram representing the relations between layers of abstraction and implementation layers (libraries) is shown in Fig.2. Each particular library provides a set of modules and components, which are implementations of entities of appropriate semantic layer. Any given library can rely on the components exported by the libraries of the previous layer and can be used as a provider of components needed for the subsequent layer implementation.

The first layer of abstraction is implemented by use of discrete event simulation environment OMNET++ [31]. OMNET++ provides the tools for simulation of network structures of different kinds and processes of message propagation in these structures.

The library INET Framework [11] is used for simulation of packet-switching networks. This library provides components implemented as OMNET++ modules and contains large variety of models of network devices and network protocols for wired and wireless networks.

Simulation of realistic computer networks is carried out by using the library ReaSE [24]. The library is an extension of INET Framework [11]. It provides tools for creating realistic network topologies which parameters are statistically identical to parameters of real computer networks topologies. ReaSE includes also a realistic model of network traffic, modeled at the packet level [16, 38]. Models of network traffic are based on the approach, presented in [33]. This approach allows generating packet level traffic with parameters, which are statistically equivalent to the traffic observed in real computer networks.

Simulation of target domain entities is committed through the set of components implemented by the authors. These components are integrated into the BOTNET Foundation Classes library (Fig.2). This library includes models of network applications belonging to botnets of various types and appropriate defense methods.

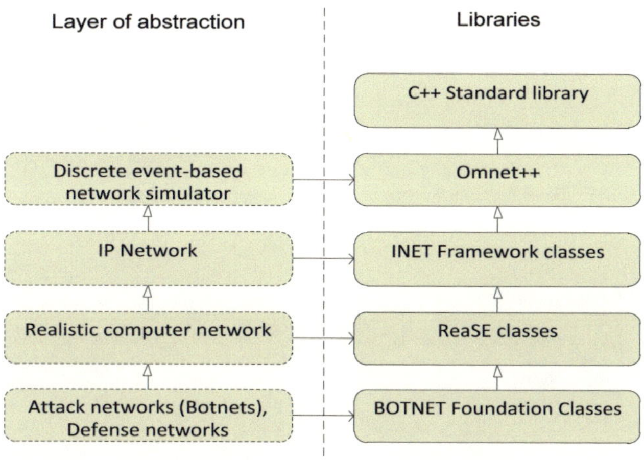

Figure 2. Relation between Abstraction and Implementation Layers

On the fourth layer of abstraction, all set of components of the target domain is divided into two groups related to attack and defense network correspondingly.

The first group contains the components (1) responsible for propagation of attack network, (2) supporting attack network on the stage of 'stealth' operation, (3) hampering detection and suppression of attack network, and (4) executing DDoS attacks.

The group of defense network includes the components (1) detecting and suppressing of attack network during every stage of its lifecycle, (2) carrying out management and control of defense network and (3) providing robustness of defense network (these components realize protocols of centralized and decentralized overlay networks).

According to the structure of the scenarios, the behavior of BOTNET models is defined by the set of conditionally independent network processes. The model of legitimate traffic is based on approach described in [33], and implemented by the components of ReaSE library [24].

4. Attack and defense models

Attack network model specifies a set of activities generated by attack network. In the current work we implemented this model by three relatively independent sub-models: the propagation model, the management and control model, and the attack phase model.

The *model of botnet's propagation* implements a scenario of expanding botnet over the computer network. The main goal of this scenario is the support of the ongoing process of involvement of new nodes into the botnet. In this paper, such scenario is presented as a model of the bot-agent code propagation by the means of the network worms of various types.

Participants of the botnet propagation scenario are the "IP Worm" and "Vulnerable App" components, which are the model of a network worm and the model of vulnerable network server, respectively (Fig. 3).

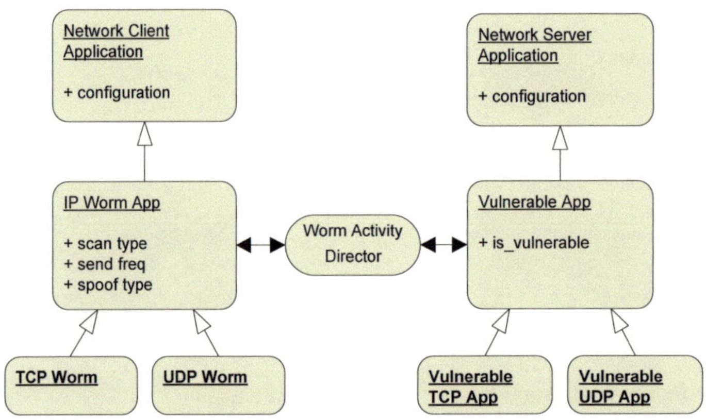

Figure 3. Static diagram of components involved in the botnet propagation scenario

The component "IP Worm" is a model of client application that responsible for sending malformed network packets in order to compromise possible vulnerable hosts. The parameters of this model are: the algorithm of victim's address generation, the method of source address spoofing, and the frequency which is used to send malformed packets. The payload of the malformed packet includes the network address of the server, which is supposed to be the command center of the growing botnet.

Component «Vulnerable App» is a model of the vulnerable server, which is prone to be infected by the receiving malformed packed.

The component interaction diagram is shown in Fig.4.

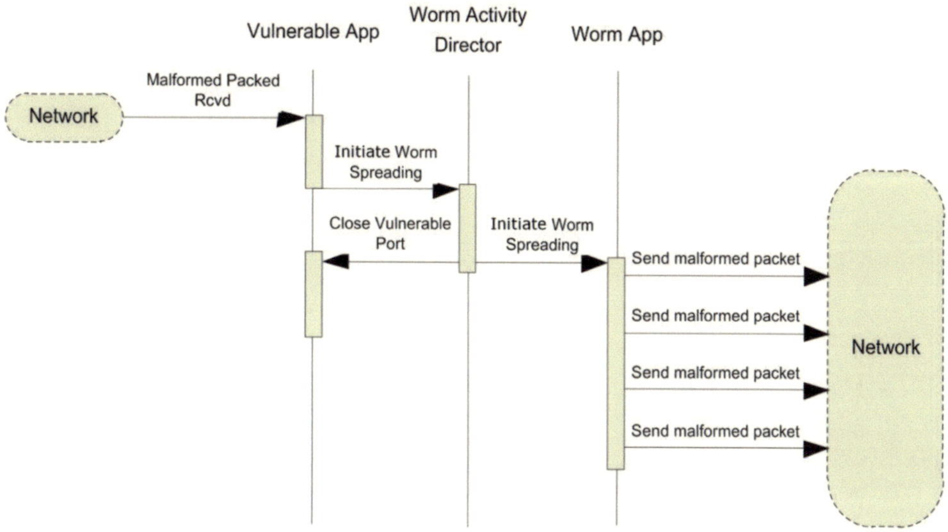

Figure 4. Component interaction diagram for the botnet propagation scenario

All communication between the models of network applications is carried out via instant messaging. The core component that responsible for the messaging support is the "Worm Activity Director". In case of receiving a malformed network packet, the model of vulnerable network service notifies the component "Worm Activity Director" immediately.

Then the component "Worm Activity Director" decapsulates the addresses of the hosts which are supposed to be command centers and sends the message which contains the information about servers to the "Worm App" component. The event of receiving such message by "Worm App" component is considered as a signal of the transition to the infecting state and as the instruction to start spreading a worm from the given host. In the current research we implemented TCP and UDP based worms and vulnerable network applications.

The *model of botnet control* implements the botnet control scenario. The goal of this scenario is to provide the persistent controllability of the whole set of botnet nodes. Such process includes the procedures for support of the connectivity of the nodes and methods that are supposed to make the botnet responsible on the commands being issued by the bot-master.

The model of botnet control represented in this paper implements two types of architectures.

The first type of the botnet is based on the IRC protocol. It is a classic implementation of a centralized botnet with a centralized command centers.

Another type of botnet is based on some implementation of P2P-protocol. Such botnets belong to a group of decentralized botnets [34]. Library component BOTNET Foundation Classes includes components that are common to both types of architectures and components specific to each of them.

Classes include components that are common to both types of architectures and components specific to each of them.

Static diagram of components involved in this scenario shown in Fig. 5.

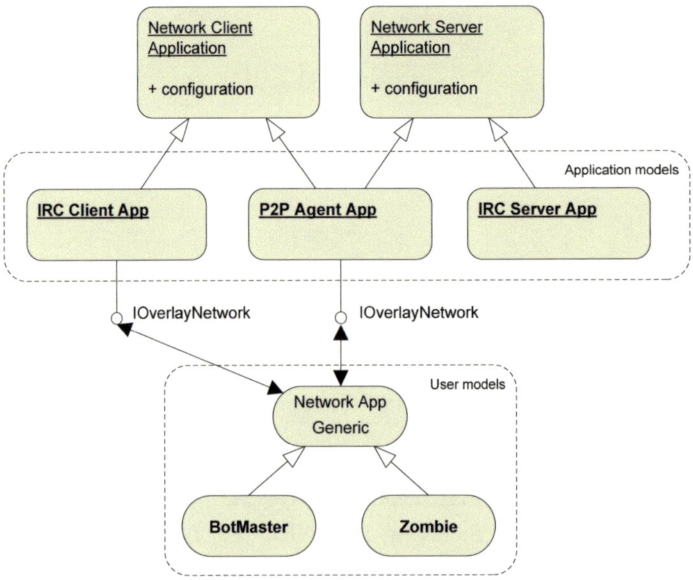

Figure 5. Static diagram of components involved in the botnet control scenario

The main components that are directly responsible for connectivity of the whole botnet, are models of network applications that implement the corresponding application protocols.

In the case of a centralized network, there is a subset of nodes – command centers – which are responsible for management of the rest of botnet nodes. The model of network service that corresponds to command center, is represented as a component "IRC Server App". This component is a particular implementation of a generalized model of the network server. It provides a partial implementation of the server side of the IRC protocol. This implementation is sufficient to reproduce the essential aspects of network behavior. Clients of such server are the "IRC Client App" components that are particular implementations of the generalized model of the network client. These components implement the client side of the IRC protocol as well.

The model of the decentralized botnet control is represented by the "P2P Agent App" component. This component is an implementation of the P2P-protocol client. Regarding to the P2P protocol specificity this component is a particular implementation of both the network server and client applications at the same time.

The essential point is that the components "IRC Client App" and "P2P Client App" are the models of network clients that implement the corresponding application layer protocols. The way to manipulate such clients is performed by the means of the component that represents the model of the user. The commonality that is inherent in the models of the clients allows distinguishing invariant interface for manipulating models of clients by the models of the user. This interface also permits to separate the business logic of the network application from a component that implements the communication protocol itself. Thus, it is possible to apply the components "IRC Client App" and "P2P Client App" over a variety of different protocols without any change of business logic of the clients.

The user models are implementations of a generic user model represented as a component "Network App Generic". The generic user model is an abstract model, which communicates in the network through the application layer protocol. The user model interacts with the protocol by the "IOverlayNetwork" interface. The specific implementations of the generic user model directly specify the logic of network activity. In the control scenario, two types of specific user models are realized: a bot-master model ("BotMaster") and a model of bot-agent, which is located on the "zombie"-nodes.

In the present work, in the botnet attack scenario an attack Distributed Denial of Service (DDoS) is simulated. The signal to begin the attack is the special command of the botnet master. The specific ways to implement this attack are "TCP Flood" and "UDP Flood". These components are directly related to the component representing the network layer protocols in the node model. Fig. 6 shows the diagram of components that implement the "TCP Flood" attack. This figure shows the structure of the node which is included in the centralized botnet.

The "zombie"-node model consist of: (1) the IRC-client model that realize communication between the node and the rest of the network, (2) the zombie-agent model that implements the communication protocol between the zombie node and the bot-master, and (3) the model of the TCP Flood component that realize the attack of TCP Flood type. The component that implements the TCP Flood attack and the IRC-client use the services provided by the module realizing the network layer protocols (TCP, IP, and UDP).

The component interaction diagram for components involved in the botnet attack scenario is shown in Fig. 7.

The bot-master initiates the command to begin the attack and sends it to zombies. This command includes the victim address in data field. Then the message containing the command is delivered to the zombies by using network protocols. The message is transmitted to the "zombie" components for processing in accordance with the logic of the control protocol.

The zombie component identifies the command, retrieves the victim address and notifies the component "IP Flood" to switch to the attack mode. The attach target is the victim node with the given address. The time to finalize the attack is determined by the logic of its implementation.

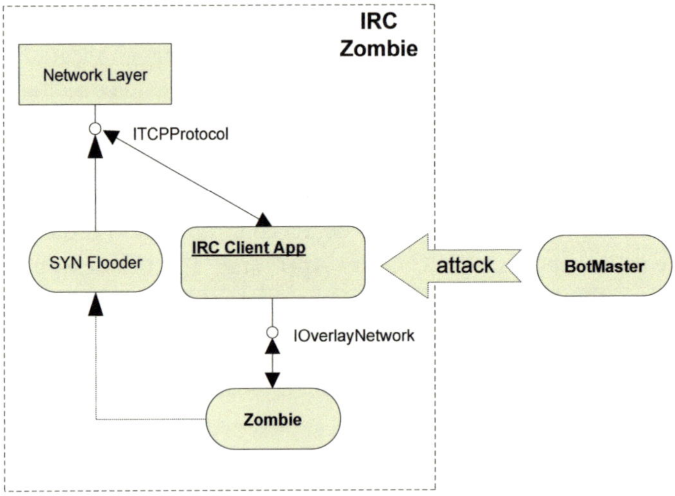

Figure 6. Diagram of components involved in the botnet attack scenario.

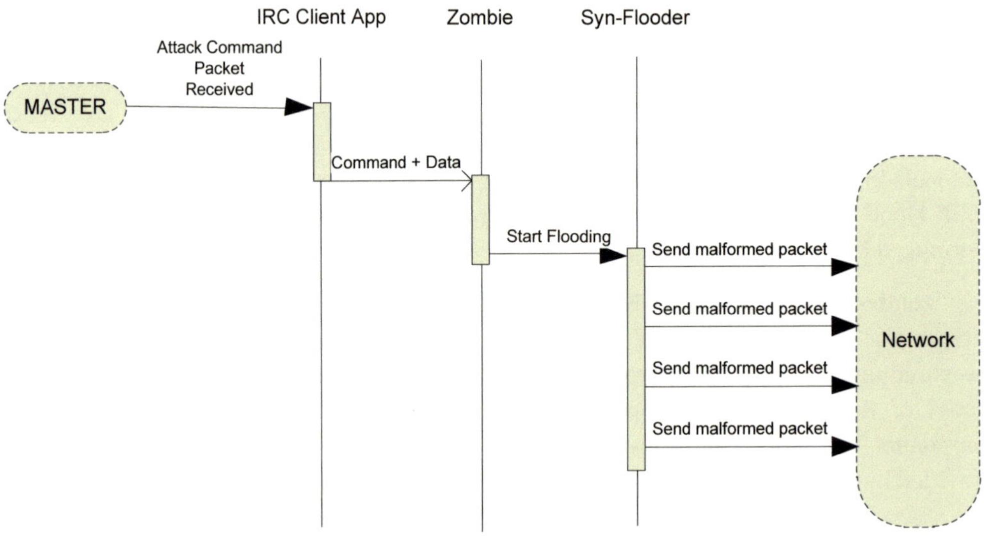

Figure 7. Component interaction diagram for components involved in the botnet attack scenario

For each activity of attack network, the *defense network* is performing the opposite activity, aiming to suppress corresponding activity of attack network. Therefore, the defense network model is implemented by three following sub-models: counteraction of attack network propagation, counteraction of attack network management and control, and counteraction of DDoS attack. In addition to actions against attacking network, protective network also performs some steps destined to ensure its own robustness.

Components that realize the entities of attack and defense networks are given in Table 1.

Module	Description
	Attack network modules
"Botnet Master"	Model of botmaster application
"Bot Client"	Model of zombie client application
"Worm"	Model of network worm application
"Vulnerable Application" "IRC client"	Model of vulnerable network application Model of IRC client application
"IRC Server"	Model of IRC server application
"P2P Agent"	Model of P2P client application
"UDP Flooder"	Model of UDP flooding application
"SYN Flooder"	Model of SYN flooding application
	Defense network modules
"Filtering router"	Model of router for filtering network traffic
"Failed Connection filter"	Traffic filter based on "Failed Connection"
"Worm Throttling filter"	Traffic filter based on "Worm Throttling"
"HIPC filter"	Traffic filter based on "Source IP Counting"
"IRC Monitor"	IRC traffic monitor
"IRC Relationship filter"	IRC related traffic filter based on "Relationship" metric [1]
"IRC Synchronization filter"	IRC related traffic filter based on "Synchronization" metric [1]
"Hop-Count Filter"	Traffic filter based on "Hop-Count Filtering"
"SIMP Filter"	Traffic filter based on "Source IP Address Monitoring"
"SAVE Filter"	Traffic filter based on "Source Address Validity Enforcement"

Table 1. Modules of BOTNET Foundation Classes

5. Implementation and parameters of experiments

An example of the simulation environment user interface in one of the experiments is shown in Fig.8. The main panel and control elements are in the upper-left corner of user interface. Main panel shows components, which are included in BOTNET models.

Control elements allow user to interact with these components. The model time control elements are presented optionally on the main panel. These elements allow, for example, to execute model step-by-step or in the fastest mode. There are also control elements, which allow performing efficient search of the appropriate instance and editing its state.

Fragment of the modeled network is also shown in Fig.8 (at the bottom left). Routers models are depicted as cylinders with arrows, and hosts models are represented as computers of different colors. Color represents the node state. Blue color is used for the incoming nodes, which have vulnerabilities.

The legitimate nodes without vulnerabilities are not colored. The view window of one of hosts (at the bottom right) and the editing window of the "router" object parameters (at the upper-right) are also shown in Fig.8.

Network topology and configuration are modeled on the two levels of details.

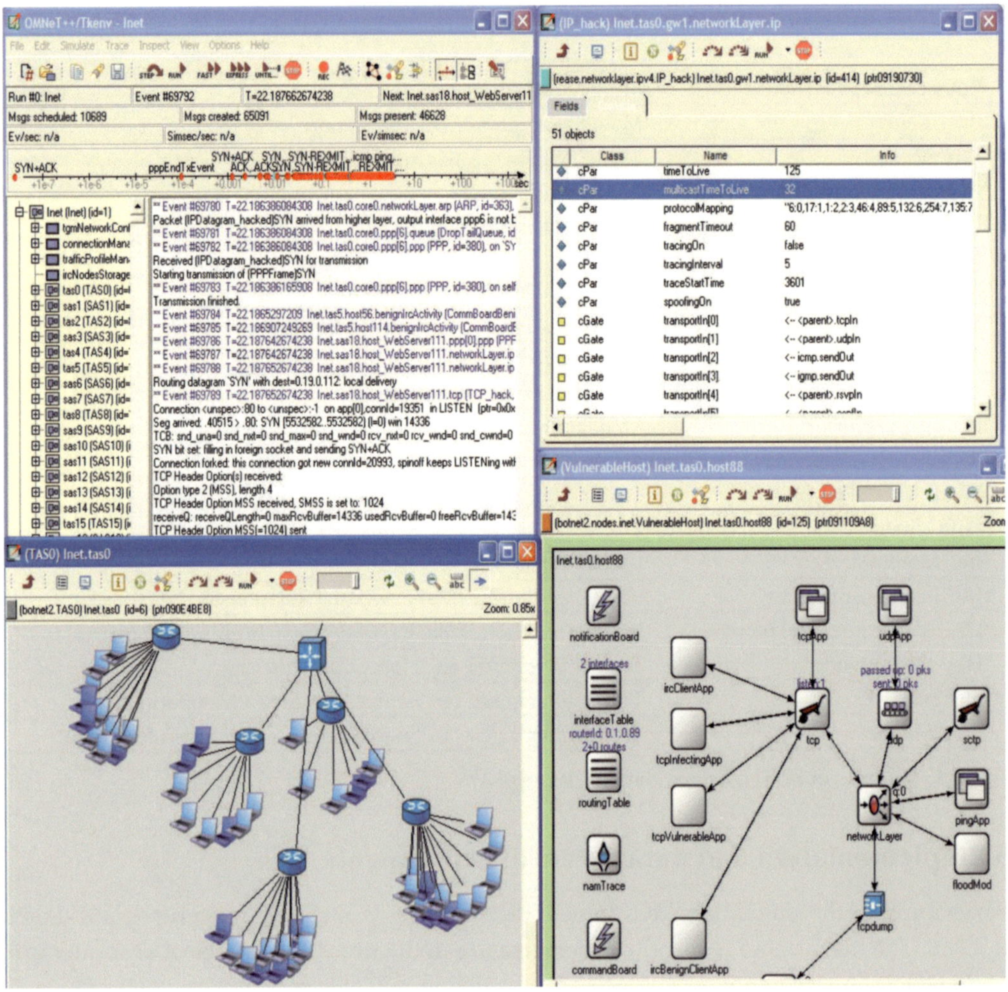

Figure 8. User Interface of Simulation Environment

On the first level the network topology is modeled on the level of the autonomous systems (AS). We used technique of positive-feedback preference (PFP) [38] to model computer network topology on the autonomous system level.

The networks which consist from 30 autonomous systems (AS-level topology) were modeled in experiments (Fig. 9). To generate the graph of the autonomous systems level the following parameters were used: threshold to take AS nodes as transit (Transit Node Threshold= 20); number of new nodes connections (P=0.4); assortative level of the generated network, which characterizes the level of nodes preference depending on their connectivity after addition of the new node to the network (Delta=0.04) [38].

Connection of transit AS is made via communication channel with bandwidth dr=10000 Mbit/s and delay d=50 milliseconds. Connection of limited AS is made with dr=5000 Mbit/s and d=20 milliseconds.

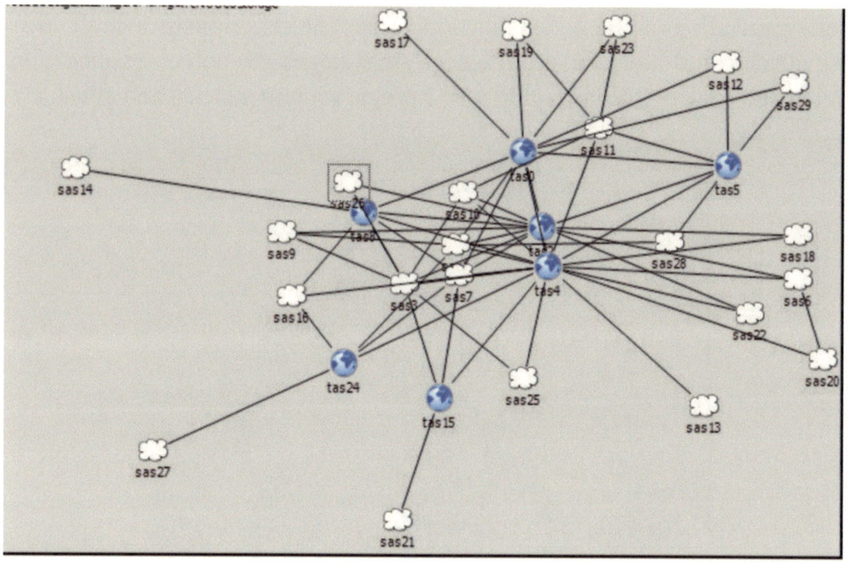

Figure 9. AS-level topology

On the second level the router-level topology is modeled for each AS (Fig. 10).

In this work we use HOT-model (Heuristically Optimal Topology) [16] with the following parameters: number of routers - from 5 to 20; the part of the core routers in the total number of routers - 1%; number of hosts on the router - from 5 to 12; connectivity level of core routers - 0.2.

Core routers are connected via communication channel with bandwidth dr=2500 Mbit/s and delay – 1 milliseconds, communication of gateways with core routers - dr=1000 Mbit/s and delay - 1 milliseconds, connection of gateways with edge routers - dr=155 Mbit/s and delay - 1 milliseconds, connection of edge router with servers - dr=10 Mbit/s and delay - 5 milliseconds. Connection of edge router with client nodes is as follows: to node - dr=0.768 Mbit/s and delay - 5 milliseconds, from node - dr=0.128 Mbit/s and delay - 5 milliseconds.

On the base of the parameters provided above, different networks were generated, including network with 3652 nodes (which is used for experiments described). 10 of these nodes are servers (including one DNS-server, three web-servers and six mail servers). 1119 nodes (near 30% from the total number) have vulnerabilities.

Also the node "master" is defined in the network. It works as the initial source of worm distribution and the initiator of botnet management commands. All nodes in the subnets are connected via edge routers. Root router "gateway" is defined in every subnet. Subnets are united via this router. User models, which send requests to the servers, are installed on the client nodes.

It is the way to create legitimate traffic. Model of the standard protocol stack is installed on each node. This stack includes PPP, LCP, IP, TCP, ICMP, ARP, UDP protocols. Models of the network components (which implement appropriate functionality) can be installed additionally depending on the nodes functional role. The experiments include investigation of botnet actions and defense activities on the stages of botnet propagation, botnet management and control (reconfiguration and preparation to attacks) and attack execution.

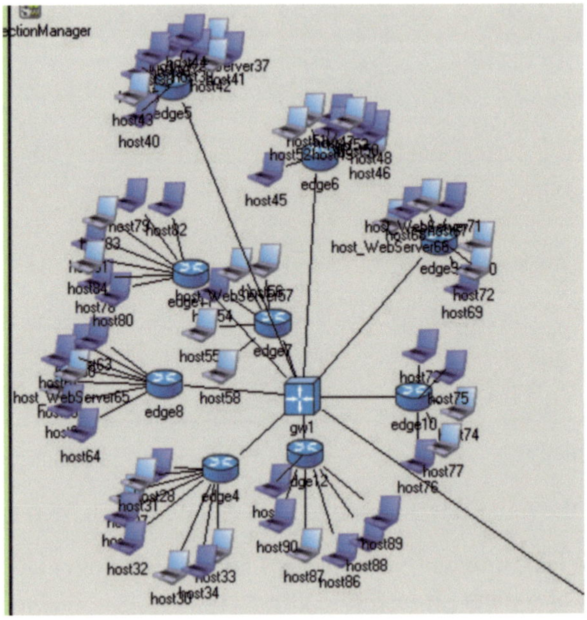

Figure 10. Router-level topology

6. Experiments

As part of our research, a set of experiments was performed. They demonstrate the operability of the developed simulation environment and main characteristics of botnets and defense mechanisms investigated.

a. Botnet propagation and defense against propagation

At the 100th second of the model time, the bot master initiate scanning the network for vulnerable hosts using one of network worm techniques. At the same time it connects to the public IRC server and creates new communication channel, thus turning into kind of "command center". We adjust the frequency of network scanning to 6 packets per second in our experiment. Random scanning on a range of predefined IP addresses is used. In case of some host getting compromised it becomes the "zombie". "Zombie" connects to public IRC server, which is "command center", and reports to bot master of its successful integrating to the botnet infrastructure and readiness to process further orders. Also "Zombie" starts to scan the network for vulnerable hosts the same way as bot master did initially.

To protect against botnet propagation the protection mechanism based on "Virus Throttling" is used. It has the following parameters - the source buffer contains 300 traffic source addresses; the buffer operates by FIFO principle. For each new source address one slot of the buffer is allocated. The buffer includes up to 5 authorized destination addresses. If the buffer is full, one of its slots can be released every 5 seconds by FIFO method and it is allowed to connect to a new remote host. This protection mechanism is installed on routers.

Several experiments were performed. Fig.11 shows the dependencies of the number of infected hosts from the botnet propagation time for cases without protection and with protection set at 30%, 50% and 100% of the routers.

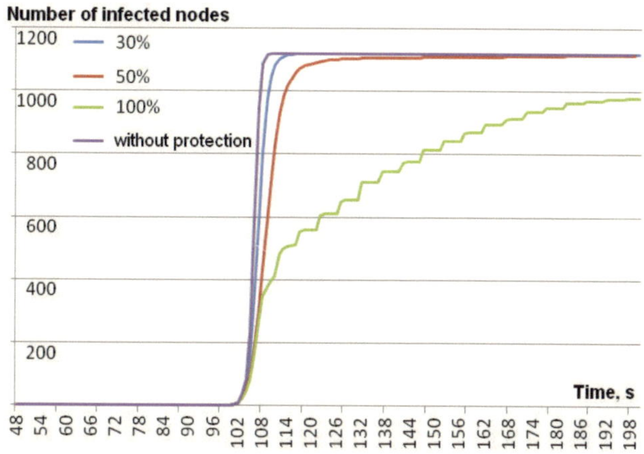

Figure 11. Number of Infected Hosts when using Virus Throttling

We analyzed in the experiments the dependencies of number of false positive rate (FP, when the legitimate packet is recognized as malicious), false negative rate (FN, when the malicious packet is not detected), and truth positive rate (TP, when the malicious packet is detected) from the botnet propagation time.

It was shown that the numbers of FP and FN are just slightly different under a small number of established protection mechanisms (30%) and limiting the source buffer up to 300 addresses. This occurs because Virus Throttling passes the packets from infected nodes, which were previously included in the source buffer, but were jammed with new infected node addresses.

When the number of protection mechanisms increased, the number of FN is significantly reduced.

Fig.12 shows the dependencies of the volume of total and filtered traffic, as well as the numbers of FP and FN rates from botnet propagation time using Virus Throttling at 30% (a), 50% (b) and 100% (c) routers, respectively.

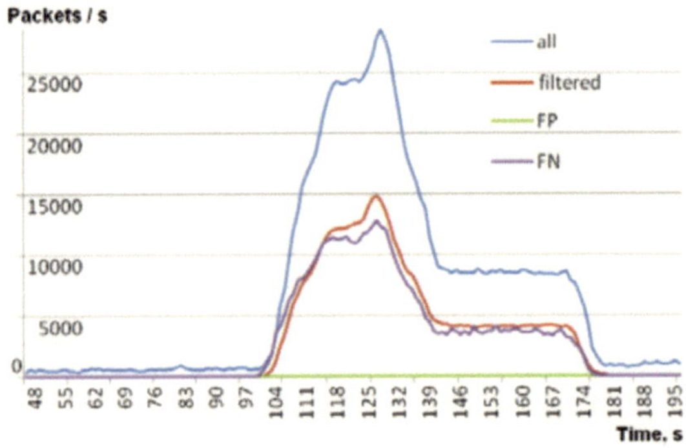

(a)

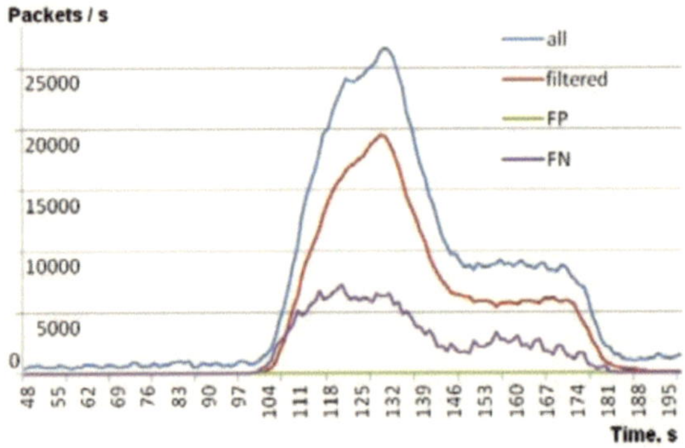

(b)

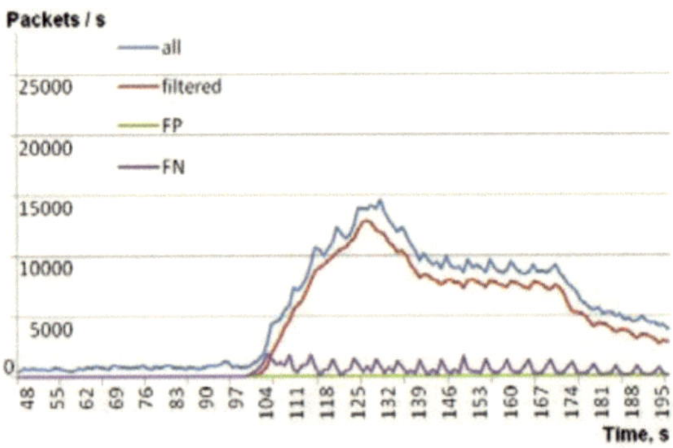

(c)

Figure 12. Main Characteristics of Virus Throttling

Fig.12 shows that when we increase the number of nodes with Virus Throttling from 30 to 50% the filtered traffic also increases, although the total amount of traffic generated by worms decrease slightly. In the case of full (100%) coverage of Virus Throttling the volume of the traffic generated by network worms and the amount of FN is significantly reduced.

Fig.13 shows the dependencies of the percentage of filtered legitimate traffic related to all legitimate traffic from the botnet propagation time, when Virus Throttling are used at 30%, 50% and 100% of the routers.

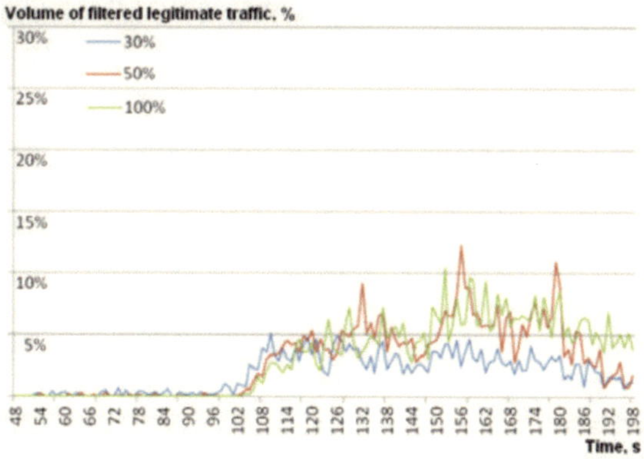

Figure 13. Volume of Filtered Legitimate Traffic when using Virus Throttling

To investigate several other protection mechanisms, we performed the same set of experiments as for Virus Throttling. For example, for "Failed Connection" technique, relative high levels of TP in all dependencies indicate that this technique allows filtering a large number of malicious packets.

However, Failed Connection does not allow significantly constraining the botnet propagation under current parameters of experiments. Such characteristics, as the relation of the number of vulnerable hosts to legitimate ones, the method of vulnerable hosts scanning and threshold for decision making, have a great impact on the quality of this technique.

b. Botnet Management and Protection against Botnet on this Stage

On this stage of botnet life cycle we investigated mainly the protection technique proposed by M. Akiyama et al. [1]. This technique involves monitoring of IRC-traffic, passing through the observer node, and subsequent calculation of the metrics "Relationship", "Response" and "Synchronization", based on the content of network packets. Metric "Relationship" characterizes the distribution of clients in IRC-channel. Too high value of this metric is considered as abnormal.

For example, the threshold for this metric can have a value of 30, 100 or 200 clients per channel. If the threshold is exceeded, the packets related to this IRC channel are filtered. The metric "Response" is calculated as the distribution of response time to the broadcasting request. The metric "Synchronization" characterizes the synchronism in group behavior of IRC clients. Consider the examples of different experiments.

IRC traffic monitoring and relationship metric calculation. IRC traffic is monitored by using "observer" components, which are installed on the core routers of network segments. Information about IRC channel and its clients is defined by analysis of IRC packets. Then, based on data obtained, the relationship metrics of observed channels are calculated in real time. It is assumed that the data, obtained from observer components, will strongly depend on the location of the observer in relation to main IRC flows, merging near the network segment that contains the IRC server.

Table 2 shows a part of observed relationship metrics for IRC channels in various network locations. There are data for the botnet control channel (Irc-bot) and two channels for legitimate IRC communication (Irc-1 and Irc-2). The number of clients in the Irc-channel 1 is 10; the number of clients in Irc-channel 2 is 9. For legitimate channels, we observe either full detection of all channel clients or complete lack of detection. This is due the legitimate IRC communication is done through the exchange of broadcast messages and, thus, if any observer is situated on the path of the IRC traffic, it finds all the clients of the channel.

#Sensor	#Irc-bot	#Irc-1	#Irc-2
sensor sas17	97,91%	100,00%	100,00%
sensor tas0	95,82%	100,00%	100,00%
sensor tas4	26,82%	100,00%	100,00%
sensor tas2	26,00%	100,00%	100,00%
sensor sas1	15,00%	100,00%	100,00%
sensor sas18	7,27%	0,00%	0,00%
sensor sas26	5,45%	100,00%	0,00%
sensor sas11	5,45%	0,00%	0,00%
sensor tas8	5,27%	100,00%	0,00%
sensor tas5	5,27%	0,00%	0,00%
sensor sas20	5,09%	100,00%	0,00%
sensor sas13	5,00%	0,00%	0,00%

Table 2. Relationship Metrics of IRC Channels

We see strong differentiation of observed metrics, depending from the observer network position. This is due to peculiarities of communication of botnet clients in the IRC control channel. Instead of using broadcast messages directed to all participants in the channel, bots exchange information only with a small number of nodes, belonging to botnet masters. We observe almost complete detection of botnet control channel for two routers in table 2. Analysis of the topology of the simulated network shows that the segment sas17 (sensor_sas17) has an IRC server node. The segment tas0, located in proximity to the segment sas17, is a transit for traffic between the IRC server and the most of IRC bots.

Thus, we can suppose that a defense mechanism, fulfilled on a small number of routers which are transit for the main IRC traffic, can be as effective as the defense mechanism installed in more number of routers. We can also assume that a defense mechanism, having a small covering of the protected network, generally will not be efficient, because only a small part of IRC control traffic passes the vast majority of routers.

IRC traffic monitoring and synchronization metric calculation. In these experiments the IRC traffic is monitored in different network locations. Based on monitoring results, the synchronization metrics are calculated. Let us consider the synchronization metrics determined by monitoring the traffic on the core router of network segment tas0 (Fig.14).

From 200 seconds of simulation time, every 100 seconds we can observe sharp spikes of traffic volume related to the botnet control IRC channel. These bursts are caused by response messages from zombies on a request from the botnet master.

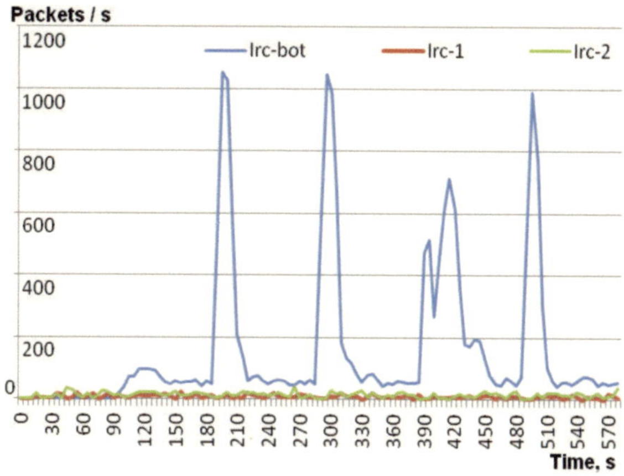

Figure 14. Synchronization Metrics for tas0

Network segment tas0 is located in proximity from the network segment which includes IRC-server. Thus, a significant part of IRC control traffic is transmitted through the router of network segment tas0. For this reason, the bursts of control channel traffic are markedly expressed against the traffic of legitimate communication.

Traffic on a network segment router sas13 was measured (Fig.15) to evaluate the impact of the proximity of the observation point from the IRC server on the severity of bursts of control traffic (and thus on the discernibility of synchronization metric).

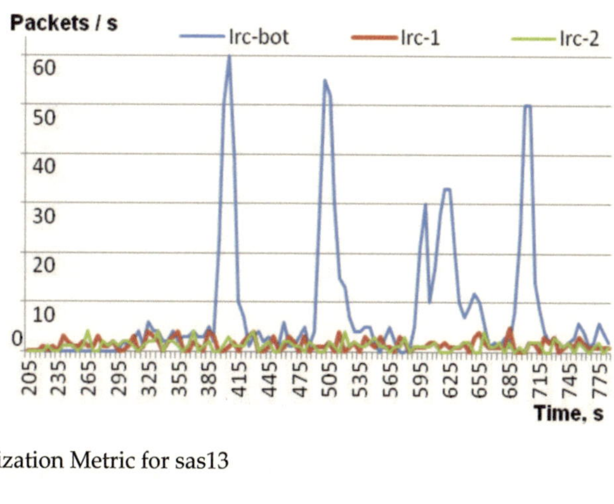

Figure 15. Synchronization Metric for sas13

Traffic measurements show a general decrease of traffic level in the observation point sas13, as well as a good visibility of traffic spikes on the core router of this network segment. Thus, the results of experiments demonstrate the applicability of synchronization metric to detect the IRC control traffic.

IRC traffic filtering based on relationship metric. This filtering method is based on the assumption that the IRC channels with a very large number of clients are anomalous. We carried out a series of experiments where the relationship metric was used for different configurations of filtering components and different critical levels of relationship. It was shown that the efficiency of IRC traffic detection and filtering, based on relationship metric, increases sharply when the routers, which are transit for IRC control traffic, are fully covered by filtering components.

IRC traffic filtering based on synchronization metric. This filtering method is based on the assumption that the short synchronous messaging in a single IRC channel is anomalous. The observed synchronization metric is calculated as the number of IRC packets, passing through the observation point, for a fixed period of time. In the experiments fulfilled, the filtering criterion is a fivefold increase in traffic for 20 seconds followed by a return to its original value. The results of experiments allow concluding about low quality of the method in the current configuration, since false positive rate has a rather high value.

c. DDoS attacks and defense against them

The module of DDoS attacks is parameterized for experiments described as follows: type of attack – SYN flooding; flooding frequency – 10, 30 or 60 packets per second; total number of packets to send by a single host – 1000. Attacks take some Web server as a target, so TCP port 80 is the destination port during attack stage. Spoofing of source IP address is fulfilled in some experiments. We adopt address range that is subset of address range of the whole network to implement spoofing.

Two kinds of defense mechanisms are considered in the description of experimental results: SAVE and SIM.

At the 400th second of model time, bot master initiates the beginning of the attack stage by sending broadcasting network message through the IRC server. This message is transmitted to all "zombie" hosts involved into the botnet. Other data, enveloped into this message, contains specification of IP address and port of the target host. Every zombie, received this message, is able to extract such information and use it as a parameter of own DDoS related activity.

Fig.16 shows the number of packets targeted to the victim host relative to the model time while SAVE method is active. Different portion of routers is used as hosts for defense method deployment. The metrics for 30%, 50% and 100% of router coverage are shown.

The false positive rate, false negative rate and correct detection rate relative to model time are shown in Fig.17. Such metrics are observed for the traffic passing through the core router of the network which victim host belongs to. The only SIM method was enabled. Fig.18 depicts the relative estimation of filtered legitimate traffic against the model time. Relative estimation of the traffic is calculated as a ratio of the number of filtered packets to the number of all packets passed through the SIM defense mechanism. Three cases for different protection coverage (30%, 50% and 100%) were considered.

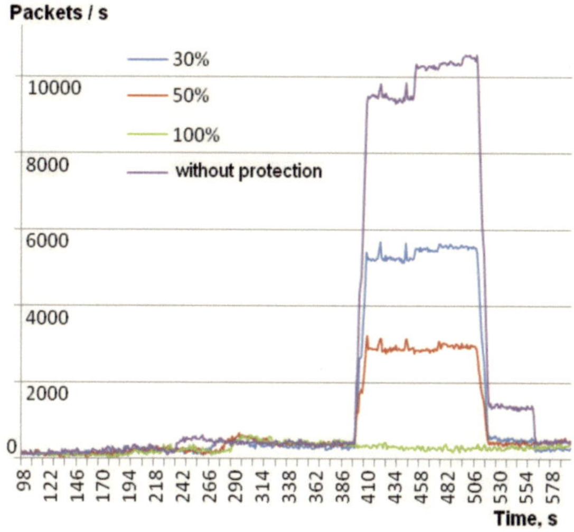

Figure 16. Number of Incoming Packets on Target Host when SAVE Method is enabled

The SIM defense mechanism reveals a high level of TP and a very low level of FN in all cases (Fig.16). A tiny spike of FN observed only at the beginning of attack stage (Fig.17). The level of FP increases gradually due to the fact of continual increment of dropped packets with unspecified IP-addresses, since the beginning of attack stage. It is noted that the ratio of filtered legitimate packets can reach up to 30-40% of legitimate traffic (Fig.18).

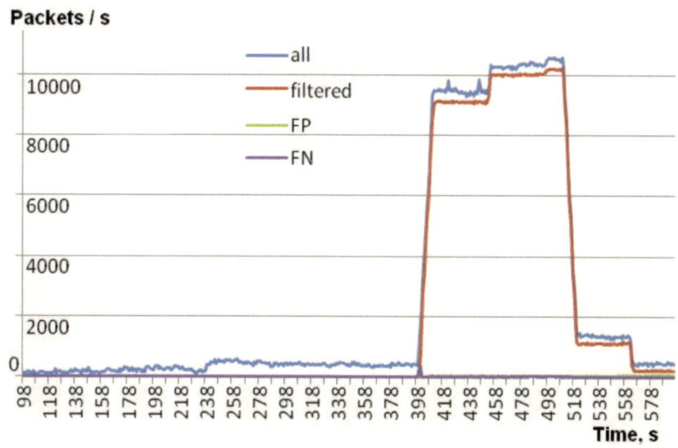

Figure 17. Main metrics of SIM

d. Comparison of with the Results of Emulation

To verify the developed simulation models, we emulated the functioning of small networks consisting of many nodes on real computers combined to a network using Oracle VM Virtual Box. On emulated computers the typical software was installed, and the work of legitimate users and malefactors was imitated. To emulate the botnet such hosts as "master", "control center" and "vulnerable computers" were selected. Furthermore, the software for monitoring of network traffic was installed on the computers.

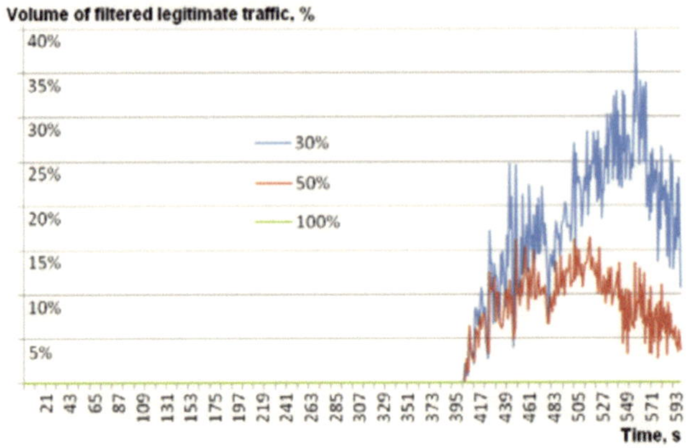

Figure 18. Volume of filtered legitimate traffic

Using the developed network testbed, we compared the results obtained on the basis of simulation models with the results of emulation. In case of discrepancies in the results the corresponding simulation models were corrected.

To test the adequacy of the simulation models, the network consisting of 20 virtual nodes was built.

The examples of parameters which were evaluated for the real network are as follows: packet delay, packet loss, the rate of infection of vulnerable hosts, the number of bots participating in the attack, the load of the victim node during DDoS-attack, etc.

In the normal state of the network, the packet delay for legitimate packets to reach the victim node was from 3 to 7 milliseconds, the packet loss was less than 1%. When we emulated a worm spreading, the rate of infection of 18 nodes was from 2.2 to 2.4 s. When performing DDoS-attack, the victim node received from 174 to 179 packets per second, and packet loss increased to 4%. In the case of simulation with the same parameters, the packet delay was 5 milliseconds with the dispersion - 2 milliseconds and packet loss - 1%. The rate of infection of 18 nodes was about 2.4 s. The number of packets used for DDoS-attacks was about 180.

7. Conclusion

The paper suggested a common approach to investigative modelling and packet-level simulation of botnets and defense mechanisms against them in the Internet. We proposed a generalized architecture of simulation environment aiming to analyze botnets and defense mechanisms. On the base of this architecture we designed and implemented a multilevel software simulation environment. This environment includes the system of discrete event simulation (OMNeT++), the component of networks and network protocols simulation (based on INET Framework library), the component of realistic networks simulation (using the library ReaSE) and BOTNET Foundation Classes library consisting of the models of network applications related to botnets and defense against them.

The experiments investigated botnet actions and protection mechanisms on stages of botnet propagation, botnet management and control (reconfiguration and preparation to attacks), and attack execution. We analyzed several techniques, including Virus Throttling and Failed Connection, to protect from botnet on the propagation stage. Botnet propagation was performed via network worm spreading. We researched techniques of IRC-oriented botnet detection to counteract botnets on the management and control stage. These techniques are based on the "Relationship" metric of particular IRC-channels, metric of the distribution of response time to the broadcasting request ("Response") and the metric of botnet group behavior synchronization ("Synchronization"). We also analyzed techniques, which work on the different stages of defense against DDoS attacks. These techniques include SAVE (Source Address Validity Enforcement Protocol), SIM (Source IP Address Monitoring) and Hop-count filtering.

The purpose of this paper is to provide an environment for simulation of computer networks, botnet attacks and defense mechanisms against them. This simulation environment allows investigating various processes in computer networks - the performance of communication channels and servers, the operation of computer network nodes during different attacks on them, the effect of protection mechanisms on the computer network, the best strategies for location and implementation of protection mechanisms.

The developed simulation environment allows changing the main parameters for conducting experiments. These parameters can be adjusted to simulate different types of worms, DDoS attacks, command centers' operation, as well as various protection mechanisms with a wide range of values.

By changing the values of the parameters used to model the life cycle of botnets and protection mechanisms against them, we can generate different types of botnets. For example, it is possible to simulate the spread of botnets for a few milliseconds or the case of their blocking at the first stage of the operation.

The experiments fulfilled were based on typical values of the parameters that can demonstrate the overall dynamics of the development and operation of botnets and the ability to implement different protection mechanisms. The conclusions derived from the simulation results are generalizable to other cases where values of these parameters are outside the range or different from those investigated.

The developed environment allows building the models based on the real network topologies with highly detailed units included in the network to provide the high fidelity of the models.

We suppose that suggested approach can be used to investigate operation of different types of botnets, to evaluate effectiveness of defense mechanisms against botnets and other network attacks, and to choose optimal configurations of such mechanisms.

Future research is connected with the analysis of effectiveness of botnet operation and defense mechanisms, and improvement of the implemented simulation environment. One of the main tasks of our current and future research is to improve the scalability and fidelity of the simulation. We are in the process of experimenting with parallel versions of the simulation environment and developing a simulation and emulation tesbed, which combines a hierarchy of macro and micro level analytical and simulation models of botnets and botnet defense (analytical, packet-based, emulation-based) and real small-sized networks.

Author details

Igor Kotenko, Alexey Konovalov and Andrey Shorov
Laboratory of Computer Security Problems, St.-Petersburg Institute for Informatics and Automation of Russian Academy of Sciences, St. Petersburg, Russia

Acknowledgement

This research is being supported by grants of the Russian Foundation of Basic Research (project 10-01-00826), the Program of fundamental research of the Department for Nanotechnologies and Informational Technologies of the Russian Academy of Sciences (2.2), State contract #11.519.11.4008 and partly funded by the EU as part of the SecFutur and MASSIF projects.

8. References

[1] Akiyama M, Kawamoto T, Shimamura M, Yokoyama T, Kadobayashi Y, Yamaguchi S. (2007) A proposal of metrics for botnet detection based on its cooperative behavior, SAINT Workshops, pp. 82-82.
[2] Bailey M, Cooke E, Jahanian F, Xu Y, Karir M (2009) A Survey of Botnet Technology and Defenses, Cybersecurity Applications Technology Conference for Homeland Security,.
[3] Binkley JR, Singh S (2006) An algorithm for anomaly-based botnet detection", Proceedings of the 2nd conference on Steps to Reducing Unwanted Traffic on the Internet, Vol.2.
[4] Chen S, Tang Y (2004) Slowing Down Internet Worms, Proceedings of the 24th International Conference on Distributed Computing Systems.
[5] Dagon D, Zou C, Lee W (2006) Modeling botnet propagation using time zones, Proc. 13th Annual Network and Distributed System Security Symposium. San Diego, CA.
[6] Feily M, Shahrestani A, Ramadass S (2009) A Survey of Botnet and Botnet Detection", Third International Conference on Emerging Security Information Systems and Technologies.
[7] Gamer T, Mayer C (2009) Large-scale Evaluation of Distributed Attack Detection, 2nd International Workshop on OMNeT++.
[8] Grizzard JB, Sharma V, Nunnery C, Kang BB, Dagon D (2007) Peer-to-Peer Botnets: Overview and Case Study.

[9] Huang Z, Zeng X, Liu Y (2010) Detecting and blocking P2P botnets through contact tracing chains, International Journal of Internet Protocol Technology archive, Vol.5, Issue 1/2.

[10] Hyunsang C, Hanwoo L, Heejo L, Hyogon K (2007) Botnet Detection by Monitoring Group Activities in DNS Traffic, 7th IEEE International Conference on Computer and Information Technology CIT, pp.715-720.

[11] The INET Framework is an open-source communication networks simulation package for the OMNeT++ simulation environment. Available: http://inet.omnetpp.org/. Accessed 2012 Marth 24.

[12] Kotenko I (2010) Agent-Based Modelling and Simulation of Network Cyber-Attacks and Cooperative Defence Mechanisms", Discrete Event Simulations, Sciyo, pp.223-246.

[13] Kotenko I, Konovalov A, Shorov A (2010) Agent-based Modeling and Simulation of Botnets and Botnet Defense", Conference on Cyber Conflict. CCD COE Publications. Tallinn, Estonia, pp.21-44.

[14] Krishnaswamy J (2009) Wormulator: Simulator for Rapidly Spreading Malware, Master's Projects.

[15] Kugisaki Y, Kasahara Y, Hori Y, Sakurai K (2007) Bot detection based on traffic analysis, Proceedings of the International Conference on Intelligent Pervasive Computing, pp.303-306.

[16] Li L, Alderson D, Willinger W, Doyle J (2004) A first-principles approach to understanding the internet router-level topology", ACM SIGCOMM Computer Communication Review.

[17] Li J, Mirkovic J, Wang M, Reither P, Zhang L (2002) Save: Source address validity enforcement protocol", Proceedings of IEEE INFOCOM, pp.1557-1566.

[18] Mao C, Chen Y, Huang S, Lee H (2009) IRC-Botnet Network Behavior Detection in Command and Control Phase Based on Sequential Temporal Analysis, Proceedings of the 19th Cryptology and Information Security Conference.

[19] Mazzariello C (2008) IRC traffic analysis for botnet detection, Proceedings of Fourth International Conference on Information Assurance and Security.

[20] Nagaonkar V, Mchugh J (2008) Detecting stealthy scans and scanning patterns using threshold random walk", Dalhousie University.

[21] Naseem F, Shafqat M, Sabir U, Shahzad A (2010) A Survey of Botnet Technology and Detection, International Journal of Video & Image Processing and Network Security, Vol.10, No. 1.

[22] Owezarski P, Larrieu N (2004) A trace based method for realistic simulation, Communications, 2004 IEEE International Conference.

[23] Peng T, Leckie C, Ramamohanarao K (2004) Proactively Detecting Distributed Denial of Service Attacks Using Source IP Address Monitoring, Lecture Notes in Computer Science, Vol.3042, pp.771-782.

[24] ReaSE - Realistic Simulation Environments for OMNeT++. Available: https://i72projekte.tm.uka.de/trac/ReaSE. Accessed 2012 Marth 24.

[25] Riley G, Sharif M, Lee W (2004) Simulating internet worms, Proceedings of the 12th International Workshop on Modeling, Analysis, and Simulation of Computer and Telecommunication Systems (MASCOTS), pp.268-274.

[26] Ruitenbeek EV, Sanders WH (2008) Modeling peer-to-peer botnets, Proceeding of 5th International Conference on Quantitative Evaluation of Systems, pp. 307-316.

[27] Schuchard M, Mohaisen A, Kune D, Hopper N, Kim Y, Vasserman E (2010) Losing control of the internet: using the data plane to attack the control plane, Proceedings of the 17th ACM conference on Computer and communications security, pp.726-728.

[28] Sen S, Spatscheck O, Wang D (2004) Accurate, scalable in-network identification of p2p traffc using application signatures, Proceedings of the 13th international conference on World Wide Web, pp. 512-521.

[29] Simmonds R, Bradford R, Unger B (2000) Applying parallel discrete event simulation to network emulation, Proceedings of the fourteenth workshop on Parallel and distributed simulation.

[30] Suvatne A. Improved Worm Simulator and Simulations. Master's Projects, 2010.

[31] Varga A. (2010) OMNeT++. Chapter in the book "Modeling and Tools for Network Simulation", Wehrle, Klaus; Günes, Mesut; Gross, James (Eds.) Springer Verlag.

[32] Villamarín-Salomón R, Brustoloni JC (2009) Bayesian bot detection based on DNS traffic similarity, Proceeding SAC '09 Proceedings of the 2009 ACM symposium on Applied Computing.

[33] Vishwanath KV, Vahdat A (2006) Realistic and responsive network traffic generation, Proceedings of the Conference on Applications, technologies, architectures, and protocols for computer communications.

[34] Wang P, Sparks S, Zou CC (2007) An advanced hybrid peer-to-peer botnet, Proceedings of the First Workshop on Hot Topics in Understanding Botnets.

[35] Wang H, Zhang D, Shin K (2002) Detecting SYN flooding attacks, Proceedings of IEEE INFOCOM, pp.1530–1539.

[36] Wehrle K, Gunes M, Gross J (2010) Modeling and Tools for Network Simulation, Springer-Verlag.

[37] Williamson M. (2002) Throttling Viruses: Restricting propagation to defeat malicious mobile code", Proceedings of ACSAC Security Conference, pp.61–68.

[38] Zhou S, Zhang G, Zhang G, Zhuge Zh (2006) Towards a Precise and Complete Internet Topology Generator", Proceedings of International Conference Communications.

Chapter 7

Using Discrete Event Simulation for Evaluating Engineering Change Management Decisions

Weilin Li

Additional information is available at the end of the chapter

http://dx.doi.org/10.5772/50579

1. Introduction

Today's hyper-competitive worldwide market, turbulent environment, demanding customers, and diverse technological advancements force any corporations who develop new products to look into all the possible areas of improvement in the entire product lifecycle management process. One of the areas facing both practitioners and scholars that have been overlooked in the past is Engineering Change Management (ECM).

On the one hand, even though the demand has increased for more effective ECM as an important competitive advantage of product development companies, the existing ECM literature focuses mainly on the following topics: i) administrative evaluation that supports the formal EC approval, implementation, and documentation process, ii) ECM in product structure and material resource planning, and iii) change propagation and knowledge management. In addition, with a few exceptions [1, 2, 4, 12, 18, 19, 20, 26], almost all the previous research or empirical studies were qualitatively discussed in a descriptive nature.

On the other hand, despite of a rich body of concurrent engineering literature that emphasizes the iterative nature of New Product Development (NPD) process, "these models see iterations as *exogenous* and *probabilistic*, and do not consider the source of iteration" [23], which causes the identified rework too general, and therefore not sufficient for an effective ECM study. As a result, there is a lack of research–based analytical models to enhance the understanding of complex interrelationships between NPD and ECM, especially from a systems perspective.

The vision behind this chapter is to ultimately bridge this gap between these two bodies of literature by recognizing the main characteristics of both New Product Development (NPD) and ECM processes, quantifying the interrelated connections among these process features in a Discrete Event Simulation (DES) model (Arena), experimenting with the model under different parameter settings and coordination policies, and finally, drawing decision-making suggestions considering EC impacts from an overall organizational viewpoint.

2. Background

2.1. Problem definition

ECM refers to a collection of procedures, tools, and guidelines for handling modifications and changes to released product design specifications or locked product scope [4, 6, 22, 35]. ECs can be classified into two main categories [4, 5, 11, 13, 27]:

- ***Emergent EC*** (EEC) originates from the problems or errors detected from activity outcomes (i.e., design data and information) that have already been frozen and formally released to the downstream phase. EECs are assumed to occur according to a certain probability determined by the conceptualized *solution uncertainty*,
- ***Initiated EC*** (IEC) requested by sources outside the project's control such as changing market conditions, arising customer requirements, new legislation, or emerging technology advances any point along the NPD process in response to the conceptualized *environmental uncertainty*.

Under this classification scheme, design iterations within an NPD process and *problem–induced* EECs are very similar, but occur in different situations. Both of them aim at correcting mistakes or solving problems through repetitively achieving unmet goals that have been set initially. EECs are requested rework to prior activities whose outcomes have already been finalized and released to the next phase. However, NPD iterations take place before any design information is formally released to downstream phases, and therefore it generally takes less time to handle iterations due to both a smaller rework scope and a shorter approval processing time. For simplicity, term "***rework***" will be used to refer to both iterations and EECs, unless specific distinction is required. From another standpoint, *opportunity–driven* IECs arise from new needs and requirements, which result in the adding of functionality to a product [10], or enlargement of the original design solution scope. A formal assessment and approval process is desirable in handling both types of ECs due to the associated complexity and potential risks [13, 35].

2.2. Context

ECM problems cannot be studied in isolation. But rather, they need to be addressed within a broader context, including the following three principle facets: i) complex systems, ii) current engineering and uncertainty, and iii) rework and change propagation.

2.2.1. Complexity

A new product is designed and developed via an NPD process through the efforts from a group of specialists under dynamic internal and external environment. This DES model brings together the four main elements of complexity associated with design and product development [10], namely, product, process, team (/designer), and environment (/user), on the decision of how iterations and ECs emerge and thus impact NPD project performance, and how should they be effectively managed by applying different coordination policies.

Highly engineered ***product*** is a complex assembly of interacting components [21, 25]. In automobile industry, a fairly typical modern vehicle is composed of more than ten thousand manufactured component pieces, supplied by thousands of outside suppliers. In the face of such great quantities of components, complex products are impossible to be built all at once. They are decomposed into minimally coupled major systems, and then further broken into smaller sub–systems of manageable size and complexity, and finally down to separate components or parts for individual detailed engineering design. On the other hand, the integration of interdependent decompositions within and across system(s) into the final overall solution as well adds up to the level of complexity and requires substantial coordination efforts [31].

Similarly, a large complex Product Development (PD) ***process***, through which all the stages of a product's lifecycle occur, is itself a complex system involving hundreds or thousands of interrelated or interacting activities which transforms inputs into outputs. As shown in the PD literature, tremendous research effort has been devoted into exploring the complexity of PD processes, especially in studying both of the advantages and disadvantages of parallel development process (also known as concurrent engineering) or spiral development process (which is applied more often in software industry) as compared with the traditional staged (also known as waterfall or sequential) development process. Some prior research particularly stressed structuring and managing the process through efforts in minimizing the interdependencies among tasks via process sequencing optimization [8, 9, 34].

Also, multi–disciplinary ***teams*** participating in an NPD project are typically composed of numerous decision makers from different functional areas (e.g., marketing, engineering, manufacturing, purchasing, quality assurance, etc.) with varied skill sets (e.g., degree of specialization, depth of knowledge, qualifications, work experience, etc.), responsibilities, and authorities working together and contributing to the achievement of the final product solution. These teams exhibit another set of complex and non–linear organizational behaviors in communication, collaboration, and integration when considering local task decisions as well as task interactions in determining aggregate system performance [28].

Last but not least, an NPD project interacts with its internal (e.g., simultaneous concurrent development of other products within the same organization) and external (e.g., customers/market, competitors, suppliers, and other socio–economic factors such as government regulations, etc.) ***environments*** throughout the project cycle. The dynamic and sometimes even chaotic competitive environmental factors also contribute significantly to the complexity in the coordination of NPD projects.

2.2. Concurrency and uncertainty

The concept of ***concurrent engineering*** is characterized by i) the execution of PD tasks concurrently and iteratively, and ii) the cross–functional integration through improved coordination and incremental information sharing among participating groups. It has been widely embraced by both academia and industry for the well documented advantages of NPD cycle acceleration, risk minimization by the detections of design errors in early stages, and overall quality improvement (e.g., [3, 17, 27]). It is one of the process features that are captured and thoroughly analyzed by the DES model proposed here.

Complexity drives ***uncertainty***. Uncertainty is an inherent nature of NPD projects stemming from all aspects of complexity associated with efforts creating a new product as discussed above. The presence of inherent uncertainty in NPD processes is much greater and, interestingly, much more complicated than those in processes of other kinds (e.g., business or manufacturing processes), even though the latter also possess certain degree of inherent unpredictability. Types of uncertainty in engineering design include *subjective uncertainty* derived from incomplete information, and *objective uncertainty* associated with environment [37]. Moreover, concurrent processing of NPD activities will further increase the uncertainty of an NPD project by starting activities with incomplete or missing input information. In this model uncertainty is explicitly differentiated into three types: i) low–level *activity uncertainty* represented by the stochastic activity duration, ii) medium–level *solution uncertainty* that dynamically calculates rework probability, and iii) high–level *environmental uncertainty* captured by the arrival frequency and magnitude of IECs.

2.3. Rework and change propagation

Evidences show clearly that excessive project budget and schedule overruns typically involve significant effort on rework [14, 15, 16, 26, 29, 30, 32]. Moreover, it is claimed by Reichelt and Lyneis [32] that "these phenomena are not caused by late scope growth or a sudden drop in productivity, but rather by the late discovery and correction of rework created earlier in the project." In this study, primary characteristics of NPD projects will be transformed into a DES model to study their relative impacts on the stochastic arrivals of ***rework*** (i.e., iterations or EECs).

Rework probability, if included in previous PD process models, is typically assigned a fixed number and remains statically along the process [4, 8, 9, 15, 26]. In reality, however, it is not always the case. Rework probability will be calculated in the proposed DES model by dynamic, evolving solution uncertainty influenced by important feedback effects from other interrelated system variables such as design solutions scope, resource availability, etc. And also, any type of rework is usually discussed on an aggregate level, instead of being categorized into iterations, EECs, and IECs as discussed in this study.

A change rarely occurs alone and multiple changes can have interacting effects on the complex change networks [13]. ***Change propagation*** is included by considering both of dependent product items and interrelated NPD activities. A complex product usually consists of several interrelated major systems, and each further contains interconnected subsystems, components, and elements. The interactions, in terms of spatial, energy, information, and material [31], that occur between the functional and physical items will cause EC of one product item propagate to the others. Besides highly dependent product configuration, product development activities are also coupled. An EC may propagate to its later activities within the current phase or after. For example, an EC that solves a design fault may trigger further changes to downstream activities in design or production phase.

3. Causal framework

Before the actural construction of a computer simulation model that is quantitatively augmented by algebraic relationships among interrelated variables, causal loop diagrams are first constructed to study how external factors and internal system structure (the interacting variables comprising the system and the cause-and-effect relationships among them) contribute qualitatively to specific behavioral patterns.

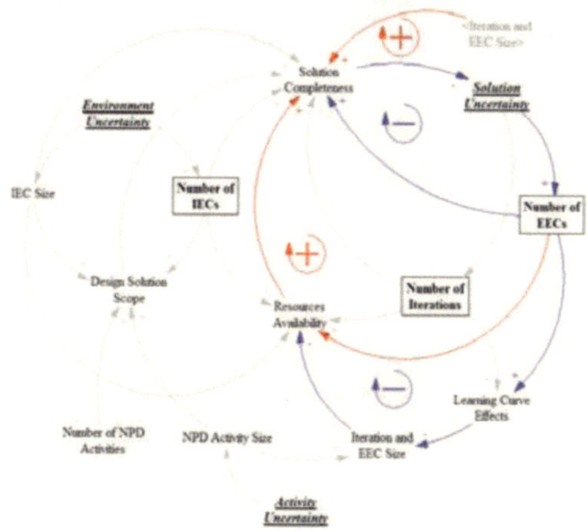

Figure 1. Feedback Loops of EEC Occurrence

Four feedback loops of various lengths (i.e., the number of variables contained within the loop) that drive EEC occurrence are illustrated in *Fig. 1* for purpose of demonstration. Five interdependent variables[1] are considered to form these loops: i) *EEC size,* ii) *solution completeness,* iii) *solution uncertainty,* iv) *Learning Curve Effects (LCE),* and v) *resource availability.*

3.1. Balancing (negative) loops

***Balancing Loop 1* (# of EECs → Solution Completeness → Solution Uncertainty → # of EECs)** depicts the reduction in the number of incoming EECs as a result of handling EECs. This phenomenon is due to the fact that processing of more EECs leads to an increase in solution completeness of the NPD project; and thus solution uncertainty decreases. Given the assuption that EEC probability is exponentially decreasing as the project's solution uncertainty decreases, the influence is along the same direction, and therefore number of EEC occurrence decreases.

The reasoning behind ***Balancing Loop 2* (# of EECs → Learning Curve Effects → EEC Size → Resource availability → Solution Completeness → Solution Uncertainty → # of EECs)** is that an increase in occurrence of EECs leads to a reduction in later EEC durations compared with the original level (i.e., the basework duration of that particular activity) because of increasing LCE. As a result, resource availability increases since less time is taken

[1] See *Subsection 4.3.3* for detailed mathematical definition of variables ii) and iii).

for completing EECs, which in turn accelerates the rate of solution completeness and thus leads to the decreasing occurrence of EECs.

3.2. Reinforcing (positive) loops

While the explanation of Balancing Loop 2 is based upon the indirect positive impact of EEC occurrence on resource availability through the reduction of later EEC durations owing to learning curve effects, ***Reinforcing Loop 3*** **(# of EECs → Resource availability → Solution Completeness → Solution Uncertainty → # of EECs)** can be interpreted by the direct negative influence of EEC occurrence on resource availability: the more EECs occur, the more resource will be allocated to process them. As opposed to Loop 2, a decrease in resource availability decelerates the rate of solution completeness, and thus causes an increasing occurrence of EECs.

Despite the indirect effects of EEC size reduction on an accelerating solution completeness rate that results in an increase in the resource availability, a decrease in EEC size also has a direct negative impact on solution completeness because of less contribution to close the information deficiency towards the final design solution, which is shown in ***Reinforcing Loop 4*** **(# of EECs → Learning Curve Effects → EEC Size → Solution Completeness → Solution Uncertainty → # of EECs).**

3.3. Summary

The above four closed feedback loops depict how the initial occurrence of EECs will lead to the subsequent modification of occurrence frequency by taking into account other interrelated variables and presenting simple cause–and–effect relationships between them. A combination of both positive and negative feedback loops indicates that the complex and dynamic interrelationships among variables make the prediction of occurring patterns of iterations/EECs not so straightforward. This phenomenon points out the necessity of constructing a simulation model that can help further quantitative analyses.

4. Model description

4.1. General assumptions

This model has two constituent sections: *NPD Section with Reworks* and *IEC Section*. Primary model assumptions underlying are listed below.

1. The overall structure of NPD process can be systematically planned beforehand in an activity–based representation according to historical data from previously accomplished projects of similar products and teams' expertise as well. All NPD phases and activities, their expected durations and units of resource required, and interdependencies relationships among them are obtainable and remain stable as the NPD project evolves. Therefore, optimization of process sequencing and scheduling is not pursued by this study.

2. There is no overlapping between activities within a same phase. An NPD activity only receives finalized information from its upstream activity within one phase, but downstream action can start with information in a preliminary form before all activities in upstream phase are completed. In addition, there is no information exchange in the middle of an activity.
3. Demand on resource for NPD activity is assumed to be deterministic fixed. However, the activity duration varies stochastically subject to activity uncertainty and LCE which vary depending on the number of attempts to that particular activity.
4. The dynamic progress of an NPD entity is reflected in the work flow within and among NPD phases. Workflow routing is probabilistically altered by either intra–phase iterations or inter–phase EECs according to the dynamically updated rework probabilities, which are calculated based on the current value of solution uncertainty.
5. Each IEC is initially associated with a directly affected NPD activity (and a directly affected product item when product structure is modeled), and may further propagate to any downstream activities based on randomly assigned probabilities. IECs are modeled within a parallel co–flow structure similar to its NPD counterpart. The IEC work flow is restricted by the precedence constraints.

4.2. Notations

Based upon these general assumptions made, notations of important model parameters and variables which will be later used in mathematical formulation are introduced.

4.2.1. Model parameters

- I: number of NPD phases
- J_i: number of NPD activities within phase i (for $i = 1, 2, \dots, I$)
- M: number of participating departments
- R_m: total number of resources available from department m (for $m = 1, 2, \dots, M$)
- r_{ijm}: units of resource required from department m to complete activity j (for $j = 1, 2, \dots, J_i$) in phase i
- d_{ij}:[2] time expected to complete activity j in phase i when resource requirement is met
- D_{ij}: mean value of d_{ij}, $D_{ij} = \beta k$

4.2.2. Model variables

- i_t/j_t: the latest–finished activity basework j_t in phase i_t at time t
- n_t: number of reworks finished at time t
- x_1/y_1: the first rework for activity y_1 in phase x_1
- x_{n_t}/y_{n_t}: the latest–finished rework for activity y_{n_t} in phase x_{n_t} at time t
- $(R_m)_t$:[3] the cumulative functional effort of the ongoing rework(s) at time t

[2] The Erlang distribution $ERLANG\ (\beta, k)$ is used as a description of NPD activity duration

[3] An aggregate term consists of ongoing rework(s)/rework propagations each one corresponding to its current stochastic functional effort value

- L_t: number of IECs finished at time t
- g_{l_1}: the activity in which IEC l is initiated
- $g_{l_{G_l}}$: number of activities IEC l propagates to ($G_l \leq I \times J_i$)
- s_{lgm}: resources required from department m to complete IEC l (for $l = 1, 2, \dots, L_t$) to activity g (for $g = g_{l_1}, g_{l_2}, \dots, g_{l_{G_l}}$)
- w_{lg}:[4] time expected to complete IEC l to activity g
- $(I_m)_t$:[5] the cumulative functional effort of the ongoing IEC(s) at time t

4.3. Design solution scope

Design Solution Scope (DSS) is defined as the overall extent of an NPD project in terms of total effort required (person–days), by completing of which the entire set of product goals will be met. It depends not only on the number of constituent activities, but also the expected duration and units of resources needed to produce the desired outputs of each activity. In a sense, design solution scope indicates one facet of the NPD project complexity with regards to its content (as a function of activity duration d_{ij} and demand for resource r_{ijm}). Of course, project complexity can also be reflected from the perspective of its architecture (i.e., the coupling among product components or the process precedence constraints), which will be discussed more in later sections on the topics of overlapping and rework probabilities.

The estimated functional effort to complete the whole NPD project is obtained as follows:

$$EN_m = \sum_{i=1}^{I} \sum_{j=1}^{J} e_{ijm} = \sum_{i=1}^{I} \sum_{j=1}^{J} (r_{ijm} \times d_{ij}) \quad (1)$$

Let's assume that L_t is the total number of incoming IECs that are finished at time t, g_{l_1} is the activity to which a randomly occurring IEC l (for $l = 1, 2, \dots, L_t$) is directly related, and $g_{l_{G_l}}$ is the last activity along the IEC propagation loop. Through the estimation of IEC duration w_{lg} and s_{lgm} number of resource required from department m, the functional effort needed to process IEC l to activity g (for $g = g_{l_1}, g_{l_2}, \dots, g_{l_{G_l}}$) is $e_{lgm} = s_{lgm} \times w_{lg}$. By a double summation over both l (of the entire set of completed IECs) and g (including the original incoming IEC and a sequence of its propagations), the cumulative functional IEC effort at time t can be represented as

$$(EI_m)_t = \sum_{l=1}^{L_t} \sum_{g=g_{l_1}}^{g_{l_{G_l}}} e_{lgm} + (I_m)_t = \sum_{l=1}^{L_t} \sum_{g=g_{l_1}}^{g_{l_{G_l}}} (s_{lgm} \times w_{lg}) + (I_m)_t \quad (2)$$

Note that besides the first term $\sum_{l=1}^{L_t} \sum_{g=g_{l_1}}^{g_{l_{G_l}}} e_{lgm}$ which describes the total functional effort spent on those already completed IECs, another aggregate term $(I_m)_t$, which represents the cumulative functional effort of the ongoing IEC(s) at time t, is used to avoid the inherently tedious expression of such stochastic, probabilistic, and discrete events in a mathematical formula. The difficulties encountered here in translating such occurrences into a precise math equation, again, confirm the advantages of using computer simulation as the research methodology in studying the interrelated and dynamic ECM problems.

---

[4] The Triangular distribution $TRIANGULAR\,(Min, Mode, Max)$ is used as a description of IEC duration

[5] An aggregate term consists of ongoing probabilistically dependent IEC(s)/IEC propagations each one corresponding to its current stochastic functional effort value.

Based on EN_m and $(EI_m)_t$, a dynamic NPD property, functional design solution scope $(S_m)_t$, can be obtained as appeared in Eq. (3) by making the following assumptions:

$$(S_m)_t = EN_m + (EI_m)_t \tag{3}$$

1. DSS of an NPD project reflects the amount of effort needed to meet the entire set of product goals, including both original pre–defined goals when the project is initiated and those additional ones determined as the project evolves.
2. Both iterations and EECs are mandatory error–correction oriented to achieve the same pre–defined goals, and thus there is no overall resultant increase in DSS. However, they will be taken into account when calculating the actual cumulative functional effort.
3. IECs are carried out to accomplish additional product goals in response to outside requirements such as altering market demands, growing customer needs, new legislations, or rapid advances in technology. IEC arrivals cause increase in DSS.

4.4. NPD framework with iterations and EECs

From an *"information processing"* view, the generic activity network proposed in [3, 4] is adopted as the fundamental modeling structure. By doing so, the NPD process can be decomposed into I numbers of *Phase* P_i $(i = 1, 2, \ldots, I)$ with certain degrees of overlapping. Each phase is further made up of J_i sequentially numbered *Activities* P_iA_j $(j = 1, 2, \ldots, J_i)$ to represent several chronological stages in design and development process. The present study assumes that there is no overlapping among activities within each phase. That is, within a single phase an NPD activity begins only after the completion of its predecessor. However, NPD phases can be overlapped by letting the successor phase begin with only preliminary information before activities in the upstream phase are all finished.

The completion of an NPD activity for the first time is called ***NPD basework***. Any later attempt, no matter in the form of *intra–phase iteration* or *inter–phase EEC*, is referred as ***rework***. When work flow is routed back by probability, it is assumed that some of the previously completed activities have encountered errors and the farthest upstream one will be identified as the "starting point" of rework loop. All downstream activities are supposed to be "corrupted" and have to be reattempted before moving on. *Fig. 2* illustrates this I–phase and J_i–activity NPD framework.

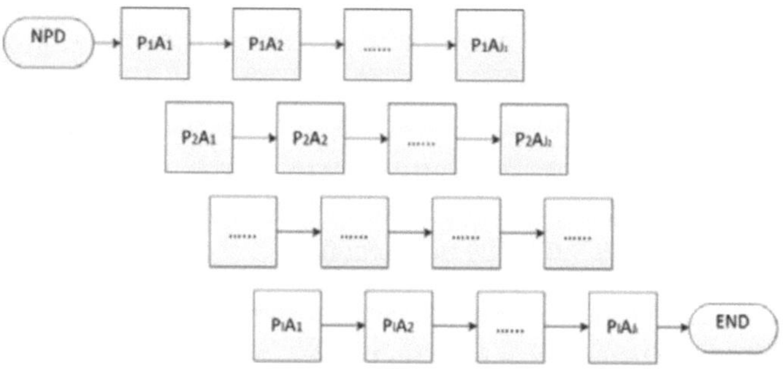

Figure 2. I–phase & J_i–activity NPD framework

4.4.1. NPD activity duration and learning curve effects

Low–level activity uncertainty is represented by random variation of activity duration around its estimate. For each NPD activity, its duration d_{ij} is sampled from a pre–determined probability distribution. The Erlang distribution $ERLANG\ (\beta, k)$ is used as a description of the activity duration. Employment of the Erlang distribution to represent activity interval is based on the hypothesis that each NPD activity consists of k number of random tasks, everyone individually having an identical exponentially distributed processing time with mean β. These mutually independent tasks can be considered as the lowest un–decomposable unit of the NPD process. Number of tasks k comprising each activity and the anticipated task duration β should be estimated by process participants and provided as model inputs.

According to the learning curve theory, the more often an activity is performed, the less time it requires to complete it and thus the lower will be the cost. This well recognized phenomenon is included as a process characteristic to improve the comprehensiveness of this DES model. Following the assumptions made in [9], LCE is modeled in the form of a linearly diminishing fraction ($0 < L_f < 1$) of the original duration whenever an activity is repeated until the minimum fraction ($0 < L_{min} < L_f < 1$) is hit and the rework processing time remains unchanged afterward. That is to say, learning curve improves through each round of rework until it reaches the minimum fraction of basework duration which is indispensible for activity execution. Let n be the number of times an activity is attempted, LCE can be expressed as:

$$LCE = \max\left(\left(L_f\right)^{N_{ij}-1}, L_{min}\right) \tag{4}$$

Therefore, the processing time of a rework to an NPD activity depends on two variables: the stochastic basework duration d_{ij} of the activity and the number of times N_{ij} it is attempted. Any types of NPD rework, no matter intra–phase iterations or inter–phase EECs, are assumed to be subject to the same LEC.

4.4.2. Overlapping and cross–functional interactions

Overlapping is defined as the partial or full parallel execution of nominally sequential development activities [25]. The underlying risk of overlapping raised by Krishnan that "the duration of the downstream activity may be altered in converting the sequential process into an overlapped process" [24] is addressed here in a slightly different way from directly increasing downstream duration and effort by a certain calculated value (e.g., [33]). The more number of activities start with information in a preliminary form or even missing information, the less is the design solution completeness, which will in turn affect rework probabilities as discussed in detail in the next section.

The concept of cross–functional integration among different functional areas during an NPD process is defined as ***Departmental Interaction*** (DI). One of the m departments takes major responsibility for the phase in its own area with specialized knowledge, and is called *major* *department* during that phase. However, the other $m-1$ departments, defined as *minor departments*, also need to participate but with less resource requirements. Cross–functional integration enables a decentralized NPD process by facilitated communications among involving departments. Recourse consumption in the form of departmental interaction is, again, an estimate from process participants. Resources can represent staffs, computers /machines, documentations, or any other individual servers. It's assumed that each resource is qualified to handle all the NPD activities within all phases.

4.4.3. Solution uncertainty

In the process modeling literature, NPD is often considered as a system of interrelated activities that aims to increase knowledge or reduce uncertainty of the final design solution [7, 24, 37]. This DES model assumes that any knowledge or experience accumulation through an NPD activity, no matter accepted to be transferred to the next activity/activities or rejected and requested for a rework, will contribute to the common knowledge base of the NPD project towards its final design solution. No development effort is ever wasted. In this context, knowledge/experience accumulation is simply measured by the cumulative effort that has been committed to the project in terms of person–days.

Functional solution completeness is defined as a criterion to reflect the effort gap between the actual cumulative functional effort accomplished to date and the evolving functional design solution scope $(S_m)_t$. The exact expression for $(C_{ijm})_t$ is determined by the amount of overlap between NPD activities. The more concurrency a process holds, the more complicated the expression will be. Eq. (5) is an illustration of solution completeness at time t for the easiest case: a sequential process. $(C_{ijm})_t$ is improved by knowledge or experience accumulation through performing NPD basework (indicated by the first term in Eq. (5)) and rework (the second term), and handling IECs (the third term). Again, a generalized abstract term $(R_m)_t$ is used here to represent the cumulative functional effort of the ongoing rework(s) at time t.

$$\left(C_{ijm}\right)_t = \frac{\left(\sum_{i=1}^{i_t-1}\sum_{j=1}^{J} e_{ijm}+\sum_{j=1}^{j_t} e_{i_t jm}\right)+\left(\sum_{x=x_1,y=y_1}^{x=x_{n_t},y=y_{n_t}}\left(\sum_{i=x+1}^{i_t}\sum_{j=1}^{j_t} e_{ijm}+\sum_{i=x}^{I}\sum_{j=y}^{j_t} e_{ijm}\right)+(R_m)_t\right)+(EI_m)_t}{(S_m)_t} \quad (5)$$

On the contrary, ***functional solution uncertainty*** $(U_{ijm})_t$ reflects the degree of functional effort absence towards the design solution scope. Therefore, the solution uncertainty of activity j in phase i at time t is $(U_{ijm})_t = 100\% - (C_{ijm})_t$.

4.4.4. Rework probability

After each activity, there is a rework review decision point that decides whether the activity output is acceptable and the NPD project entity gets through or it needs to flow back for a rework according to a weighted rework probability determined by the latest levels of functional solution uncertainty. A critical assumption we made is that the *iteration probability* of an activity is negatively proportional to the NPD project's latest level of solution uncertainty. That is, chance of an activity gets to iterate before it is released to the next phase will increase as the project unfolds with more information available and its solution uncertainty decreases. Two arguments are presented to backup this assumption:

1. As the project unfolds, more information will be available to justify further iteratively refinement of the design solution for each component [37].
2. Since a product architecture often consists of multiple conflicting targets that may be difficult to meet simultaneously and thus requires further trade–offs, "design oscillations" on a system level may occur due to the interdependencies among local components and subsystems even after the achievement of individual optimum [10, 28].

The functional iteration probability is formulated by a negative exponential function of uncertainty as appeared in Eq. (6), where $0 < \alpha < 1$ is a process–specific ***Iteration Probability Constant*** (IPC) that should be determined beforehand as a model input.

$$(PI_{ijm})_t = \alpha^{(U_{ijm})_t + 1} \tag{6}$$

Since NPD activities are decentralized through cross–functional integration among participating departments, so is the decision making process of carrying out rework. The overall iteration probability of activity j in phase i is the weighted mean by the number of resources each department commits to the activity.

$$(PI_{ij})_t = \frac{\sum_{m=1}^{M}(r_{ijm} \times (PI_{ijm})_t)}{\sum_{m=1}^{M} r_{ijm}} \tag{7}$$

Similarly, *EEC probability* is characterized by an ***EEC Probability Constant*** (EPC) $0 < \gamma < 1$. However, as opposed to iteration probability, it is assumed to be exponentially decreasing as the project's solution uncertainty decreases. That is to say, the chance of revisiting NPD activities, whose outputs have already been frozen and released to their successor phase, is the highest after the first activity of the second phase and continuously reduces according to the continually increasing design solution completeness.

$$(PE_{ijm})_t = \gamma^{(C_{ijm})_t + 1} = \gamma^{2 - (U_{ijm})_t} \tag{8}$$

$$(PE_{ij})_t = \frac{\sum_{k=1}^{n}(r_{ijm} \times (PE_{ijm})_t)}{\sum_{k=1}^{n} r_{ijm}} \tag{9}$$

Given the overall rework probability, the next step is to identify which upstream activity generates the design error disclosed by rework review and therefore becomes the starting point of rework loop. For simplicity, it is assumed that each upstream activity gets an equal chance of initiating an intra–phase iteration loop or an inter–phase EEC loop.

4.4.5. *Rework criteria and rigidity of rework review*

According to the rationale explained in previous subsections and causal loop diagrams created, the occurrences of both iterations and EECs are governed by a combination of balancing and reinforcing loops. Take *Loop 3* as an example, less resource availability resulted from increasing EEC arrivals will decelerates the rate of solution completeness, and further increase the occurrence of EECs.

To avoid the dominance of such reinforcing loops which will eventually lead to a net effect of overall divergence with no termination condition, ***rework criteria*** are established as the first step of rework review after the completion of an activity to check whether the cumulative functional effort committed to the deliverable is high enough to provide a satisfying outcome, and therefore let the NPD entity pass rework evaluation. If the cumulative devoted effort fails to meet the pre–determined criteria (i.e., the cumulative effort is less than the expected amount), the entity will be evaluated at the rework decision–point and go for iteration or EEC according to the rework probability calculated by solution completeness. If the committed effort is higher than the pre–set amount, the NPD entity will conditionally pass rework evaluation and continue executing next activity/activities.

Unger and Eppinger [36] define ***rigidity*** by the degree to which deliverables are held to previously–established criteria as metrics to characterize design reviews. By putting it in a slightly different way, rigidity of rework review is considered in this DES model as the strictness of pre–defined rework criteria with respect to the amount of cumulative effort committed to a particular NPD activity.

4.5. IEC framework

Unlike iterations and EECs, IECs are studied through a different DES model section other than the NPD framework. The IEC framework explores how IECs emerging from outside sources after the NPD process begins are handled and how an initiating IEC to a specific activity of a product item will cause further change propagation in its downstream activities and other dependent product items.

4.5.1. IEC processing rules

IECs affecting activities in different NPD phases are assumed to arrive in randomly after the NPD project starts. A checkpoint is inserted before the processing of an IEC to verify whether the directly affected NPD activity has started yet. The incoming IEC will be hold until the beginning of processing of that particular activity.

During NPD rework reviews, the upcoming NPD activity will also be hold from getting processed if there are IECs currently being handled with respect to any of its upstream activities until new information from these IECs becomes available (i.e., the completion of IECs). Purpose of such an inspection is to avoid unnecessary rework as a result of expected new information and updates. However, the NPD activity will not pause in middle of its process due to the occurrence of IECs to any of its upstream activities.

Fig. 3 summaries the entire rework review process after the completion of each activity that includes three major steps as discussed before:

1. Check if there are currently any IECs being handled with regards to any of its upstream activities. If the condition is true, wait until new information from all of these IECs becomes available; if condition is false, go to the next step;

2. Compare the cumulative devoted functional effort so far to the pre–determined rework criteria. If the condition is true, the work flow conditionally pass the rework review and directly proceeds to next activity/activities; if the condition is false, go to the next step;
3. As a result of cross–functional negotiation and integration, calculate rework probability according to the current levels of functional solution uncertainty. NPD project entity either flows back to the identified activity that contains design errors for rework or proceeds to the activity/activities by probability.

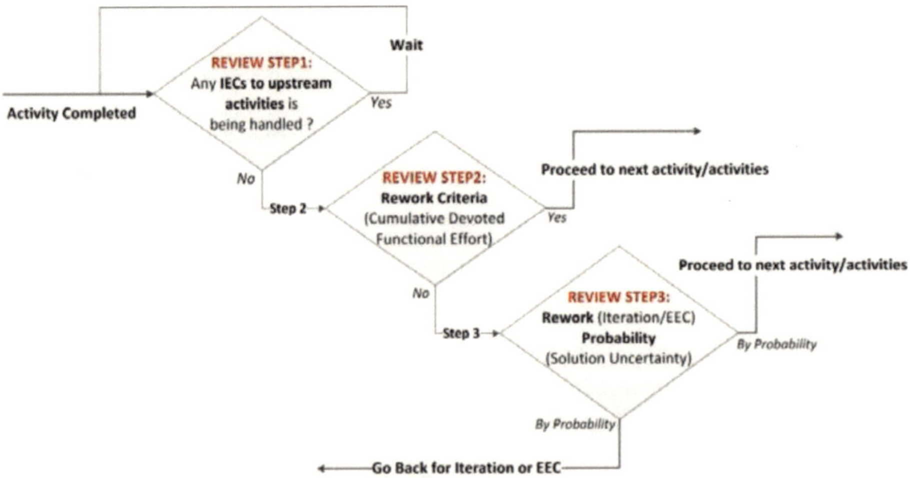

Figure 3. 3-Step NPD Rework Review Process

4.5.2. Frequency and resource consumption of IEC

Compared with NPDs that are much more likely to adhere to a planned schedule, IECs can occur without any plans. Therefore, the Exponential distribution is used to represent IECs' arrival interval. IEC's processing time is assumed to follow the Triangular distribution, where there is a most–likely time with some variation on two sides, represented by the most likely (Mode), minimum (Min), and maximum (Max) values respectively. The Triangular distribution is widely used in project management tools to estimate activity duration (e.g., Project Evaluation and Review Technique, Critical Path Method, etc.). The amount of resources required for an IEC to be processed is ***IEC effort***. When there are not enough resources available for both processes, resource using priority needs to be assigned to either NPD or ECM to seize necessary resource first.

4.5.3. IEC propagation

Change Propagation (CP) is assumed to be rooted in both interrelated *activities* of a PD process and closely dependent constituent product *items*. That is, modifications to an initiating activity of one product item are highly likely to propagate to other activities within the same or different stages along the PD process, and may require further changes across to other items that are interconnected through design features and product attributes [23].

This phenomenon is simulated by two layers of *IEC propagation loop*. Firstly, CP review decisions are performed after the completion of an IEC and then propagate to one of its downstream activities by predefined probabilities. We assume uni–directional change propagation based on process structure. That is, an IEC to one NPD activity will propagate only to its successor activities within the current or next phase. For example, an IEC to enhance a particular design feature may result in substantial alterations in prototyping and manufacturing. On the other hand, innovations in manufacturing process will only cause modifications within production phase but not changes in design.

Secondly, the first–level activity IEC propagation loop is then nested within an outer loop determined by particular dependency properties of the product configuration. Once an IEC to one product item and its CPs to affected downstream activities are completed, it will further propagate to item(s) that is/are directly linked to it.

5. Numerical application

A numerical example is presented in this section to illustrate how this DES model can actually be applied to facilitate ECM policy analysis. A combination of different process, product, team, and environment characteristics are tested through design of experiments. NPD project lead time, cost (or engineering effort in some cases), and quality are generated by the model as the three key performance measurements of the project under study to evaluate overall product development efforts.

5.1. NPD section

The NPD section is demonstrated by a simple application of three representational phases of an NPD process: i) concept design and development (***Concept***), ii) detailed product design (***Design***), and iii) production ramp up (***Production***). Each phase consists of three sequentially numbered and chronologically related activities. The information flow between every two activities is indicated by solid arrows as shown in *Fig. 4*.

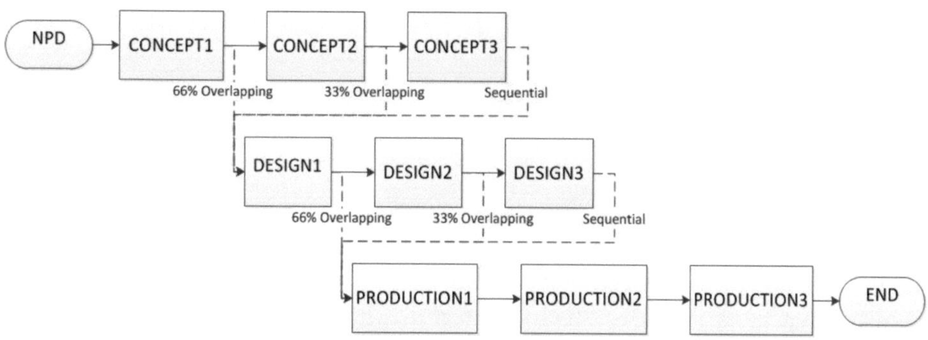

Figure 4. NPD Framework with Iterations and EECs

Through this 3–phase and 3–activity framework, various overlapping ratios of an NPD process: 0%, 33%, 66%, or mixed (e.g., 0% overlap between Concept and Design and 33%

overlap between Design and Production), can be constructed by connecting intra–phase activities via different combinations of dashed arrows.

5.2. Overlapping strategy

An NPD process with 0% overlapping is also called a *sequential* process, in which the downstream phase is allowed to start only after receiving the output information from the upstream phase in its finalized form. That is, different phases comprising an NPD process are connected in a completely linear fashion.

Besides its capability of representing a sequential process, this framework can also be assembled into *concurrent* processes by allowing the parallelization of upstream and downstream activities. For a 33% overlapped process, the first activity of downstream phase begins simultaneously with the last activity of upstream phase. For a 66% overlapped NPD process, the first activity of the following phase starts simultaneously with the second activity of the preceding phase.

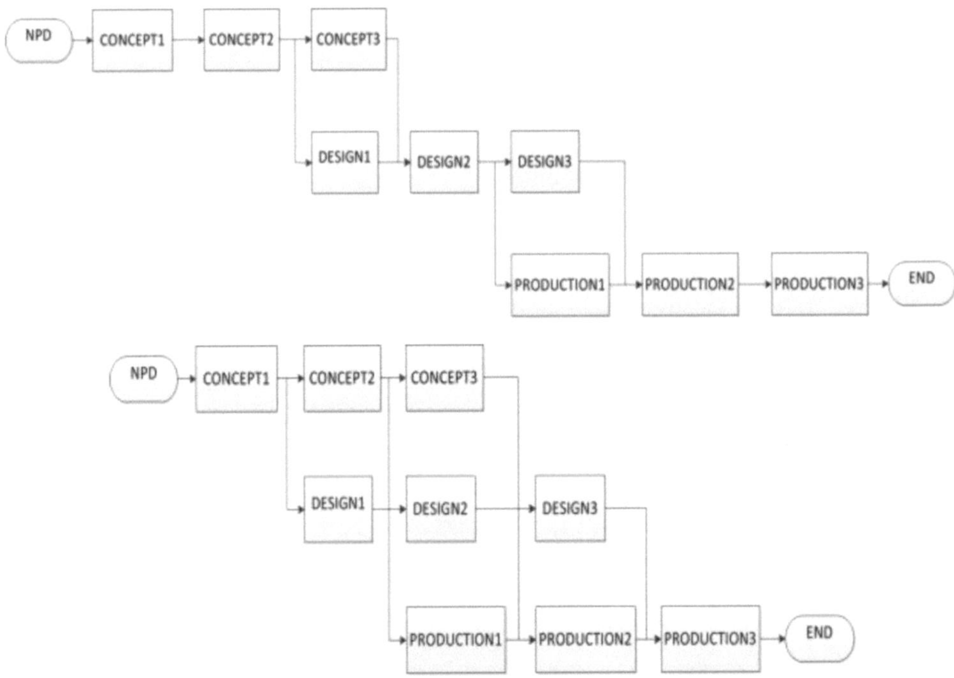

Figure 5. NPD Framework with Iterations and EECs

Obviously, as compared to its counterpart in a sequential process, the solution uncertainty of downstream activity increases due to the fact that it begins before the completion of all upstream activities using only preliminary output information, while the solution uncertainty of the upstream activity remains unchanged. That is, only the solution uncertainty of overlapped activities in succeeding phases will be affected under the current model assumptions.

5.3. NPD process parameter

When considering the activity duration estimates, it is further assumed that the mutually independent and exponentially distributed duration has a mean of $\beta = 2$ days for activities in all three phases. Furthermore, the number of tasks that compose activities within one phase remains the same, but increases from phase to phase to represent the increasing content and complexity of design and development activities as the NPD project unfolds: $k = 4$ for activities in Concept phase; $k = 6$ for Design phase; and $k = 10$ for Production phase. Note that when LCE are taken into account, random variables described by the Erlang distribution $ERLANG(\beta, k)$ only represent processing intervals of NPD basework. Rework duration is also subject to N_{ij}, the number of times that an activity is attempted, in the form of

$$LCE = max\left(\left(\frac{1}{2}\right)^{N_{ij}}, 0.1\right)$$

To match the three major phases of the illustrated NPD process, it is assumed that there exist three different functional areas: *marketing*, *engineering*, and *manufacturing*, that participate in the overall NPD process through integrated DI. Based on the model assumption that each activity consumes a total number of 100 resources units to complete, DI is defined as follows: 60 units requested from major department and 20 units requested from each of the other two minor departments. To estimate the final project cost, the busy usage cost rates are set as *$25/hour* and idle cost as *$10/hour* for all resources.

Different rigidities of rework review, which are represented by various rework criteria ratios (i.e., relationships between rework criteria and the evolving functional design solution scope $(S_m)_t$) will be explored more in depth through "what–if" analysis.

5.4. IEC section

Fig. 5 gives an overview of the IEC model section applying 33% overlapping strategy. It is assumed that an IEC will propagate to one of its downstream activities in the current or next phase with equal chances, and this propagation will continue in the same manner until the end of IEC propagation loop when no more change is identified. For the purpose of demonstration, a full list of potential downstream change propagations of each IEC is provided on the right side of the *IEC Propagation* decision point. In the actual simulation model, verbal description is replaced by connectors between the IEC propagation decision point and the corresponding IEC process modules.

Take the IEC to activity Concept1 as an example, change propagation will result in a maximum of six follow–up IECs (i.e., IECs to C2, C3/D1, D2, D3/P1, P2, and P3) and a minimum of two (i.e., IECs to C3/D1/D2 and D3/P1/P2/P3). For simplicity, it is also assumed that each IEC, no matter in which activity it is occurred, equally consumes 10 resource units from each of the three departments to get processed.

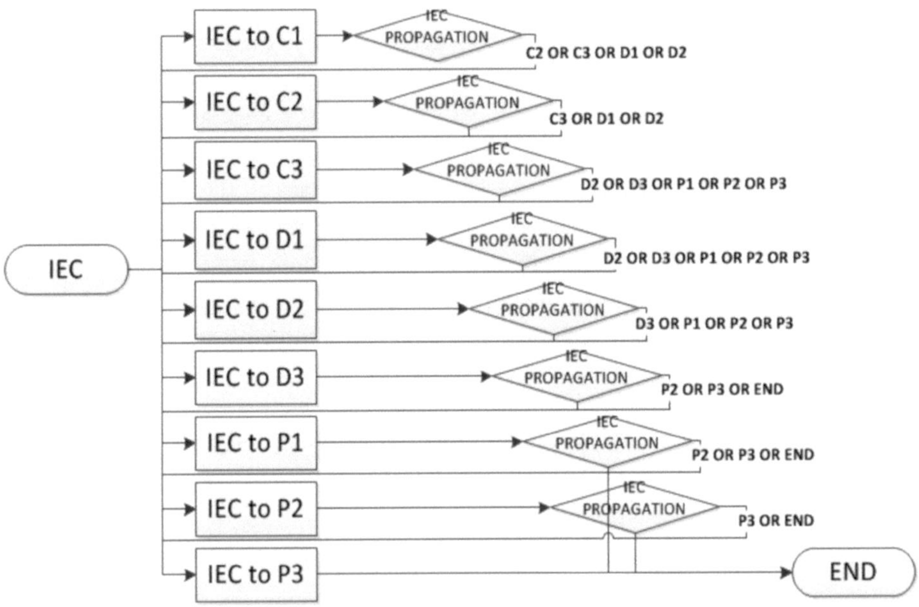

Figure 6. NPD Framework with Iterations and EECs

5.6. Summary of model inputs and outputs

Table 1 summarizes the complete list of model input parameters/variables and their corresponding values. There are altogether 14 model inputs that represent key NPD and ECM decision parameters, among which 7 are chosen as *design factors* or *constraints* (highlighted rows in gray) and their effects on the project performance measures (i.e., model outputs) will be tested at specific *levels* (highlighted text in bold), while others will be held constant when the design of experiment is conducted.[6]

It is important to know that all these values are set in a way to facilitate relative comparison of project performance among various scenarios using "what–if" analysis instead of aiming to reproduce the real behavior patterns of an NPD project of any kind. To successfully implementation of the proposed simulation model for a specific use or situation, these inputs should be appropriately calibrated depending on different circumstances.

At the end of each simulation run, Arena automatically generates a variety of both default and user specified model output statistics, which include time, cost, Work in Process (WIP), count, etc. Information is displayed under different categories (e.g., Entity, Process, Queue, Resource, and User Specified). Some of the key model *responses* are listed in the table below.

[6]These held-constant factors, such as number of phases and activities comprising the process, number of involving departments, duration estimates of NPD activities and IECs, etc., are peculiar to specific development project as . For purposes of the present experiment these factors are not of interest.

Input Data	**Value**
List of phases and activities comprising process	$I = 3\ (Concept - Design - Production)$; $J_i = 3\ (e.g. Concept1 - Concept2 - Concept3)$
List of involving departments	$M = 3\ (Marketing; Engineering; Manufacturing)$
Overlapping Strategy ***(OS)***	***Low***: 0%; ***Medium***: 33%; ***High***: 66%
NPD Activity Duration *(days)*	$d_{1j} = ERLANG(2,4), D_{1j} = 8;\ d_{2j} = ERLANG(2,6), D_{2j} = 12;\ d_{3j} = ERLANG(2,10), D_{3j} = 20;\ j = 1,2,3$
Learning Curve Effects ***(LCE)***	$\boldsymbol{no\ LCE; LCE} = max\left(\left(\frac{1}{2}\right)^{N_{ij}}, 0.1\right)$
NPD Activity Functional Resource Consumption	$r_{1j1} = 60, r_{1j2} = r_{1j3} = 20;\ r_{2j1} = 20, r_{2j2} = 60, r_{2j3} = 20;\ r_{3j1} = r_{3j2} = 20, r_{3j3} = 60;\ j = 1,2,3$
Functional Resources Constraints ***(FRC)***	$\boldsymbol{R_m} = 70, 80, \ldots, 190, 200;\ m = 1,2,3$
Cost of Resource	$Busy/Hour = \$25; Idle/Hour = \$10$
Rework Likelihood ***(RL)***	***Low***: $\alpha = \gamma = 0.3$; ***High***: $\alpha = \gamma = 0.45$
Rework Criteria ***(RC)***	***Stepped Linear; Linear; Convex–Up; Concave–Up***
IEC Arrival Frequency (Inter–arrival Times) *(days)*	***Low***: *Random (Expo)20*; ***Medium***: *Random (Expo)10*; ***High***: *Random (Expo)5*
IEC Duration Estimates *(days)*	$w_{lg} = TRIA(1.6, 2, 3.2), g = 1,2,3;$ $w_{lg} = TRIA(2.4, 3, 4.8), g = 4,5,6;$ $w_{lg} = TRIA(4, 5, 8), g = 7,8,9;\ l = 1,2,\ldots,L_t$
IEC Functional Resource Consumption	$s_{lgm} = 10\ and\ 20,\ l = 1,2,\ldots,L_t;\ g = 1,2,3;\ m = 1,2,3$

Table 1. Model Inputs

Output Data	**Definition**
NPD Project Lead Time	The total time of an NPD entity accumulated in process activities and delays (time elapsed between start of Concept phase and end of Production phase).
Project Cost	The total of busy costs (i.e., costs while seize) for all staffing and resources for both NPD and IEC entities.
Total Cost	The total expenditure on both busy and idle (i.e., costs while scheduled, but not busy) resources for NPD and IEC entities.
Cumulative Functional Effort	The accumulated departmental workload (in units of person–days) accounted for both NPD and IEC entities.
Cumulative Total Effort	The accumulated total effort accounted for both NPD and IEC entities (i.e., the sum of all the cumulative functional efforts).
Quality	Ratio of the final design solution scope over the original design solution scope.

Table 2. Model Outputs

6. Results

Impacts of the following managerial strategies and coordination policies on the responses of interest are investigated, and the root causes behind the performance of measurement system are explored:

a. Impact of NPD process characteristics such as LCE, Rework Likelihood (RL) and *Overlapping Strategy* (OS);
b. Impact of rework review rigidity – *Rework Review Strategy (RRS)*[7];
c. Impact of IEC arrival frequency;
d. Combined impact of IEC arrival frequency and size – *IEC batching policy;*
e. Impact of functional resource constraints – *resource assignment Strategy;*
f. Impact of change propagation due to interconnected product configuration.

Due to space limit, only partial results of policy analysis a are presented to demonstrate how the proposed DES model can be used as a valuable tool for evaluating ECM decisions. 200 *replicates* are generated under each combination of LCE, RL, and OS, and thus result in altogether 2400 simulation runs, each using separate input random numbers. Performance data generated by the model are then exported to a Excel worksheet, in which individual project performance measures are recorded and various data graphs are generated.

Mean values of the experiment outcomes are displayed in Table 3. Columns ***(i)*** and ***(ii)*** record in an absolute sense the mean values of the observed lead time and project cost from 200 replications of each scenario, while columns ***(I)*** and ***(II)*** show the percentage change of (i) and (ii) relative to the baseline case results ***(BL1)***, respectively.

It is important to note that managerial suggestions are not made merely based on the final output performance measures obtained for each scenario. Rather, attention is focused on the comparison of these numbers to their corresponding baseline results, which helps to provide us intuitive understanding of the impacts of reworks on project performance under different process features and parameter settings. Through the interpretation of results presented in *Table 3*, several concluding observations can be issued:

1. When rework is not involved, the project performance stays consistent: the higher the activity overlapping ratio, the less the lead time. It can be obtained by summing up the durations of activities along the critical path. At the same time, since total person–days effort required for completing the project remains unchanged no matter which OS is applied, final project cost for all levels of *OS* (i.e., ***(a)***, ***(b)***, and ***(c)***) in the baseline case should be very much similar, which is confirmed by the running results. This can be considered as a simple model verification check[8].
2. Effects of LCE: by comparing the mean values of lead time and project cost of scenarios ***(A)*** with scenarios ***(B)*** under different combinations of RL and OS levels, it can be

---

[7] The first two strategies are analyzed with only the NPD section of the model.

[8] Model is continuously verified by the reading through and examining the outputs for reasonableness and justification under a variety of scenarios and settings of parameters.

concluded that the evaluation of learning curve effects unambiguously results in a remarkable decrease in both NPD lead time and cost.

3. Effects of RL: by comparing ***(i)*** and ***(ii)*** of scenarios **(1)** with scenarios **(2)** under different combinations of LCE and OS levels, it can be concluded that a higher likelihood of rework in NPD activity undoubtedly causes an increase in both lead time and cost.
4. Effects of OS w/o LCE: by comparing lead time and project cost of scenarios ***(A)*** in a relative sense, we find that an increasing overlapping ratio aggravates the impact of NPD rework on both responses. That is, when NPD rework is included in the model but no LCE is considered, the greater the overlapping ratio, the higher the percentages of increase in both lead time and project cost as compared to baseline case. In addition, we notice the time–cost tradeoffs between a sequential process and a 66% overlapped process from columns ***(i)*** and ***(ii)***. This observation agrees to the general acknowledgement that overlapping may save time but is more costly.
5. Effects of OS w/ LCE: Situation is not that predictable when LCE is taken into account and formulated as $LCE = \max\left(\left(\frac{1}{2}\right)^{N_{ij}-1}, 0.1\right)$ in the model. Significant increase of both time and cost due to rework is alleviated by the evaluation of LCE. Under low RL circumstances ($\alpha = \gamma = 0.3$), a highly overlapped process excels in both response variables in an absolute sense. However, there is not clear trend shown in the comparative values. Particularly, at high level of RL ($\alpha = \gamma = 0.45$), we observe that a 33% overlapped process leads to both absolute (compared with the results of 0% and 66% in scenario ***(B)–(2)***) and relative (compared with the 33% baseline results ***(BL1)–(b)***) maximum values for lead time and project cost.
6. By comparing columns ***(I)*** and ***(II)***, we observe a project behavioral pattern that the percentage increase of project cost is always higher than that of lead time at the occurrence of rework. That is to say, compared with lead time, project cost is more sensitive to rework. And the difference between the two percentages of increase is largest when a sequential NPD process is adopted. The only exception is scenario ***(B)–(1)–(c)*** with the percentage increase of project cost 0.9% lower than that of lead time.

After investigating project cost performance that reflects the overall effort devoted to the NPD project, how the amount of functional effort contributed by each participating department is affected by different LCE, RL, and OS levels is further examined.Three major conclusions can be drawn by breaking down the overall committed effort into functional effort contributed by each department:

1. From *Fig. 7-a*, we observe that differences between the committed effort from the major department (i.e., Mfg Effort) of downstream phase (i.e., Production phase), and the efforts devoted by the other two departments (i.e., Mkt Effort & Eng Effort) drop dramatically from a sequential process ***(a)*** to concurrent processes ***(b)*** and ***(c)*** regardless of LCE or RL levels.
2. Moreover, from a relative perspective (*Fig. 7-b*), the percentage increase of Mfg Effort versus baseline is higher than those of Mkt and Eng Efforts in all sequential processes but ***(A)–(2)–(a)***, in which Mfg Effort %Change = *72.5%* and is slightly lower than Mkt

Effort %Change = *75.6%*. However, in concurrent processes, an inverse relationship but of a much greater magnitude (especially at high RL level) is observed. That is, by starting downstream activities early with only preliminary information, concurrent engineering tends to alleviate the impacts of rework on activities in Production phase while intensifying those on activities in the two upstream phases. Although the concept of *cross–functional integration* has already been applied to the sequential process that allows engineers from Mfg Dept to be engaged early in both Concept and Design phases, which differentiates it from a traditional waterfall process, the impact of rework mostly occur in Mfg Dept. A concurrent process tends to shift rework risks and even out committed efforts among various functional areas owing to another critical characterization of concurrent engineering: *parallelization of activities*.

3. Mkt Effort undergoes the highest percentage of increase from when RL changes from low to high regardless of LCE or OS levels. Then is the Eng Effort. Mft Effort has the least amount of fluctuation across different scenarios.

LCE	*RL* (α, γ)	*OS*	**(i) Lead Time (Days)**	**(I) Time %Change c/w BL1**	**(ii) Project Cost** ($\$ \times 1000$)	**(II) PC %Change c/w BL1**
(BL1) Baseline	No Rework	**(a)** 0%	119		7,168	
		(b) 33%	101		7,168	
		(c) 66%	81		7,169	
(A) *No LCE*	**(1)** ***Low*** $\alpha = \gamma = 0.3$	**(a)** 0%	158	32.0%	**10,781**	48.2%
		(b) 33%	160	58.9%	11,778	61.9%
		(c) 66%	**131**	62.6%	12,107	66.6%
	(2) ***High*** $\alpha = \gamma = 0.45$	**(a)** 0%	176	47.2%	**11,948**	64.2%
		(b) 33%	192	90.4%	14,542	99.8%
		(c) 66%	**162**	100.1%	14,927	105.4%
(B) $LCE = max\left(\left(\frac{1}{2}\right)^{N_{ij}-1}, 0.1\right)$	**(1)** ***Low*** $\alpha = \gamma = 0.3$	**(a)** 0%	141	17.6%	9,542	33.1%
		(b) 33%	129	28.1%	9,436	31.6%
		(c) 66%	**106**	31.0%	**9,185**	28.1%
	(2) ***High*** $\alpha = \gamma = 0.45$	**(a)** 0%	152	27.2%	**10,370**	44.7%
		(b) 33%	158	56.6%	12,044	68.0%
		(c) 66%	**121**	49.2%	11,037	54.0%

Table 3. Project Performance under the Impact of OS, RL and LCE

To better visualize the correlations between lead time and effort, scatter plots of 200 model replicates' lead time and total effort outcomes under different levels of OS and RL are demonstrated in *Fig. 8*. Red lines in the plots indicate the lead time and total effort required for BL1 baseline cases (an "ideally executed" project without accounting for rework).

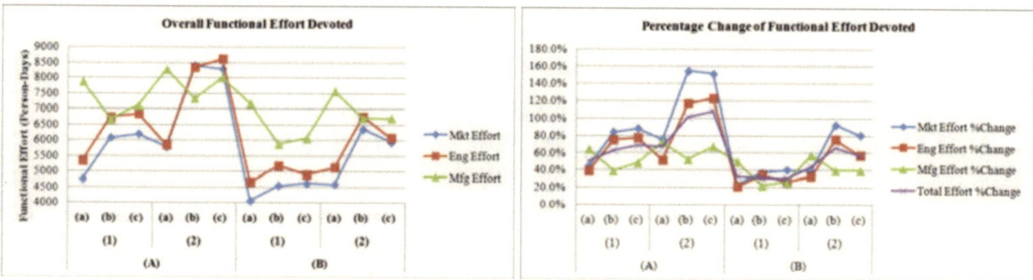

Figure 7. (a/b). Overall/ Percentage Change of Functional Effort Devoted

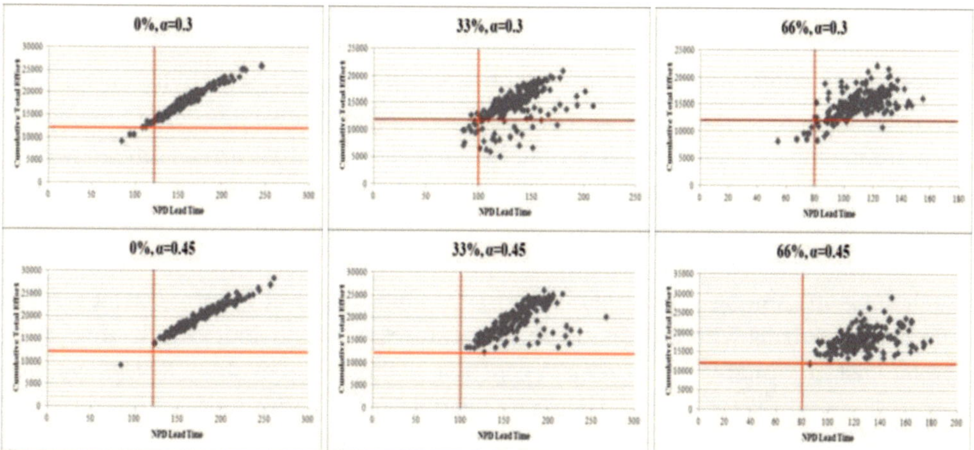

Figure 8. (a/b). Scatter Plots of the RL Impact on Different OS

We can clearly observe that a majority of replications exceed the lead time and effort of ***BL1*** by a considerable amount because of rework. Furthermore, as overlapping ratio and rework probability constants (α for IPC and γ for EPC) increase, there is also a notable increase in the number of replicates that are off the trend line. This phenomenon reveals that a high overlap ratio of upstream and downstream activities, combined with a high likelihood of unanticipated activity rework that requires additional resources will result in a strong tendency for NPD projects to behave in an unstable and unpredictable manner and lead to unforeseen departures from the predetermined baseline plan. Also note that, there exist possibilities where total effort or lead time or both are smaller than those required for the respective baseline cases, which is due to the stochastic nature of the model inputs (i.e., random inputs of activity duration, rework probabilities, etc.).

7. Conclusion

This research proposes a comprehensive discrete event simulation model that captures different aspects of PD project–related (i.e., product, process, team, and environment) complexity to investigate their resultant impacts on the occurrence and magnitude of iterations and ECs that stochastically arise during the course of an NPD project, and how the multiple dimensions of project performance, including lead time, cost, and quality, are consequently affected. In addition to the integration of several critical characteristics of PD projects that have been previously developed and tested, (e.g., concurrent and collaborative development process, learning curve effects, resources constraints), this research introduces the following new features and dynamic structures that are explicitly modeled, verified, and validated for the first time:

1. This DES model *explicitly distinguishes between two different types of rework by the time of occurrence*: intra–phase iterations and inter–phase EECs. Moreover, *engineering changes are further categorized into two groups by their causes of occurrence,* emergent ECs "that are necessary to reach an initially defined standard in the product" [13], and initiated ECs in response to new customer requirements or technology advances.
2. *Uncertainty is differentiated and conceptualized into three categories.* Activity uncertainty is reflected in the stochastic activity duration using probability distributions, and environmental uncertainty is primarily modeled by the arrival frequency and magnitude of IECs. In particular, solution uncertainty is an important model variable that dynamically determines the rework probability which will be discussed next.
3. This study provides presumably the first attempt to integrate cause–and–effect relationships among project variables into a DES model of PD projects. Traditional DES model deals with only static project features in "open–loop, single–link" causal relationship format [14] that remain constant as the model evolves. *Rework probability is no longer pre–determined* and remains fixed over the entire time frame of the NPD process as appeared in most of previous studies. Instead, it is calculated in real time by the model itself. That is to say, rework probability is now included in a *feedback structure* that changes over time in response to the project's evolving uncertainty levels.
4. The specific three–step *rework review process structure*, together with the *rigidity of rework reviews*, allows more explicit and detailed modeling of this critical aspect of ECM, which is not attempted by previous studies. Decision points are used with rules to conditionally process ECs. They also give the users flexibility to define one or more rules in priority evaluation order.
5. *The traditional restrictive assumption of a stable development process with no environmental disturbance is also relaxed* by introducing the random occurrence of IECs, which will lead to an enlarged design solution scope of the final product and thus affecting the project solution uncertainty.

Results show under different conditions of uncertainty, how we should apply various kinds of strategies and policies, including process overlapping, rework review, IEC batching, resource allocation, to not only achieve benefits but also recognize potential tradeoffs among lead time, cost and quality. The study concludes with the following observations or understandings that either have been identified previously in the existing literature or disclosed for the first time with the help of newly added and verified model features:

1. Significant increase of both time and cost due to rework is alleviated by the evaluation of LCE.
2. The percentage increase of project cost is always higher than that of lead time at the occurrence of rework and IECs. That is, compared with lead time, project cost is more sensitive to rework/IECs.
3. By starting downstream activities early with only preliminary information, concurrent engineering tends to alleviate the impacts of rework on activities in downstream phases while intensifying those on activities in the upstream phases. It also tends to shift rework risks and even out committed efforts among various functional areas. In addition, departments that are majorly involved in upstream phases undergo higher fluctuation in effort.
4. A high overlap ratio of upstream and downstream activities, combined with a high likelihood of unanticipated activity rework that requires additional resources will result in a strong tendency for NPD projects to behave in an unstable and unpredictable manner and lead to unforeseen departures from the predetermined baseline plan.
5. Adopting a more restrictive *RRS* (Convex–Up) leads to a longer NPD lead time and higher project cost. There is no obvious distinction between Stepped Linear and Linear *RRSs*. Also, the evaluation of *LCE* reduces the impacts of *RRS*.
6. When only the IEC process propagation among development activities is examined, high correlations between lead time, cost, and quality are observed. However, when the effects of IEC product propagation among dependent product components/systems, the correlation between lead time and project cost, and the one between lead time and quality drop significantly.
7. Batching of IECs possesses a competitive advantage in lead time over handling IECs individually. This superiority is the greatest when a sequential PD process is adopted, and reduces as overlapping ratio increases. However, there is neither IEC policy shows "dominant" advantage in project cost or quality.
8. Potential tradeoffs among NPD lead time and total cost are clearly identified when resource assignment decision is to be made. A higher level of OS leads to a shorter NPD lead time and less total cost given the same amount of functional resource allocation. However, the benefits of lead time reduction by assigning more resources are the most obvious in a sequential process, and activity overlap reduces the degree of obviousness the benefits have. The higher the OS, the less the benefits.
9. Linearity between lead time and quality is observed in all three OS levels: the higher the functional resource availability, the shorter the lead time, and the lower the quality. The linearity slope increases as the *OS* increases. The percentage of decrease in quality versus baseline case is the largest in a sequential process and decreases as *OS* increases.
10. The evaluation of IEC product propagation leads to a general increase of the multiple dimensions of NPD project performance from baseline case, except a counterintuitive decrease in NPD project lead time for a less coupled product configuration under a high environmental uncertainty and a high *RL*.

Three possible main directions of future studies beyond the work presented here are summarized as follows:

1. Model features including: i) different relationships between solution uncertainty and rework probability, ii) more detailed modeling of dynamic rework review criteria (in replace of the current static one), and iii) parallel rework policy need to be tested to assess their impacts on project performance measures.
2. The review of literature has indicated a lack of development process models that are capable to be extended and implemented into a multi–project environment while still keeping detailed aspects of project complexity. Building blocks of the model framework can be reconfigured and applied at various detail levels. From a single project level to the entire organizational level, it opens possibilities for further analyses of multi–project management, such as work force planning strategies, coordination policies of interdependent parallel projects, etc.
3. This DES model can also be further extended across organizations. By relaxing the single organization restriction of the current model and including inter–organizational influences, how engineering changes propagate along supply chain and affect NPD project performance can be explored.

Author details

Weilin Li
Syracuse University, The United States

8. References

[1] Balakrishnan, N., A. K. Chakravarty. (1996). Managing Engineering Change: Market Opportunities and Manufacturing Costs. *Production and Operations Management*. 5 (4):335–356.

[2] Barzizza, R., M. Caridi, R. Cigolini. (2001). Engineering Change: A Theoretical Assessment and A Case Study. *Production Planning & Control*. 12 (7):717–726.

[3] Bhuiyan, N., D. Gerwin, V. Thomson. (2004). Simulation of the New Product Development Process for Performance Improvement. *Management Science*. 50(12):1690–1703.

[4] Bhuiyan, N., G. Gregory, V. Thomson. (2006). Engineering Change Request Management in a New Product Development Process. *European Journal of Innovation Management*. 9(1):5–19.

[5] Black, L. J., N. P. Repenning. (2001). Why Firefighting Is Never Enough: Preserving High–Quality Product Development. *System Dynamic Review*. 17(1):33–62.

[6] Bouikni, N., A. Desrochers. (2006). A Product Feature Evolution Validation Model for Engineering Change Management. *Journal of Computing and Information Science in Engineering*. 6(2):188–195.

[7] Browning, T. R. (1998). Modeling and Analyzing Cost, Schedule, and Performance in Complex System Product Development. Doctoral thesis. Massachusetts Institute of Technology. Cambridge, MA.

[8] Browning, T. R., S. D. Eppinger. (2002). Modeling Impacts of Process Architecture on Cost and Schedule Risk in Product Development. *IEEE Transactions on Engineering Management*. 49(4): 428–442.

[9] Cho, S. H., S. D. Eppinger. (2005). A Simulation–Based Process Model for Managing Complex Design Projects. *IEEE Transactions on Engineering Management*. 52(3):316–328.

[10] Clark, K. B., T. Fujimoto. (1991). Product Development Perfornmance: Strategy, Organization, and Management in the World Auto Industry. Boston, Mass.: Harvard Business School Press.

[11] Clarkson P. J. and C. Eckert. (2004). Design and Process Improvement: A Review of Current Practice. Springer. 1st edition.

[12] Earl C., J. H. Johnson and C. Eckert. (2005). "Complexity" in *Design Process Improvement – A Review of Current Practice*. 174-196, Springer, ISBN 1-85233-701-X, 2005

[13] Eckert, C., P. J. Clarkson, W. Zanker. (2004). Change and Customisation in Complex Engineering Domains. *Research in Engineering Design*. 15(1):1–21.

[14] Ford, D. N. (1995). The Dynamics of Project Management: An Investigation of the Impacts of Project Process and Coordination on Performance. Doctoral thesis. Sloan School of Management. Massachusetts Institute of Technology. Cambridge, MA.

[15] Ford, D. N., J. D. Sterman. (1998). Dynamic Modeling of Product Development Processes. *System Dynamics Review*. 14(1): 31–68.

[16] Ford, D. N., J. D. Sterman. 2003. Overcoming the 90% Syndrome: Iteration Management in Concurrent Development Projects. *Concurrent Engineering: Research and Applications*. 11(3):177–186

[17] Ha, A. Y., E. L. Porteus. (1995). Optimal Timing of Reviews in Concurrent Design for Manufacturability. *Management Science*. 41(9):1431–1447.

[18] Hegde, G. G., Sham Kekre, Sunder Kekre. 1992. Engineering Changes and Time Delays: A Field Investigation. *International Journal of Production Economics*. 28(3):341–352.

[19] Ho, C. J. 1994. Evaluating the Impact of Frequent Engineering Changes on MRP System Performance. International Journal of Production Research. 32(3):619–641.

[20] Ho, C. J., J. Li. 1997. Progressive Engineering Changes in Multi–level Product Structures. Omega: International Journal for Management Science. 25(5):585–594.

[21] Hobday, M. (1998). Product Complexity, Innovation, and Industrial Organization. *Research Policy*. 26(6):689–710.

[22] Huang, G. Q., K. L. Mak. (1999). Current Practices of Engineering Change Management in Hong Kong Manufacturing Industries. *Journal of Materials Processing Technology*. 19(1):21–37.

[23] Koh, E. CY., P. J. Clarkson. (2009). A Modelling Method to Manage Change Propagation. In *Proceedings of the 18th International Conference on Engineering Design*. Stanford, California.

[24] Krishnan, V., S. D. Eppinger, D. E. Whitney. (1997). A Model–Based Framework to Overlap Product Development Activities. *Management Science*. 43(4):437–451.

[25] Krishnan, V., K. T. Ulrich. (2001). Product Development Decisions : A Review of the Literature. *Management Science*. 47(1):1-21.

[26] Lin, J., K. H. Chai, Y. S. Wong, A. C. Brombacher. (2007). A Dynamic Model for Managing Overlapped Iterative Product Development. *European Journal of Operational Research*. 185:378-392

[27] Loch, C. H., C. Terwiesch. (1999). Accelerating the Process of Engineering Change Orders: Capacity and Congestion Effects. *Journal of Product Innovation Management*. 16(2):145–159.

[28] Loch, C. H., J. Mihm, A. Huchzermeier. (2003). Concurrent Engineering and Design Oscillations in Complex Engineering Projects. *Concurrent Engineering: Research and Applications*. 11(3):187–199.

[29] Lyneis, J. M., D. N. Ford. (2007). System Dynamics Applied to Project Management: a Survey, Assessment, and Directions for Future Research. *System Dynamics Review*. 23(2/3): 157–189.

[30] Park, M., F. Peña–Mora. (2003). Dynamic Change Management for Construction: Introducing the Change Cycle into Model-Based Project Management. *System Dynamics Review*. 19(3):213-242.

[31] Pimmler, T. U., and S. D. Eppinger. (1994). Integration Analysis of Product Decompositions. In *Proceedings of the ASME Design Theory and Methodology Conference*, 343–351. Minneapolis, Minnesota: American Society of Mechanical Engineers.

[32] Reichelt, K., J. Lyneis. (1999). The Dynamics of Project Performance: Benchmarking the Drivers of Cost and Schedule Overrun. *European Management Journal*. 17(2):135-150.

[33] Roemer, T. A., R. Ahmadi. (2004). Concurrent Crashing and Overlapping in Product Development. *Operations Research*. 52(4): 606–622.

[34] Smith, R. P., S. D. Eppinger. (1997). A Predictive Model of Sequential Iteration in Engineering Design. *Management Science*. 43(8):1104–1120.

[35] Terwiesch, C., C. H. Loch. 1999. Managing the Process of Engineering Change Orders: The Case of the Climate Control System in Automobile Development. Journal of Product Innovation Management. 16(2):160–172.

[36] Unger, D. W., S. D. Eppinger. 2009. Comparing Product Development Processes and Managing Risk. International Journal of Product Development. 8(4):382–401.

[37] Wynn, D. C., K. Grebici, P. J. Clarkson. 2011. Modelling the Evolution of Uncertainty Levels during Design. International Journal on Interactive Design and Manufacturing. 5:187–202.